Stairs

Christian Peter
Christine Peter
Daniel Reisch
Katinka Temme

DETAIL Practice

Authors

Christian Peter
Christine Peter
Daniel Reisch
Katinka Temme

Publisher

Editing (German Edition):
Steffi Lenzen (Project head)
Eva Schönbrunner, Sophie Karst

Editorial team (German edition):
Jana Rackwitz, Katrin Pollems-Braunfels,
Michaela Linder, Duy Mac

Cover Design:
Kai Meyer, Munich

Drawings:
Marion Griese

Translation into English:
Julian Jain, Berlin

Copy-editing (English edition):
Stefan Widdess, Berlin

Proofreading (English edition):
Meriel Clemett, Bromborough, UK

An Edition DETAIL book

ISBN 978-3-95553-397-7 (Print)
ISBN 978-3-95553-398-4 (E-Book)
ISBN 978-3-95553-399-1 (Bundle)

Printed on acid-free paper made from cellulose bleached without the use of chlorine.

Typesetting & production:
Simone Soesters

Printed by:
Grafisches Centrum Cuno GmbH & Co. KG, Calbe
1st edition, 2018

This book is also available in a German language edition
(ISBN 978-3-95553-372-4).

Bibliographical information of the German National Library
The German National Library lists this publication in the German National Bibliography; detailed bibliographical data are available on the internet under http://dnb.d-nb.de.

DETAIL Business Information GmbH
Messerschmittstr. 4, 80992 Munich, Germany
Tel: +49 89 381620-0
www.detail-online.com

FSC www.fsc.org
MIX
Paper from responsible sources
FSC® C043106

Contents

Preface

A new book on stairs?

Books on stairs play an important part in the reference libraries of many architectural practices. Every year, many new publications appear on this topic, including collections of current and/or historical project examples, combined with a rapidly growing flood of images.

Providing an alternative to "picture books" of this sort, this book demonstrates a new approach to the subject of stairs, highly fascinating in symbolic, spatial and constructional terms:

When a new building with a stair is conceived, the question which arises in the first instance is about the stair's spatial and aesthetic expression. The type of construction and the material initially take a backseat. When considering reference objects, the first step thus focuses on design principles and spatial aspects, including questions such as: How is the stair placed in the space? Is the stair a work unto itself, or does it humbly recede into the background to avoid impairing the spatial impression and harmony? Does the stair, in its material and form, continue the concept of the building, or dominate the space as a "foreign object" or an autonomous body?

These and further questions directly lead to a "typology of the stair" according to categories that initially focus on the design. What is new in doing so is the classification into five pairs of terms that develop dialectically, and help to more distinctly distinguish the typologies from each other, to allow for clear-cut classification. At the outset, the design and construction typologies are more precisely differentiated and their development historically elucidated in individual chapters.

The section on theory is followed by a collection of ten projects, presenting in detail one stair of every category, respectively. A matrix summarises the five pairs, pointing out further references in a user-friendly manner.

The stair as space-defining element makes a substantial contribution to the perceived atmosphere or spatial impression.

For the selection of projects, it was important that the respective stair harmonises with its surrounding space, jointly conveying this atmosphere. Deliberately, it was not the most topical examples that were selected, but rather those where the stair and the building sensibly and qualitatively collaborate coherently.

The book concludes with a planning guide that explains the different parts of stairs, construction elements, the types of construction, as well as the materials for the load-bearing part of a stair, including materials for coverings and handrails, in a logical step-by-step manner.

The result is a handbook in step with actual practice, which outlines the planning procedure incrementally, with reference to aesthetic and constructional questions, thus closing a didactic gap.

Christian Peter, Christine Peter, Katinka Temme, Daniel Reisch

Munich, August 2017

Methodology

1

2

The planning of stairs normally sets wide-ranging and partly highly complex requirements. Alongside functional, structural and building physics-related prerequisites (see "Planning guide", p. 94ff.), the design-based and aesthetic aspects in particular are paramount here.

The position and conception of a stair have diverse effects on space. Therefore, one can justifiably speak of a stair as being a significant as well as decisive space-defining element. Moreover, for stairs, more than for all other spatially effective elements, basic mathematical rules also play a role, i.e. the rise/run ratio underlying a stair, which determines its appearance, and hence the surrounding space.

Due to their three-dimensional structure, stairs dominate space. Though doors and windows exhibit a depth effect, they are less space-containing since they are arranged on the outer contours, and hence act as part of the spatial shell. Stairs – especially in a central arrangement – more emphatically determine the overall impression. Constructed in a usually orthogonal arrangement, they shape the atmosphere on account of their diagonally effective corporeality.

By way of a so-called Laurin stair (a stair whose rise increases with height), visitors to the 2014 Venice Biennale of Architecture were able experience how individual proportions affect one's own perception: depending on the gradient of the steps, combined with different degrees of bodily strain, different ways of walking automatically ensue (fig. 1). This clearly shows that a stair is an architectural element which the user directly experiences via his/her own body.

Due to its potentially highly dominant spatial effect, as well as the direct bodily experience for every user, a stair is decisive for the conception of spaces. In order to allow planners to classify stairs in the design and construction process, a categorisation into different types is presented in this publication.

A stair as part of a building design is subject to numerous dependencies. The project examples selected for the book correspondingly demonstrate that stairs can achieve different effects and can create a variety of spatial impressions. For the sake of orientation, this variety can essentially be categorised into five dialectic conceptual pairs: "Jacob's ladder and Sculpture" (p. 8ff.); "Stage and Landscape" (p. 18ff.); "Aesthetics of technology vs Longing for the archetype" (p. 26ff.); "Volume vs Continuity" (p. 34ff.); as well as "Furniture and Addition" (p. 40ff.), with these basic types often also appearing and being applied in a combined manner in practice.

1 Laurin stair, Venice Biennale (IT) 2014, Institut für Scalalogie OTH Regensburg
2 Stair typology, Venice Biennale (IT) 2014, Institut für Scalalogie OTH Regensburg

Jacob's ladder and Sculpture

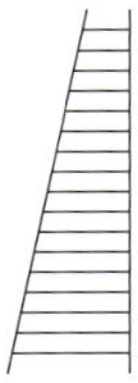

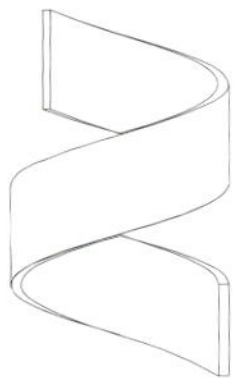

1 Jacob's ladder, Morocco 1984, Hansjörg Voth
2 Jacob's ladder, mine tip Norddeutschland, Neukirchen-Vluyn (DE) 2009
3 Jacob's ladder, mine tip Beckstraße, Bottrop (DE) 1995, Wolfgang Christ
4 The stair as stair by itself. Endless Stair, London Design Festival 2013, London (GB) 2013, dRMM Architects
5 Kukulcán pyramid, Chichén Itzá (MX) 8th–11th century
6 Bridge, stair, viewing platform: Stair sculpture, Rotterdam (NL) 2013, Next architects

1

2

3

Viewed historically, stairs initially served the purpose of providing a purely functional vertical link between two or more floors. The "stair per se" was primarily always about simple constructional requirements (see also "Longing for the archetype", p. 29ff. as well as "Construction typology", p. 48ff.). Just as important was an "economy of space", i.e. to give up as little space as possible for a stair. Rapidly, however, the function of a stair was symbolically inflated. In church construction, the stair was henceforth considered as a metaphor for the connection between the earthly, secular, and the celestial, sacred. In secular building, it represents wealth and power. In conjunction with this upgrading, an abundance of forms as well as decorative design details established themselves in stair construction.

Numerous art works show the transcendental power inherent in stairs even today, and how congenial the categories "Jacob's ladder" and "Sculpture" are with each other. The German artist Hansjörg Voth takes up these topics in his Jacob's ladder sculptures in the desert of Morocco, translating them into an impressive artistic expression (fig. 1).

Applying the motif of the stair as an element of suspense between two levels also, however, works particularly well in landscape architecture, such as on the Rheinelbe and Norddeutschland mine tips (fig. 2). The tetrahedron "Haldenereignis Emscherblick", too, on the Beckstrasse mine tip (fig. 3) successfully symbolises the desire of the people to reach the holy of holies in heaven, or at least come closer to the clouds. This scenic outpost was conceived as a landmark during the International Building Exhibition (IBA) Emscher Park (1989–99) by the architect Wolfgang Christ from Darmstadt, in close collaboration with the structural engineer Klaus Bollinger.

However, these "Jacob's ladders" are, in fact, anything but ladders: the stairs become independent artistic objects, walkable sculptures, and hence "landmarks" of an entire region.

At this point, at the latest, it becomes apparent that the architectural element of the stair can transcend the purely functional role of access, and can stand in a dialogue of art – architecture – metaphysics. The stair has the function of connection, it is an "object" to be detailed independently as well as a spatial body, though it also serves as a place of longing to reach the light or a higher level (figs. 4, 6).

Linguistically, you 'step up the game' and climb a 'career ladder'; in popular music, titles such as "Stairway to Heaven" characterise these age-old yearnings.

Jacob's ladder

In various cultural circles, Jacob's ladders have a long tradition, especially shaped by faith. In spite of the different religious backgrounds, they are, however, employed in basically similar ways. In doing so, they usually represent the orientation towards the divine on account of their elongated and rising linearity. For this reason, these orchestrated step formations often terminate in a place special to faith, which is usually consecrated, or in the "embodiment of the divine", the sky. In addition, in many cases, the physical effort expended when walking up these flights of steps is also meant to express a gesture of humility and cleansing by the climber.

4

5

The step pyramids of the Maya
The pyramids of the Maya are stepped multiple times and contain a temple space inside. With the pyramids, the Maya celebrated their affinity to the gods. The forecourt was used for ceremonies and games. In the design of the Maya pyramids, the impact of the stair as the measure of all things in space, as mentioned at the beginning, is also recognisable (fig. 5). There is much speculation about the number of steps and the ratio of the rise to the stair run; frequent interpretations see a calendrical relationship to the proportions of the stair. This shows the mathematical calculation basis of a stair since the demonstrable objective is, in particular, to generate harmony between the number of steps and the gradient, having both a structural as well as an aesthetic effect.

Jacob's ladders in the Asian region
The sacred mountains in China are one of the main constituents of the religious tradition of Taoism and Buddhism: the mountain is a basic cosmic element, and represents the connection between heaven and earth, which is also shown by the trigram in "The Book of Changes" [1]. The Chinese term for pilgrimage, "cháobài shèngshān", literally means "to pay one's respects to a sacred mountain". The ascent thus is a conscious religious act, with the stair, in this sense, embodying a human being's approach to the heavenly. Some of these sacred mountains can even only be climbed by steep ladders or stairs (fig. 7), emphasising the distance between the earthly and the divine.
In Buddhism, on the other hand, the stair represents the threshold of a boundary, to be passed over consciously, between the

6

real and the divine world. This makes it an important symbolic part of "o-mairi" ("going to the shrine or visiting the temple"). All parts of a shrine complex are ritual. The stairs, like the gates, serve to mark this threshold (fig. 8).

The sacred stair – Jacob's ladder in the Christian tradition
Jacob's ladder is the origin of the metaphysical stair in the Christian world. It is the symbol for the ascent and descent between Earth and the heavens. The Old Testament, in the Book of Genesis, chapter 28, narrates the story of Jacob who, during his escape from his brother Esau, on the way to Haran, sees a ladder in his dream, which stands on the Earth and reaches to the heavens, and on which God's angels ascend and descend. At the very top, he sees God the Lord himself standing there, who introduces himself as God of Abraham and Isaac, promising him land and offspring. Even though the image of the ladder prevails in the occidental pictorial tradition, the Hebrew word "sullām" can also be translated as stair, steps or ramp, thus providing diverse interpretations of the term Jacob's ladder. The pictorial imagination underlying the biblical story is probably based on the temple stair of an ancient Near Eastern ziggurat, which leads up from the Earth to the holy of holies [2] (fig. 9).

Numerous Jacob's ladders can be found in sacred buildings, where the biblical text was realised as built form. Due to its special importance, the Scala Regia must be mentioned here (fig. 10). It connects St. Peter's Basilica in Rome with the Raphael Rooms and the Sistine Chapel. Built in the 16th century by Antonio da Sangallo the Younger, it was rebuilt by Gian Lorenzo Bernini in 1663–1666.

7

8a

a Gate (torii)
b Stone stair (kaidan)
c Path to the main shrine (sandō)
d Water basin for washing the hands and mouth (chōzuya or temizusha)
e Lanterns (tōrō)
f Stage for Kagura performances (kagura-den)
g Administration office (shamusho)
h Prayer plaques (ema)
i Auxiliary shrine (setsumatsusha sessha / massha)
j Lion-dogs (komainu)
k Hall of worship (haiden)
l Fence / enclosure of the shrine (tamagaki)
m Main shrine (honden)

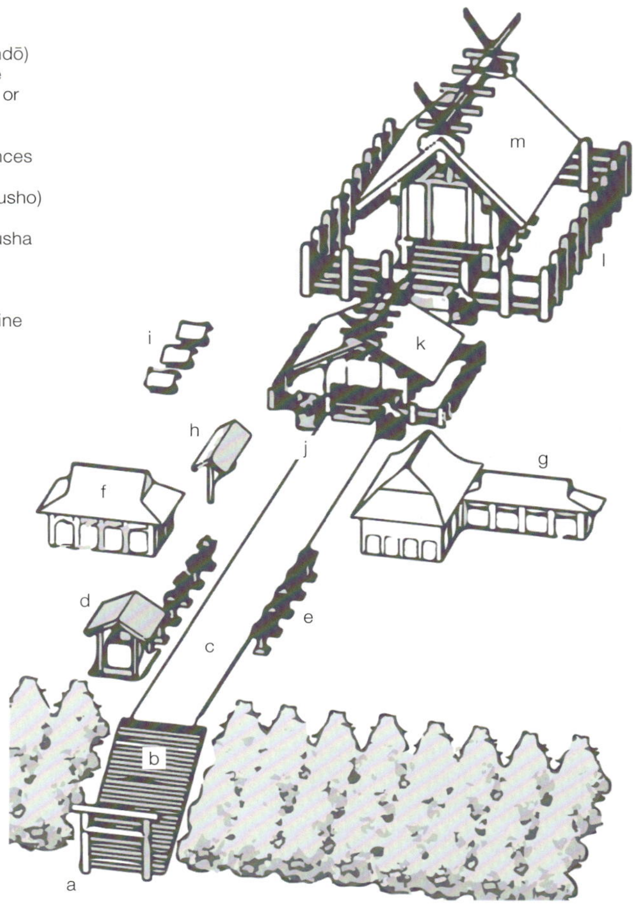

8b

7 Hua Shan – Sacred mountain, Shaanxi (CN)
8 The stair in Buddhism
a Engaku-Ji Temple, Kita-Kamakura (JP) 1282
b Exemplary structure of a Shinto shrine complex
9 Jacob sees Jacob's ladder in a dream, woodcut by Julius Schnorr von Carolsfeld (1860), Berlin, Sammlung Archiv für Kunst und Geschichte
10 Historical photo of the Scala Regia, Rome (IT) 1663–1666, Gian Lorenzo Bernini

9

Bernini had the stair taper down towards the rear, in order to optically elongate the space. This topic of the manipulation of spatial perception repeatedly appears in the Christian-religious context of the Vatican: the trapezoidal complex of St. Peter's Square, with its fourfold row of columns in the colonnade (1656–1667) by Bernini, likewise emphasises the funnel-shaped effect of the square towards St. Peter's Basilica.

Another outstanding example of implementing the biblical template are the Holy Stairs (Scala Sancta) by the master builder Domenico Fontana, which are also located in Rome. They lead up to the Sancta Sanctorum chapel on the site of the Lateran, and supposedly come from the palace of Pontius Pilate. Jesus is said to have set foot on them in the trial prior to his crucifixion. According to tradition, they were brought from Jerusalem to Rome by Constantine's mother, St. Helena, in 326. In remembrance of the sufferings of Christ, the stair is only supposed to be stepped on in a kneeling posture. Wooden cladding has protected the marble steps from wear and tear since 1723. In order to obtain an indulgence, pilgrims must ascend the steps on their knees saying the Lord's Prayer on each step [3].

The symbolism of historical stairs
In summary, it can be said that these historical stairs were especially applied symbolically in order to consciously address the distance between two levels, and hence create an atmosphere of distance, deference and power. At the same time, a stair stands for the connection of two levels, which is accompanied by the desire to overcome a "threshold". The spatial impact of these hierarchy-generating stairs is underpinned by compositional tricks, such as the already mentioned enhanced taper, as well as a "false" perspective, which is created by a sequence of vertical elements such as columns. Likewise, the gradient (i.e. step height) is often exaggerated, so that one has to make a physically demanding and conscious effort to negotiate them. As in Rome, the already mentioned pyramids of the Maya elevated the deities, not only in an imaginary sense, by means of an extremely steep stair with a large step height.

Contemporary Jacob's ladders
Though our age is largely secularised, Jacob's ladders continue to be employed for special building tasks. Steven Holl very deliberately uses this motif for the stair extension of the Department of Philosophy at New York University: the light breaks spectrally and through perforated handrails, which adds a metaphysical layer to the space and epitomises the constructional philosophy. The stair winds up in a marginally offset manner, so that a positional change always brings about an interesting change of perspective. In doing so, in a generic sense, the different positions in philosophy are metaphorically implemented (fig. 11).

10

12

11

Continuity and orientation towards the light are the outstanding features of Jacob's ladders in a contemporary context, too. In the residential building by Hiroyuki Arima (fig. 12), a continuous stair runs through the entire building. Alongside the living, dining and sleeping area, it refers to the outside – and even to the sky – on account of its large openings. The stair itself is a white, monolithic body which terminates exactly at the ceiling level, followed by a few glass steps, which provide access to the music pavilion located on the roof of the building. As such, a clear distinction is made between the white space and the glazed sky, i.e. between the earth-linked (living) and the dematerialised (music).

In the residential building in Estrela by Aires Mateus, the stair spans the space in a linear fashion, thus referring to the two longitudinal facades in order to draw on the light there. In doing so, the space to be accessed takes a back seat, the moment of suspense lies in the movement from bottom to top. The light of the opposite facade openings directs users aloft (fig. 13).
In the building in Fontinha, also by Mateus, light is also the elementary design medium. The stair is flooded with light in such a manner that it has the effect of being a logical consequence of the spatial thoroughfare. The stair and its associated space seem as if they have been extracted from the overall volume, creating an exceedingly suspenseful spatial impression (fig. 14).

The stair as Jacob's ladder illustrates the relationship of the stair to space particularly well: the play between the stair as positive (being an additive) spatial element, and the hence negative stairwell, can inspire in design. Similar to the designs by Aires Mateus, which are

11 "Jacob's ladder" at the Department of Philosophy at New York University (NYU), New York (US) 2007, Steven Holl Architects
12 "Jacob's ladder", residential building, Dazaifu (JP) 1995, Hiroyuki Arima
13 Residential building, Estrela (PT) 2016, Aires Mateus
a Section, scale 1:400
b Stair in its spatial context
14 Residential building, Fontinha (PT) 2013, Aires Mateus
a Section, scale 1:400
b Stair in its spatial context
15 Stone house, Brione (CH) 2005, Wespi/de Meuron
a Section, scale 1:400
b Lighting via the skylight
16 Haus mit einer Wand [House with one wall], Zurich (CH) 2007, Christian Kerez
a Floor plans (ground floor and upper floor), scale 1:400
b Hierarchy in space

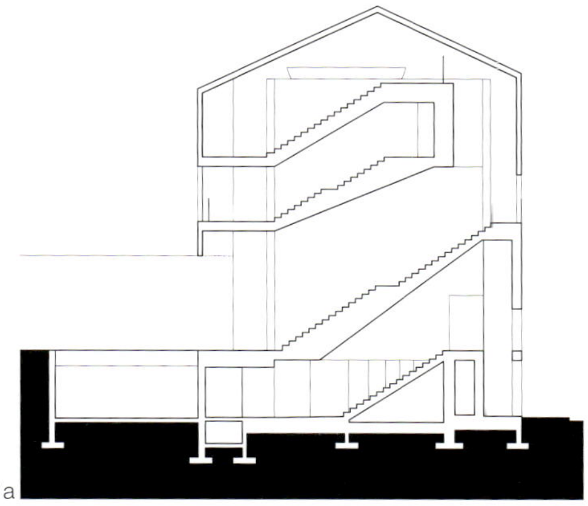
13 a

b

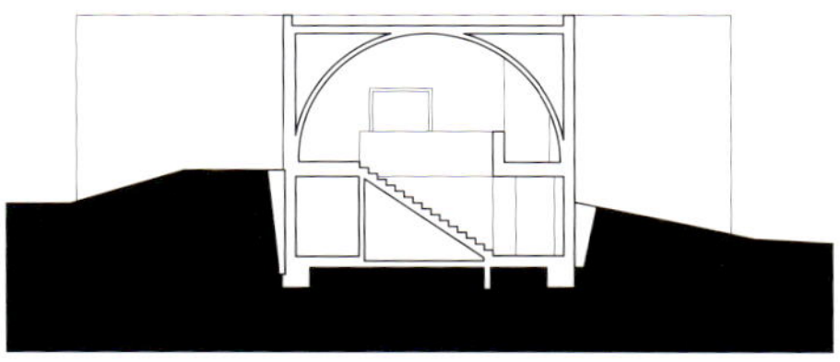
14 a

b

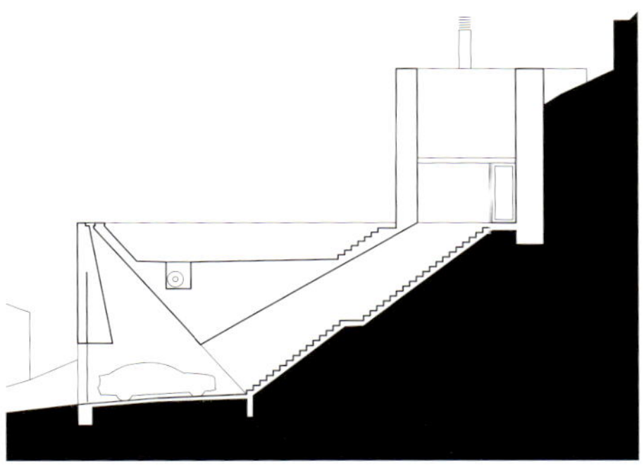
15 a

b

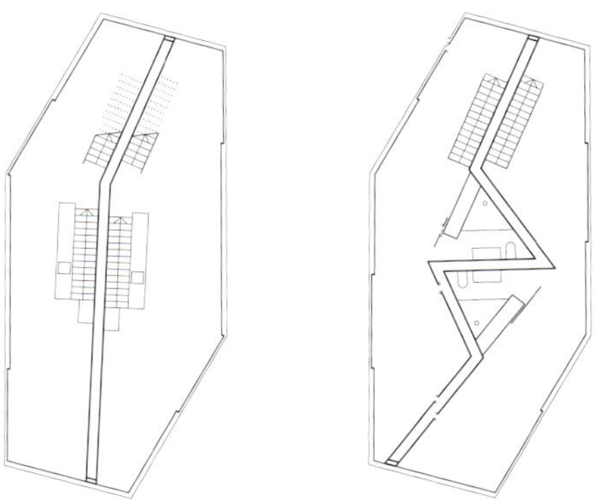
16 a

b

determined by the sectional figure, an impressive, funnel-shaped space is created in the stone house in Brione by Wespi de Meuron, which is, above all, defined by the form and the culmination towards the skylight (fig. 15). The stair and the building are so archaic in their materials that the space seems as if it is hewn in stone.

The stair in the "House with one wall" by Christian Kerez belongs to the category of Jacob's ladders since it runs through the entire house in a cascade, and "organises" the house together with the wall that gives its name to the building. The stair dominates the otherwise loft-like free space. However, it is so closely linked to the wall that one cannot speak of an independent quality and hence classification as a sculpture (fig. 16). In fact, however, the stair, here forms an important guide and spatial ordering principle, leading straight to the light.

The stair as Jacob's ladder thus demonstrates continuity and an upwards orientation, often also towards a band of light or skylight. In the residential building by Buchner Bründler Architekten, the stair is already recognisable in the outer volume (fig. 17 a). Its orientation towards the light is enhanced by the curvature of the space at the upper pedestal (fig. 17); due to this, the light seems celestial and mysterious and the stair itself captivates on account of its graceful soberness (fig. 18 b).

Sculpture
Stairs can be categorised as sculpture when they exhibit strong individuality with regard to their form, materials, construction and conception, i.e. when they stand in clearly perceivable contrast to the rest of the spatial concept. In doing so, the stair seems like a single body, without,

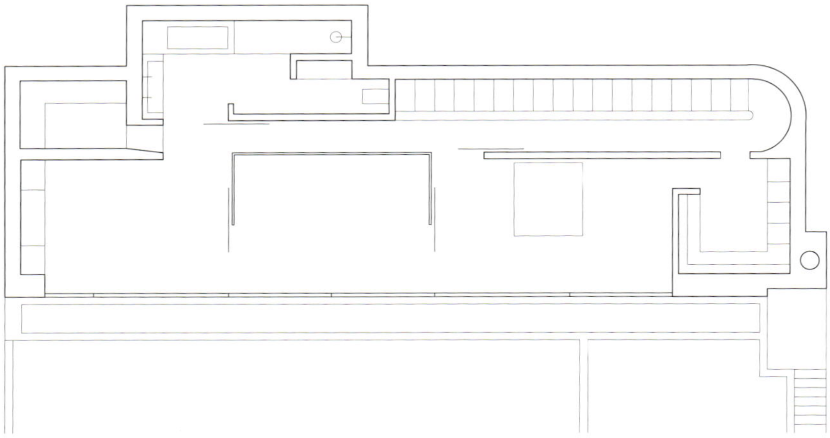

17

however, dividing the space (see "Volume vs Continuity", p. 34ff.).

The staging of power
Historically, the category of sculpture can be traced back to the development of the stair in secular buildings, which is closely linked to the continuation of the simple stair to the metaphysically charged Jacob's ladder in sacred buildings. In place of the deities, there are now, however, omnipotent rulers. They use the stair to demonstrate power and status, and for this purpose, implement pompous and sweeping stairs in their residences. Opulent and magnificent stairs require a large amount of free space in order to be effective and to unfold. As such, due to their wasteful handling of resources, these sculptural step compositions are primarily reserved for wealthy clients. They serve to orchestrate the spectacle, with the journey simultaneously representing the destination. These approaches are implemented in an almost ideal-typical manner in the stairs of the baroque period.

Stairs of the baroque period
In contrast to the spiral stairs of medieval castles and the more elaborate but spatially still restricted stairs of Renaissance palaces, stairwells in the baroque period were increasingly designed as ostentatious reception rooms. The Residence in Würzburg, with its stairwell, can be seen as the architectural culmination of this development (fig. 3, p. 49). The court architect Balthasar Neumann placed a three-flight stair with an ambulatory underneath an impressive vaulted ceiling decorated with a huge fresco from 1752/53, painted by the Venetian Giovanni Battista Tiepolo. Owing to the spatial geometry, and in connection with the painted ceiling, the impression of an endless expanse is created, which clearly reveals a connection with the characteristics of the sacred Jacob's ladders. For Balthasar Neumann, the model for the conception of the stair at the Residence in Würzburg was Schloss Weißenstein in Pommersfelden, which was built by Johann Dientzenhofer as a private summer residence for the Prince-Bishop of Bamberg and Elector of Mainz, between 1711 and 1718. The stairwell is decorated with a ceiling fresco by Johann Rudolf Byss. As in the Residence in Würzburg, the stairs are characterised by a succession of step sequences, while both stairs are not located directly at the facade, but are separated from the window openings by an ambulatory. In Pommersfelden, the ambulatory takes the form of a loggia gallery, while in Würzburg, it is – together

18a

b

17 Floor plan, scale 1:200, Residential building Chienbergreben, Gelterkinden (CH) 2012, Buchner Bründler Architekten
18 Residential building Chienbergreben
a Exterior view
b Interior
19 Interior view of the stair of the Palazzo De Sinno, Naples (IT) 18th century, Fernando Sanfelice
20 Palazzo Sanfelice, Naples (IT) 18th century, Fernando Sanfelice
a Four-flight stair
b Twin spiral stair

19

a

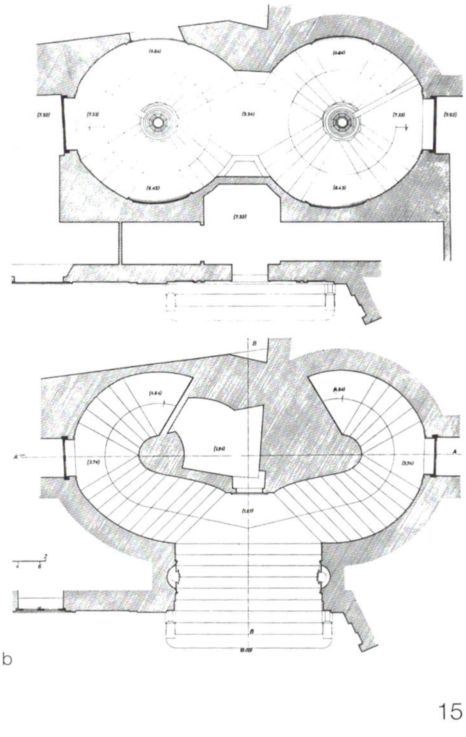
20b

with the stair – part of a gigantic hall [4]. While the two above-mentioned examples are housed inside, in specially designed stairwells, the stairs of many baroque Neapolitan palazzi, by contrast, mark the transition between indoor and outdoor areas. Due to a dense road network in Naples, building development took the form of rising blocks and contracting courtyards, where stairwells, with arches open to the outer side, were arranged in the form of courtyard loggias. These take on an important role for communication and exchange within the urban society, while they are also popular among the citizen class, and not just reserved for absolute rulers. In a comparatively confined space, spatially complex formations such as reciprocally running, interlocking, and multi-flight stairs were built. The wealth of forms of these structures is impressively comprehensive.

As an example, the works of Fernando Sanfelice (1675–1748) are to be mentioned here. He initially trained as a painter and then worked as an architect. He designed the stair of the Palazzo De Sinno in the Via Roma (fig. 19) whose stairwell lies at the end of a narrow courtyard and is hardly visible from the outside. Inside, however, a fascinating vertical path develops, which is marked by two dramatically alternating flights of stairs, the relationship between the stairs, but also by its suspenseful connection to the outside. Sanfelice's main work, however, is considered to be the two stairs in his own residence. One of them consists of two four-flight stairs that move inversely to each other and take up the entire wing of a palace block (fig. 20 a). Spatially almost even more exciting, however, is the concealed and more modest-looking stair in the flanking part of the palace. It is accessed via a single-flight curtail step, which transitions into the shape of a twin circular stair (fig. 20 b). Due to the sequence of darker, tunnel-like sections and lighter, open-top parts, users experience a diversified and impressive walk through the building [5].

The stair halls of the 19th century

In the course of the 19th century, functional aspects again assumed greater importance, alongside the task of representation in the planning of stairs. In the large-format stairs of theatre buildings which were constructed in this period, such as at the Paris Opera, designed by Charles Garnier (fig. 21, p. 16), the exemplary focus was on the practical question of how a large number of visitors could be guided through the building in a short time. There were, moreover, deliberations on how individual building parts could be logically linked with each other through the positioning of a stair. In spite of the functional aspects, the representative and festive character of the implemented stairs was not neglected. This is demonstrated by the sculptural form of the stair in Paris, but also by the attention to the design of the numerous decorative elements in the area of the flight of stairs and the balustrade elements.

The sculptural stair in a contemporary context

In spite of limited resources, sculpturally formed stairs continue to be of great importance today, even if their formulation nowadays usually turns out to be less opulent. For this reason, too, it is no longer the volume alone which is paramount in this category as is, for example, the case with Stefan Giers' walkable stair sculpture in the Lusatian lakeland (fig. 22, p.17). In contrast to the "sculptural" stairs described above, it does not fulfill an access function in the sense of connecting or reaching other levels or spaces, but exclusively serves an

21

21 Stair of the Palais Garnier opera house, Paris (FR) 1862–1874, Charles Garnier
22 Stair sculpture Landmarke Lausitzer Seenlandschaft [Landmark Lusatian Lake District], Senftenberg (DE) 2008, Stefan Giers
23 Interior stair XXS House, Ljubljana (SI) 2004, dekleva gregorič arhitekti
24 IKMZ information, communication, and media centre of the BTU Cottbus (DE) 2003, Herzog & de Meuron
25 Mumuth musical theatre, Graz (AT) 2009, UN Studio
26 Use of traditional materials in digital design, detail of stair, opera house, Harbin (CN) 2015, MAD Architects
27 Design Collective furniture shop, Qingpu (CN) 2012, Neri & Hu

(artistic) end in itself: towards Sedlitz Lake, its imposing building structure with its closed surfaces appears as a simple stele; towards the land side, on the other hand, it opens up and shows its sculptural flights of stairs.

Dekleva gregorič arhitekti demonstrate in the XXS House in Ljubljana that a complex yet at the same time extremely delicate construction can be effective as a sculpture, too (fig. 23). In the 43 m^2 holiday home in the centre of Ljubljana, the building dimensions were predetermined by an existing building. Nevertheless, all residential functions for two persons were to be integrated. The materials orient themselves in character towards the traditional house next door, which is distinguished by rough, unadulterated surfaces. For this reason, concrete, terrazzo, plywood, iron and felt dominate the interiors. The stair does not require special material elevation, it takes up little space and seems almost like a ladder. In spite of the spatial limitation, however, it manages to appear free and sculptural, thus making the space appear surprisingly large.

As defined at the outset, the stairs in the category of "sculpture" are usually independent volumes. As a result, the boundary to the artistic object is fluid. In doing so, the sculptural stair has to act as a strong element; correspondingly, all constituent parts are subordinated to this idea: the "handrail" is usually a closed wall; the construction of the steps and wall connection is invisible, while the structure is not recognisable from the outside.

The stair usually has the effect of a total work of art, with the result that the individual parts often strongly recede into the background. Frequently, the orchestration of stairs in space requires artisanal skills in order to realise the desired appearance in the first place. In the Museum Küppersmühle in Duisburg, by Herzog & de Meuron, the stair is housed in a self-contained stairwell, similar to the baroque constructions described above, in order to be free from constraints and dependencies. Only then can it have the envisaged impact: on account of the sculptural appearance of the stair, it now blends into the sequence of exhibition rooms of the converted old building almost like an exhibition object (fig. 38, p. 107).

In the buildings of Herzog & de Meuron, such as the Laban Dance Centre in London, or the library at BTU Cottbus, the stair often plays a significant role, and is accordingly worked out, often by sculptural craftsmanship. In doing so, the stairs of the library, in particular, are interesting since the interior presents itself as highly complex due to the curving facade. Here, vertical air spaces and colourfully designed bookshelf zones create a sense of order. Solid cores, but especially also the freely winding spiral stairs, connect all floors with each other. These areas are highly remarkable, both in colour-related and formal terms, and have a distinct signalling effect (fig. 24).

Likewise striking in its colour scheme is the stair in the Mumuth Musiktheater in Graz. Here, the "black box" of the theatre is combined with a series of public movement spaces (foyer and access spaces). With a view to emphasising the movement flow taking place here, the design of the stair follows the fluid moment and, owing to its winding shape, develops along the upper floors in a downright dramatic fashion. At the same time, visitors can also orient themselves by the bright red colour (fig. 25), and are guided to the

22

23

24

rehearsal rooms and the music hall. Ben van Berkel describes the new building as "a classical relationship between music and architecture – classical but with a twist" [6].

The works of MAD Architects are representative of an entire generation of young architects, for whom digital media are not only implementation tools but can also be applied in design generation. At the same time, the dedication to detailing and artisanal development is extraordinary, such as in the stair in the opera house of the northern Chinese city of Harbin, displaying high appreciation of traditional materials and construction techniques, in spite of a "modern" design vocabulary (fig. 26). This shows once again how digital tools make it possible to rethink traditional materials: the sculpture in the opera house in Harbin gives cause to pause, raises questions and generates new viewing habits. It can thus bring about a conscious involvement with the space and the viewer – just as every artistic work would claim to do.

In programmatic terms, the sculpture-stair occurs especially frequently – though not exclusively – in cultural institutions. Here, the stair creates a setting. One example for the application of this category in other areas is the store designed by Neri & Hu for the avant-garde furniture shop Design Collective in a suburb of Shanghai. The building is accessed by a steel funnel, symbolising the transition from the urban space to the exhibition space. This stair, too, seems like a part of the exhibition since its colour scheme, materials and form strongly contrast with the white interior (fig. 27). The stair creates an extremely suspenseful space: the gaze is directed upwards or downwards, and due to this changed viewpoint, new perspectives are experienced. Such a dramatic "sculpture" attracts and almost automatically arouses curiosity. Who and, above all, what is up there?

The examples show how stairs can free themselves from the supposed spatial, formal or organisational constraints of the building. Their colour scheme, form and materials, as well as their construction, can be independent of the building structure as a whole. In this way, such stairs usually seem highly autonomous or "self-confident". Though they developed from the tradition of the metaphysical Jacob's ladder, this type of sculpture departs from the sacred to refer only to itself. In doing so, however, the sculpture does not have to seem like a foreign body in space. The stair as sculpture is in itself already a total work of art, thus emancipating itself almost automatically from the rest of the spatial occurrences.

Notes

[1] I Ching: The Book of Changes, translation by Richard Wilhelm. Düsseldorf 1999
[2] https://de.wikipedia.org/wiki/Jakobsleiter_(Bibel), as on 02.05.2017
[3] https://de.wikipedia.org/wiki/Heilige_Stiege, as on 05.05.2017
[4] Mielke, Friedrich: Handbuch der Treppenkunde. Hanover 1993, p. 64
[5] Daidalos, No. 9 Treppen, September 1983
[6] www.baunetz.de/meldungen/Meldungen-Musiktheater_in_Graz_von_UN_Studio_fertig_742494.html, as on 05.05.2017

25

26

27

Stage and Landscape

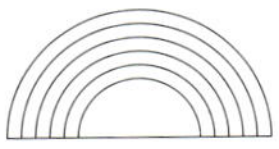

1 Culture for the bourgeoisie, Altes Museum, Berlin (DE) 1825–30, Karl Friedrich Schinkel
2 The stair as a stage in "Die Verachtung – Le Mépris", Jean-Luc Godard, STUDIOCANAL / COMPAGNIA 1963
3 A "stairwell" inspired by M.C. Escher in "Die Reise ins Labyrinth", Jim Henson, TriStar Pictures 1986
4 The dizziness is symbolised by the stair in "Vertigo", Alfred Hitchcock, Paramount Pictures 1958

1

2

Similar to the conceptual pair of the Jacob's ladder and sculpture, the categories of the stage and landscape exhibit a large number of commonalities. They are mostly used to describe stairs which serve to orchestrate daily life in exterior but also interior spaces. In doing so, the social and spatial interaction always plays a major role. While in the stairs in the category of the stage, the focus is on the entry and exit of users, those in the category of landscape focus on addressing, further developing or newly defining existing topographies into space-determining atmospheres.

The stair as a stage

Historically, divine and feudal representation still played a major role in the case of Jacob's ladder and sculpture, while the category of the stage stood for the democratisation of the stair in public space, since with the demise of the Ancien Régime, the opulently formed stair also became a real, accessible place for ordinary citizens.
One example is Karl Friedrich Schinkel's Altes Museum in Berlin. When the notion of cultural education of broad sections of society in the sense of Humboldt's educational ideal gained currency, the Prussian king Frederick William III implemented a series of new buildings, which were intended to lift the feudal boundaries of the institutions in favour of a public offering. The classicist outside stair emphasises the opening of the educational institutions for a comprehensive group of people, and thus forms a stage for the invigorated bourgeoisie (fig. 1). In the Altes Museum, the opening of the facade, and the relationship of the stairwell to the outside space, ensures continuation of this new bourgeois life, thus leading to the construction of a publicly accessible space where cultural exchange with a view towards the urban landscape can take place. Schinkel consciously quoted elements of the architecture of ancient Greece which – owing to the agora, in particular – symbolised the life of an enlightened society.

The orchestrated stair

The broad spectrum of the stair's design potential as a stage can be analysed by considering films and stage works, as stairs often display an elevated image of reality here, due to their dramaturgic application. When comparing the two media, film in particular represents an interesting object of study since it fulfils the expectations of broad sections of society, on account of its usually more realistic and less abstract quality, thus more closely corresponding to the basic understanding of the stair as a stage for all.
Whether it is Scarlett O'Hara in "Gone with the Wind" (1939), who glides towards Rhett Buttler, or Brigitte Bardot, who strides down the stair of the Casa Malaparte, made famous by Jean-Luc Godard's "Contempt" (1963) (fig. 2), the stair symbolically continues to have an impact as a stage for the original link between two contrary poles. In both films, the drama dominates the power of love. In doing so, the stair emphasises the ups and downs in the relationships between the protagonists (Scarlett vs. Rhett and Ashley, or Camille vs. Paul and Jeremy), while the growing independence of women also finds a symbolic analogy.
Apart from being a symbol for the ambivalence of human relationships, the stair in film not only finds application as a metaphor for pursued, or already achieved, social advancement, but also as a motif in thrillers or horror films. It is employed as a mystical element, as in Jim Henson's fantasy film "Labyrinth"

(1986), where David Bowie, as a goblin king, makes trouble on a stair, which is similar to a construction by M. C. Escher (fig. 3), or in the film version of Umberto Eco's "The Name of the Rose", where the stair resembles a claustrophobic labyrinth. In Alfred Hitchcock's thriller "Vertigo" (1958), the fear of heights is already eponymous. The tower stair dramatically illustrates the associated panic (fig. 4).

What all film stairs have in common is that they make a strong contextual reference to their surroundings and the story to be told. This reference is always subtly put in the spotlight to avoid deviating from the actual story. Moreover, the stairs usually have oversized widths and lengths, in order to be effective as stages. Skilful light guidance and choice of perspective additionally charge the scenery in a dramaturgical manner.

The stair as a stage for social interaction
The motif of orchestration also takes effect in many interior spaces of actually existing buildings. The stair becomes a stage for social interaction, such as in the Apollo schools by Herman Hertzberger (fig. 5, p. 20). With his building from the late 1970s, the architect demonstrated the implementation of a new understanding of education. The school was not to be a disciplinary custodial and educational institution anymore, but was to accompany pupils on the path to becoming mature, self-critical and political human beings. Not only the curricula were reformed, but also the school buildings: many concepts for "freer" schools, with open, interactive and integrative spaces were created. In the Apollo schools in Amsterdam, this free exchange takes place in the stairwell. This is not a closed-off space, but rather a spacious atrium, which is viewable from several levels, and where gatherings take place.

3

4

5

6

Benches are integrated into the fall protection, while concrete balustrades alternate with wooden elements, inviting users to lean on or against them. The stair is bipartite: a narrow, briskly walkable stair with an appropriate tread line, on the one hand, and a podium stair, which leaves out every other step, and instead offers greater depth for sitting. The agora as a place of assembly, which Schinkel had already brought into the museum, established itself in school and administration buildings.

The stair by Diller Scofidio + Renfro/FXFOWLE in the renowned Juilliard School, the music conservatory and drama school in New York City, likewise corresponds to this understanding of education and space. It is a meeting place, but also a place to linger, enabling – more or less casually – important exchange among the musicians and actors. In order to spatially support the stage character of the stair, the balustrades have a wall-like form, and connect the lower with the upper floor in a spatially dynamic trapezoidal shape. Together with the steps, they form a colour contrast to the surrounding space (fig. 6).

As in the Villa Malaparte, Vector Architects, in their "Seaside Chapel", draw attention to a special landscape context in an exceptional manner. The spectacular location on the beach is almost theatrically orchestrated through an unusual, formally elevated building and a large outside stair (fig. 7). The building stands as a logical continuation of the stair, which extends through the building and up to the terrace with its open view of the sea. Visitors to the chapel can stride up or down the stair, or simply use it as a seating surface. Indirectly incident light atmospherically charges the interior of the chapel.

5 Apollo schools, Amsterdam (NL) 1980–83, Herman Hertzberger
6 Spontaneous social meeting place, Alice Hall/Juilliard School, New York (US) 2009, Diller Scofidio + Renfro/FXFowle
7 A stage as is, Chapel in Qinhuangdao (CN) 2015, Vector Architects
8 The stair as a lounge. Showroom of the Siclo company, Mexico City (MX) 2015, Rojkind Arquitectos + Cadena y Asociados
9 Inhabited stair, orchestration of space, residential building, Tokyo (JP) 2008, Atelier Bow-Wow
10 The monolithic stair requires the user as orchestrator. Haus Fabrizzi, Conthey (CH) 2014, savioz fabrizzi architectes
11 The stair as a stage. Vals thermal bath (CH) 1996, Peter Zumthor

7

8

Apart from the stated public buildings, the stage-like "event stair" as a place of social exchange, is also found in numerous offices, shops and concepts for catering. Here, the desire for an urban meeting place merges with a clever economic concept (fig. 8).

A stage on a small scale can be found in the residential project Machiya by Atelier Bow-Wow. Here, the stair is an internal meeting place for the residents, and thus extends the confined living area of a former teahouse. Objects can be put down or consciously placed on the steps; moreover, the stair offers inviting seating options, and in this way – alongside the connection it provides between two levels – simultaneously also functions as space-saving furniture (fig. 9).

In the residential building by savioz fabrizzi architectes, the monolithic-sculptural formulation of the stair can likewise be associated with a stage. It separates the more intimate sleeping areas from the collectively used living hall. Walking down and walking up from one area to another can be appealingly observed from the cooking, dining and living area, linked by split levels (fig. 10).

The Swiss architect Peter Zumthor, in the thermal bath at Vals, created a continuous transition from the inside to the outside by the consistent and almost exclusive use of one material: local Vals gneiss. The shallow steps, leading from the access and changing room level to the thermal landscape, seem as if hewn from a mountain. The long treads create the illusion of a landscape, so that entering the thermal bath feels almost like stepping onto a stage set. Bathing is staged as a sensual pleasure (fig. 11).

What all these stage stairs have in common is that the surrounding space has to very openly orient itself towards these stairs. The stair is visible in full view, and usually lies along a wall, while the space orients itself in this direction. At the same time, in construction terms, it can be observed that the stairs, with their homogenous materials, hold back very deliberately, as in films, in order to leave the entire attention to the user, or to highlight the (supposed) simplicity of the building. It is only through the user that the spaces are orchestrated; otherwise, they remain in an abstract, sober condition, almost as an "objet d'art".

The outside stair as a stage
The motif of the stair as a stage also appears in outdoor space, especially in outside stairs, such as the Spanish Steps by Francesco De Sanctis in Rome. Though they primarily serve as a link between the Piazza di Spagna and the church of Santa Trinità dei Monti, they offer tremendous qualities for lingering, and thus are an important part of urban life: the urban (open) space becomes a "place to be" and a "place to meet". This is further suggested by the orchestration of this stair in numerous films, such as "La Dolce Vita" by Federico Fellini (1960), "The Talented Mr. Ripley" (1999), right up to "To Rome with Love" (2012) by Woody Allen. As regards urban development, the connection of the two visual axes is an aesthetic challenge here, which De Sanctis overcame with a central stair and two parallel sideward flights of stairs. As a symbol of the Holy Trinity (Trinità), the stairs merge and part three times before reaching the church.

However, it is not only stairs in urban squares which are highly popular, but also those by the water. While paying homage to nature, i.e. the view of the

9

10

11

12

13

water and, where applicable, of the surrounding (urban) landscape, as well as the view of an attractive panorama on the other side of a river, as in Basel, Cologne or Dresden, for example (fig. 12), the open space extension of the city is, however, just as important, as is the formulation of a platform for the urban bustle. Moreover, these gradations extending towards the water fulfil functional aspects and serve, for example, as a protective measure against flooding.

Thanks to their features, all these facilities often evoke ancient amphitheatres, which were actually the first stairs planned for open spaces with an added value for the user or the audience. Many of these buildings, such as the amphitheatres in Taormina or Delphi, are picturesquely situated in the landscape, offering both a clean view of the theatre stage and an impressive vista of the surrounding landscape (fig. 13). In conclusion, it is precisely in this typological category that the boundaries are highly fluid: the amphitheatre shows how a landscape can turn into a stage and a stage into a landscape.

The stair as a landscape

The typology of the "stair as a landscape" doesn't refer to stairs which merely stand in a landscape. Rather, it is about the conception of the stair itself as landscape. This can, on the one hand, mean that the landscape is continued or highlighted, or that the landscape is artificially created by a stair in the first place. Reiulf Ramstad orchestrated a stair and visitor platform made of prepatinated steel in the fantastic fjord landscape of the Trollstigen Plateau in Norway, which may, however, be viewed more as a sculpture in an impressive

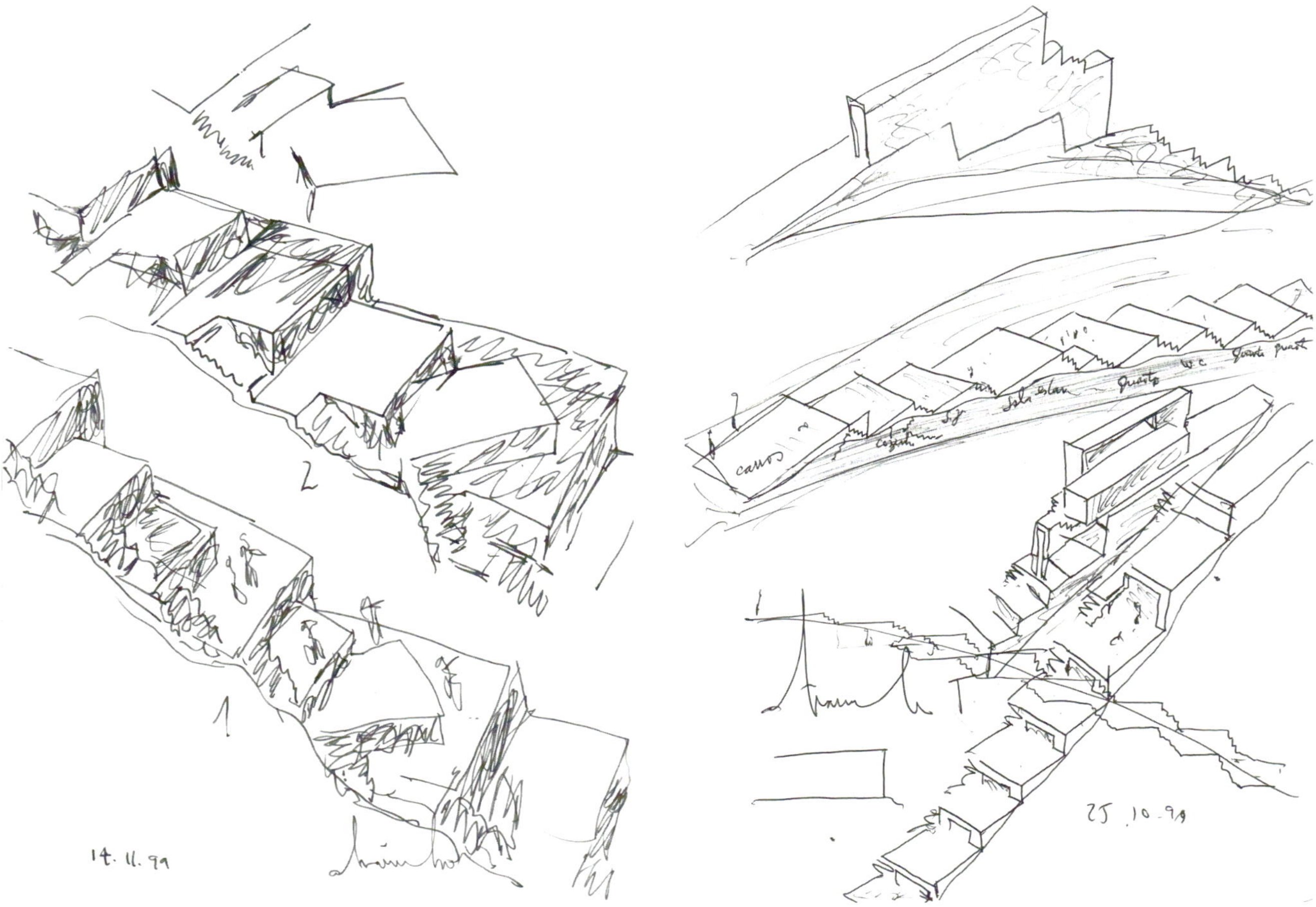

14

12 Evening mood in the extended public space in Cologne (DE)
13 Orchestrated landscape at the amphitheatre in Delphi (GR) 4th or 3rd century BC
14 Sketch illustrating the topographical design, Casa Tóló, Ribeira da Pena (PT) 2005, Álvaro Leite Siza Vieira
15 The stair "architecturalises" the slope. Casa Tóló
16 The stair merges with the landscape before the sea starts. International Passenger Terminal, Yokohama (JP) 2002, Foreign Office Architects (FOA)
17 The landscape floe turns into a public stage. Norwegian National Opera, Oslo (NO) 2007, Snøhetta

15

landscape setting (see "Jacob's ladder and Sculpture", p. 8ff.).

Orchestration of topography
The stair as landscape often takes up the surrounding topography as the main motif. With the Casa Tóló in Portugal, Álvaro Leite Siza designed a building which – in the shape of a stair – is integrated into the slope and merges with the topography (fig. 14). At the same time, the stair shapes the entire building, which almost completely recedes behind this built topography (fig. 15).

16

In the ferry terminal in Yokohama by Foreign Office Architects, by contrast, a topography is artificially formed by the building in the first place. With its stairs, the entire building appears like an extensive hilly landscape by the water, which one can wander through; gradients are transformed into step formations. To access the building, openings are embedded in the "landscape" through which users can dip into the interior of the structure (fig. 16).

In a similar manner, the opera house in Oslo by Snøhetta demonstrates that the stair – apart from connecting two or more levels – can also serve to overcome urban developmental or landscape-related level differences (fig. 17). Moreover, it illustrates that the design concept of what initially appears to be a very abstract idea of convoluted ice floes can successfully structure and shape the open area of the opera.

In the works of Carlo Scarpa, the network of relationships consisting of natural landscape, water and the artificially stepped stair likewise assumes an important role. He usually uses the stair to create a connection between the place and the overriding design concept. As such, the

17

18

19

20

21

bright marble stair in the Fondazione Olivetti metaphorically epitomises Venice's connection with the water: the steps float on the mosaic of the floor, shifting in a floe-like fashion, and finally piling up to the upper floor level (fig. 18). The glass mosaic of the floor follows a deliberate irregularity, thus creating the "effect of a moving surface [...], as if the floor was always flooded" [1].

The Dutch architecture firm OMA, with its extension of the site of the Illinois Institute of Technology in Chicago, originally created by Ludwig Mies van der Rohe, expresses the democratic and particularly North American ideal of an open campus which, similar to a marketplace, is intended to be a central meeting place for all students. Rem Koolhaas conceived the building as a city within a city, which differentiates itself – only by small differences in levels – into various, always publicly accessible areas, such as a canteen, a copy shop, a bookstore, social services, etc. Though the motif of the outside stair is a landscape planning element to begin with, it offers diverse visual axes and openings, resulting in relationships and points of contact otherwise known from an urban context (fig. 19). The stair supports the quality of stay and communication of students on account of the shallow gradient and elongated steps. The slowed pace of ascent takes up Heidegger's motif of a "philosophical walk". In the process, the physical activity supports the mental activity. The campus becomes a knowledge landscape with an "urban environment".

The Belgian architect Stéphane Beel takes up the idea of a connecting stair landscape within an urban network in his project for the M – Museum Leuven. With the extension comprising two new buildings, he not only combines the new with the old, but once again integrates the museum meaningfully into the urban context by creating several new approaches and public outdoor terraces. Moreover, Beel incorporates a pedestrian walkway through the museum and the garden, so that the site connects with the everyday life of the city. In doing so, the stairs are gentle mediators between the urban spaces and the museum spaces. The shallow gradient permits combination with a handicapped accessible ramp, making this extension of the city accessible for all residents (fig. 20).

Zaha Hadid also demonstrates in the Heydar Aliyev Cultural Center, how the stair can function as a continuation of the urban landscape. The building is shaped by softly curved forms. It takes up the natural difference in terrain level, and fluidly carries it forward inside. For this reason, the stair is a deliberately shallow threshold: instead of displaying a steep rise, the stair as landscape is also a mediator of content (fig. 21).

The buildings of Sou Fujimoto prove how the stair can be almost the sole space-defining element. His "Final Wooden House", for example, a square holiday home with an edge length of 4 m, consists of stacked cedar wood beams with identical cross sections. The building itself becomes a stair, and the stair is space and furniture, construction, landscape and a stage rolled into one (fig. 22).

Also constructed out of wood, the Hakusui nursery school in Sakura impressively shows how the exterior landscape can be continued inside as a play and recreation space for the children. Here, the elongated, shallow stair is not a stage, but offers spatial, educational and playful potential (fig. 23).

22

23

24

Reading landscapes

Similar to the "study stage" in the Apollo schools by Hertzberger, reading landscapes are also multifunctional stairs. On the one hand, they serve as a conventional stair, and on the other, offer additional space for seating surfaces, while also being observation posts and meeting places. Many of these stairs combine two different gradients and thus take up the motif of an auditorium. In contrast to a stage, however, the seating surface is not meant for an audience attending an event, for example, but provides room for a user's own activities – reading, in this case (fig. 24).

The library in Liyuan by Li Xiadong Atelier only comprises a stair and a shell. The dialogue between the stair, shaped into a reading landscape and the user creates a very special spatial atmosphere. The choice of natural materials for the facade, the cladding of the steel support structure and the stair itself, with its volumetric presence, evokes a pleasantly warm and inviting spatial impression (fig. 25). As such, the reading landscapes in particular reveal the diverse possibilities which stairs as a spatial element imply, and demonstrate the potential added value which they can provide.

18 The stair floats on the water in Venice. Fondazione Olivetti, Venice (IT) 1958, Carlo Scarpa
19 Campus - Landscape, IIT McCormick Tribune Campus Center, Chicago (US) 2003, OMA / Rem Koolhaas
20 Stair and ramp merge into an abstract work of art. Barrier-free access, "M Museum" Leuven (NL) 2009, Stéphane Beel
21 The stair becomes a landscape, the building becomes an urban landscape. Heydar Aliyev Center, Baku (AZ) 2012, Zaha Hadid Architects
22 House of wooden modules, stair as space, furniture, construction, landscape and stage, Kumamoto (JP) 2006, Sou Fujimoto
23 Stepped play landscape in the Sakura nursery, Sakura (JP) 2014, Yamazaki Kentaro Design Workshop
24 Library on the beach (Seashore Library), Qinhuangdao Shi (CN) 2015, Vector Architects
25 The stair as a multifunctional stage, reading landscape and structuring element. Liyuan Library, Huairou near Beijing (CN) 2011, Li Xiaodong's Atelier

25

Note

[1] Los, Sergio: Carlo Scarpa. Cologne 1994, p. 96

Aesthetics of technology vs Longing for the archetype

1 The stair dominates the space and upgrades the mundane use. Livraria Lello e Irmao, Porto (PT) 1906, Xavier Exteves
2 Floor plan of mezzanine, residential building Moller, Vienna (AT) 1927, Adolf Loos
3 The cool rationalism of Walter Gropius. Bauhaus Dessau (DE) 1926
4 Crown Hall IIT, Chicago, IL (US) 1956, Ludwig Mies van der Rohe

1

Technical developments steadily drove the evolution of the stair in the past. In doing so, novel construction methods also increasingly became the central design theme of stairs. The display of the aesthetics of technology had its heyday at the end of the 1990s, especially in the high-tech buildings of British architects such as Norman Foster or Richard Rogers. At the same time, a contrary movement set in, which once again strove for a rawer and more archaic expression. This was linked to the longing for easily comprehensible constructions – the longing for the archetype of the stair. This new approach clearly shows how a change of values in society can even be reflected in the design of stairs. When a society is in a positively optimistic mood, this is usually accompanied by a forward-looking, bold and progressive architectural language. In times of uncertainty, however, what has been historically handed down and proven assumes greater importance.

Aesthetics of technology

For centuries, it was the constructions and technical means that allowed the stair volumes to appear almost weightless which attracted particular interest. This endeavour was supported by new materials and production technologies with the onset of industrialisation. Highly delicate steel constructions shaped the stair architecture of the fin de siècle and the emerging Art Nouveau styles. In the Benelux countries and France in particular, this led to the development of a new space-impacting stair aesthetics.

Boldness versus pragmatism
The Livraria Lello e Irmao in Porto serves as a good example for the way in which a boldly constructed stair can dominate a design as a space-defining element, and as a feature which significantly shapes the atmosphere (fig. 1). With its detailed opulence and aesthetic diversity, the stair elevates the space. The construction is breathtaking, viewers marvel at its audacious structure. The red stair carpet additionally crowns the centrally placed element. As such, the bookstore doesn't seem like a mundane shop but fascinates as a "book palace".
Victor Horta, too, in the Hôtel Tassel in Bruges imbued the access space with special significance owing to the attention to detail of his curved flights of stairs (fig. 13, p. 51). In both historical examples, the stair thus is a means to upgrade the space and to shape it using ornamentation.

The audacity of the technical revolutions not only spurred on the designers, but accompanied the political mood from the First World War to the global economic crisis, and to the Second World War. With the need to focus on pragmatics in times of war and reconstruction, the degree of detailing in stairs also declined. This approach, however, was not seen as deficient, but was perceived as being part of a new aesthetic which highlighted the simplicity of craftsmanship. In this way, the interplay between light, space, form and colour took place in a concentrated manner, artistically reaching new dimensions.

In the works of Adolf Loos, stairs and landings, though largely unadorned and free of ornamentation, play a key role. They were fundamental prerequisites for his Raumplan [spatial plan]. In this architectural concept, Loos strove for both utmost rationality and elegant furnishings at the same time. The design principle involves constructing individual spaces at various heights depending on their significance, and arranging them on top of and next to each other

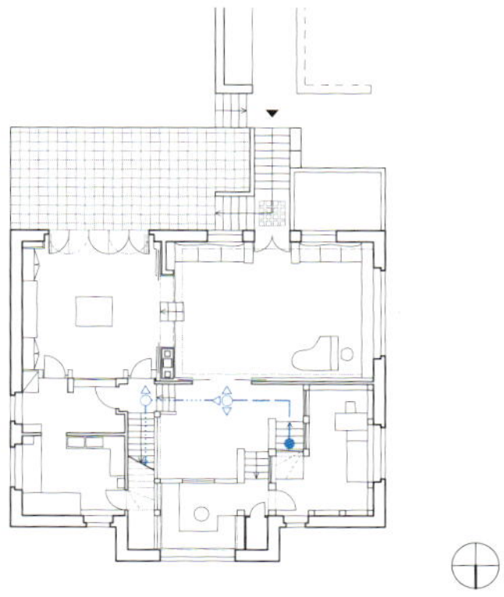

2

3

"in space". As such, he "composed" the spaces within the volume specified by the external walls and located around the central chimney axis. The resulting levels at different heights inevitably entail a variety of stairs, which define the space and rhythm (fig. 2).

The stairwells of the Bauhaus in Dessau and Weimar likewise impress on account of their meticulous composition and their technical aesthetic. Materials and colour, reduction of ornamentation, clear constructional details and generous spatial arrangements define the circulation areas here, which are used as assembly and meeting places for different disciplines (fig. 3). The social component elucidated by the Bauhaus philosophy, but also the design-related artistic level, likewise becomes clear, both in the paintings of Oskar Schlemmer and the photographs of Lux Feininger.

The finesse of floating
In line with the Bauhaus teaching and its discourse between craftsmanship and industrial series production, the pursuit of a technical aesthetic highlighting the construction is also discernible in the work of Ludwig Mies van der Rohe. In the case of Mies van der Rohe, however, the space is not anymore understood as a volume, as with Adolf Loos, but as a sequence of dissolved discs, layered vertically or horizontally, subtly delimiting the space. In doing so, Mies van der Rohe dissolved fixed spatial borders, thus freeing the tectonic structure. This effect also determines the design of the stairs. In the Crown Hall at the IIT in Chicago, his place of activity after the Bauhaus, the campus grounds are literally drawn into the building. In doing so, the stair serves as an almost indistinguishable link between the inside and the outside, where the individual steps are mounted in a very gentle and delicate manner in their appearance. Similar to Schinkel (fig. 1, p. 18), a spatial flow is set in motion here, owing to the technical possibilities of steel (fig. 4).

The stair as a means of transparency
In postmodernism, as with Art Nouveau, form and colour are once again applied more playfully. While drawing from classicism, one also takes the chance to experiment in the fields of space and material. New composite materials and adhesives as well as modern, sophisticated methods for glass production enrich the market and hence also the diversity of stair constructions. Due to the social desire for "transparency", glass as a material especially gains increasing importance. However, skilful application of non-transparent materials can also create permeability. The stair at the Institute of Molecular Genetics in

4

5 
6a 
b 

Prague, for example, appears dissolved in its constructional detailing even without the use of glass (fig. 5).

With rising growth and affluence, more and more companies are taking the chance to represent their entrepreneurial visions in structural form. However, this does not necessarily mean a return to ornamentation and décor, but rather results in a newly discovered audacity of form, appearance and construction. Companies continually adapt their market strategies. For example, Apple Stores demonstrate how a contemporary, innovative enterprise constantly reinvents itself with the aid of architecture and design. Made entirely out of glass, the stair at the Apple Store in Regent Street in London, with its constructional elegance and technical finesse, corresponds to the philosophy of the brand prevalent during the time of its creation (2004) (fig. 6a). In 2015, it was replaced by a closed stair made of natural materials with ergonomically formed wooden handrails. The showcasing of technical possibilities was replaced by current issues, such as ergonomics and sustainability (fig. 6b).

The stair minimised by technology
Technical innovations and the increasing acceptance of metal as a material also make possible new forms of stairs in residential areas. In Toru Murakami's residential building in Imabari, the load-bearing stringer of the steel stair visually recedes significantly to its central placement, thus considerably reducing the perceived thickness of the material. The intrinsically archaic material of the darker teakwood steps anticipates the residential use of the upper floors on account of the warm character of the wood, and with its filigree detailing, blends into the modern

7 

5 Transparent yet no glass, Institute for Molecular Genetics, Prague (CZ) 2008, Deyl-Šešták-architekti
6 Apple Store Regent Street, London (GB)
  a Old stair, 2004, Bohlin Cywinski Jackson
  b The new spirit in the Apple Store, 2016, Foster & Partners
7 The folded steel stair becomes an independent design feature. Residential building, Tokyo (JP) 2007, Claus en Kaan Architecten
8 Like an art object, the stair refers to the hitherto unused potential of the high spaces in the historical house. House C, Milan (IT) 2010, Francesco Librizzi studio
9 Restraint in a memorial. Memorial & Museum, Judenplatz Vienna (AT) 2000, Jabornegg & Palffy
10 Plastic as facade, stair and louvre, a new translucency. Plastic House, Tokyo (JP) 2002, Kengo Kuma & Associates

8

aesthetic of the house (fig. 33, p. 106). In the case of Claus en Kaan, the technical aestheticisation is explained by the desire for simplicity in appearance which in reality, however, possesses a high degree of constructional complexity. The apparent simplicity stands vis-à-vis elaborately produced construction details and complex manufacturing processes of the folded steel stair. Since the handrails are likewise exceedingly reduced and designed to be almost invisible, the architectural language presents itself entirely free from any decor. The link between the wall and the stair is negated in such a way that the stair merges into an almost artistic abstraction (fig. 7).

Many stairs in the category of "Aesthetics of technology" are defined by a sophisticated reduction of material thickness, combined with a complex treatment of architectural details in handrails, steps or landings. Due to the gentle handling of these details, these architectures are ideologically very close to the design vocabulary of Carlo Scarpa (fig. 18, p. 24).

Francesco Librizzi studio carried out an intervention in a historic town house in Milan from the year 1900, as Scarpa had similarly done in many of his buildings. The available area in the floor plan is small, while instead, the room height is imposing. The architects responded to this particularity in the spatial proportions with a minimal yet distinct intervention. The new stair emphasises the potential of the space, though it leaves it untouched in itself (fig. 8).

In fact, these technically apparently simple and visually minimalist stairs are often applied in a museum-related context; with their artistic restraint, combined with a craftsmanship displaying a great attention to detail, they are perhaps meant to resemble a sophisticated display case – in terms of their appearance, degree of constructional detail and impact. In other culture-related fields, however, such stairs are spatially effective as models of an overall design idea. This is demonstrated by, for example, the stair in the Museum Judenplatz in Vienna (fig. 9), or the one in the "Plastic House" for a photographer in Tokyo (fig. 10).

Even in minimalist architecture, technical achievements still reveal new design potentials: handrails are reduced to thin pipes while ornamentation soberly and coolly takes a back seat. The guiding idea of the Bauhaus – planning by applying high-quality craftsmanship while maintaining an appropriateness to the material and resource efficiency – continues to assert itself up to the present day. Having primarily been an economic decision during the Bauhaus period, it has today become a question of ecology and sustainability. Consideration of prudent, seemingly simple concepts and constructions will surely continue to remain expedient and hence sustainable.

Longing for the archetype

The element of the originally simple ladder is also significant in contemporary architecture. While "Jacob's ladder" was extensively detailed not only symbolically but also aesthetically, contemporary ladders are predominantly designed in a restrained manner and committed to an "economy of space", i.e. to the demand of using as little space as possible. In Japan in particular, where building plots are rare and therefore expensive, architects often fall back on simple and extremely steep stair forms or even the archetype of the stair – the ladder – as a method for efficient space utilisation (fig. 11, p. 30). In the English-speaking

9

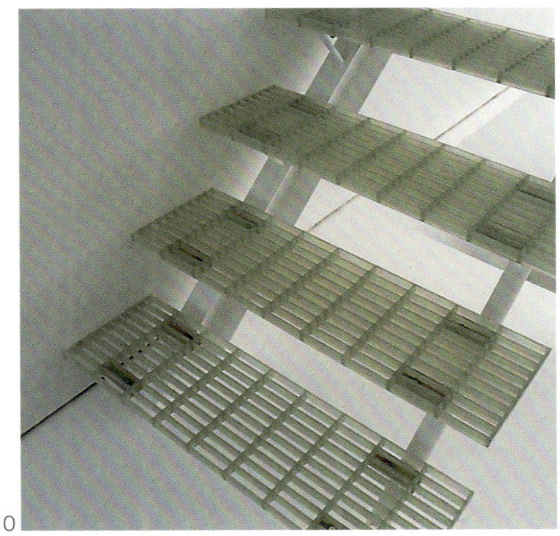
10

11 
12 
13 

and Benelux countries, the tradition of the steep stair lives on to this day. It leads the visitor to the upper floors almost immediately after entering a flat.

The narrow residential building in the centre of the city of Ghent, with a width of only 3.50 m, exemplifies this application. Due to the staggered arrangement of the building structure, the architects nevertheless ensure sufficient lighting, with a split-level layout positioning the floors spaciously and open to each other. The likewise open wooden stair ensures communication across levels and allows light to reach deep into the space from the skylight (fig. 15; fig. 11, p. 51).

The primeval stair in traditional architecture
In their archaic appearance, many contemporary stairs refer to historical examples in vernacular architecture. The simplicity of the stair as a constructional element is demonstrated particularly by the Dogon stairs in Mali: carved from a plain tree trunk with a forked branch at the upper end to find sufficient support along the mud walls (fig. 12). Further interesting examples are early settlements in what is today Mesa Verde

14 

11 A simple stair links the living and roof levels. Roof House, Kanagawa (JP) 2009, Tezuka Architects
12 Songo granary with a stair made of deadwood, Dogon (ML), without date
13 Elaborately built cave dwellings with simple wooden ladders. Cliff dwellings of the Anasazi. Mesa Verde, Colorado (US) ca. 1190–1270
14 The banister made of black steel takes up the movement of steps in a self-evident manner. Mud house Rauch, Schlins (AT) 2008, Roger Boltshauer and Martin Rauch
15 Single-family house, Ghent (BE) 2010, Dierendonckblancke architecten
a Section, scale 1:200
b The simple wooden stair links the split levels in the extremely narrow townhouse.
16 The archaic stair as a modern classic. Casa Barragán, Mexico City (MX) 1948, Luis Barragán
17 A three-storey house with a spectacular view of the ocean, the delicate stair elegantly links the floors. Casa 11 Mujeres, Zapallar (CL) 2007, Mathias Klotz
18 The concrete floor is hand-polished silky-soft. Belavali House, Kalyan Dombivli/Alibaug (IN) 2012, Studio Mumbai

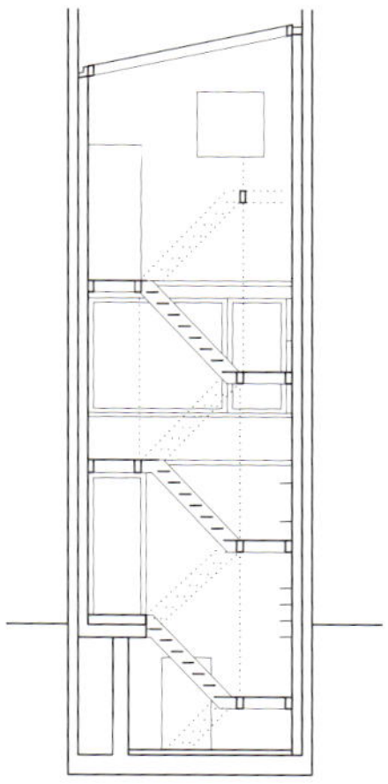

15a

b

National Park in Colorado. Here, approximately 600 partly well-preserved cliff dwellings of the Anasazi tribes were found. Cliff Palace is one of the largest of these settlements in the Mesa Verde area. An overhanging niche in the rock had already been used in 1200 AD to construct accommodations there, using available materials, such as soil, water, ash and sandstone. Wooden ladders connect all levels with each other. The simplicity and constructional clarity of these historical examples are still meaningful and continuously influence contemporary architecture (fig. 13).

Analogue and archaic: longing for the archetype

Roger Boltshauer and Martin Rauch demonstrate the potential elegance of a modern archaic stair in their mud house in Schlins, Austria (fig. 14). The steps "grow" out of the rammed earth wall while the balustrade logically results from the spiral moment. Due to its shape and arrangement in the floor plan, it refers to the historical derivation of a tower stair. Holes in the steps create an impressive play of light. In this way, the raw feel of the mud is accentuated at the same time, so that the stair supports the space and its atmosphere, instead of being purely self-sufficient. Therefore, it is more easily assigned to the beauty of the craftsmanship and the poetic simplicity of the material than to a sculpture, which would more strongly challenge the concept of the building. The sharp edges and clarity of the shapes are, however, accentuated in such a manner that a departure from traditional mud architecture in the service of a contemporary aesthetic clearly becomes discernible.

Planning strategies which very confidently handle regional building materials and traditions are gaining in importance. The related philosophy also determines the conceptual approach for planning stairs in this context.
One of the pioneers of this development is undoubtedly the Mexican architect Luis Barragán. The plain wooden stair at Casa Barragán initially seems traditional. The surrounding space, however, is distinctively modern in its form, proportion, guidance of light and colour. By linking tradition and modernity, a fascinating and timeless spatial atmosphere is thus created (fig. 16).
The Chilean architect Mathias Klotz follows the leads of Luis Baragán by transferring traditional materials into a modern design vocabulary (fig. 17).

Studio Mumbai from India, with its founder Bijoy Jain, also stands for this approach. The studio is more a workshop than an office: in an open-air hall, where dozens of material samples and building components are stored and processed, architects cooperate with craftspeople in planning and execution. The buildings created in this context are convincing due to a clear design vocabulary and contemporary, generous spaces. The selected materials, which partly come from historical building stock, display a clear connection to traditional building typologies, and underline the significance of craftsmanship for architecture. With regard to stairs, this is demonstrated at the Belavali House. The elegant banister made of tropical wood deliberately contrasts with the homogeneously designed wall and the smooth, grey-plastered steps. Here, a refined aesthetic is generated, particularly due to a sensitive use of materials (fig. 18).

In the Alpine region, a similar approach has developed for several years now: by means of a reduction of material and form, buildings are created which act

16

17

18

19 

20 

21 

through relationships (to the context, the applied material, the construction), and are thus "ingrained". This approach connects with an architectural tradition which also had an impact in Scandinavia, as with Alvar Aalto, for example: restriction to often only a single material which is detailed and processed with extraordinary refinement. The form is reduced and the entire building refrains from making a dramatic gesture (fig. 19). Everything seems unassuming at first, but the accuracy in the spatial disposition and materialisation appears highly poetic and deeply human in its scale. Perhaps it is precisely in this sense of scale and formal humility where its strength lies: like a primeval hut, this architecture protects without isolating itself. The building corresponds to human beings without exaggerating. The suitability for daily use harbours alluring beauty (fig. 20). This applies to architecture in general, but is particularly reflected in the formulation of stairs.

The conversion of an unused stable into a residential building in the village centre of Soglio, Switzerland, planned by Ruinelli Associati, demonstrates this meticulousness and sensitivity with respect to the regional context. For one thing, the local connection is taken seriously as the stern inner walls, made of tamped concrete, take up the motif of the old stone walls of the village. For another thing, the materials used reflect the surrounding building stock: untreated solid oak wood, tamped concrete and welded steel are applied on site with skilled craftsmanship and utmost precision. What is impressive here is that due to the modern detailing and refinement of traditional craftsmanship, a contemporary and timely architectural language with a strong identity has been

22a 

b 

created, which also shapes the construction of the vertical spatial access (fig. 22).

Since the 1990s, Gion Caminada has taken over various construction tasks in his hometown of Vrin (fig. 21). Preserving the cultural landscape of the Alpine region, and hence also the compact townscape, has become possible within the framework of a foundation: the inhabitants can purchase building land, and thus withdraw it from speculation. "The Alpine region combines unique natural and cultural landscapes with distinctive building forms, which have developed from a centuries-old adaptation to the geographical and climatic conditions," says Caminada. In the process, contemporary parameters are added by all means which, however, enrich the historical cultural heritage with exciting new designs and techniques.

The works of the two last-mentioned architects are shaped by the fact that the design approach runs throughout the entire building and all construction elements follow an overriding objective. This particularly applies to the stairs. Perhaps the success of buildings such as those by Gion Caminada or Armando Ruinelli makes it clear that most construction tasks are not about the extreme or about showcasing but about intimacy and retreat, home and longing. The buildings in Vrin and Soglio are examples of the return to tradition, craftsmanship, regional materials and manufacturing techniques.

Buchner Bründler also play with the primeval image of the house in their holiday home in Linescio, Ticino (fig. 23). While externally appearing like a prototypical 200-year-old stone house using the log building method in granite, it is completely hollowed out inside and spaciously designed in concrete, displaying a clear design vocabulary. Through this measure, the building stock is accepted while the interior follows its own order and philosophy. Hollowing out allows the space with the gabled roof to create a stronger impact, and the archaic image of the solid house is elevated to an aesthetic with an artistic feel.

The buildings of Thomas Kröger symbolise the longing for a withdrawal from the urban world. The revival of regionalism is driven by the fear of social upheaval and a desire for deceleration in one's own daily life. As such, the notion of home has a positive connotation, similar to the previous examples.

The stairs in the category of "Longing for the archetype" are, therefore, mostly found in holiday homes, where city dwellers return to after years of global and urban nomadism, in seemingly close contact with nature. This is insofar a gain for architecture as the largely organic, durable materials then actually react sensitively and responsibly to the context, and thus demonstrate an appreciation for the built form per se (fig. 24, 25).

23

24

25

19 All one material and yet highly differentiated in its detailing. Town hall, Säynätsalo (FI) 1952, Alvar Aalto
20 Simplicity in materials and form. Residential building "Creek House", Skåne (SE) 2014, Tham & Videgård
21 New and yet having been there all along. Butcher's shop, Vrin (CH), Gion Caminada
22 Casa RM, Soglio (CH) 2009, Ruinelli Associati
a The idea of the former stable is reflected in the materials used.
b Tamped concrete and untreated solid oak wood steps define the open stair
23 Casa d'Estate, Linescio (CH) 2008, Buchner Bründler Architekten
24 A contemporary design vocabulary and respect for the location, landscape and tradition. Country house, Uckermark (DE) 2014, Thomas Kröger
25 Peace and strength on the raw poured asphalt floor which links the living area with the sleeping areas. Werkhaus, Gerswalde (DE) 2013, Thomas Kröger

Volume vs Continuity

1

2

3

A stair can appear as an independent body and hence initiate a new or further spatial experience or can recede almost bodilessly vis-à-vis the character of a building, its materials and clear spatial order. This clearly shows how differently stairs can influence the perception and overall impact of space.

Volume

In the theory of perception, a lot of research is conducted on the psychological effect of spatial proportions and materials in interior spaces. In doing so, it has emerged that a well-proportioned, clearly structured and precisely framed space has a positive impact, since it neither overwhelms nor is aloof [1]. Due to its optical weight, the stair as a volume can therefore make an important contribution to structuring space in a pleasant way. When designing stairwells as independent volumes, two basic types are to be assumed: on the one hand, stairs which are arranged laterally, accompanying the space, and seem concealed due to mostly opaque design. Here, space usage more or less remains unaffected by the stair; on the other hand, stairs which – due to the positioning of their volumes – segment the space into several parts. Here, the stair is a means for zoning, thus replacing a partition wall. By shifting it to one side of a space and possibly having an additional vertical division in the form of a wall, the space is volumetrically downsized, while a central position divides the space. The clear conception of the space is, however, preserved in both cases. What needs to be emphasised in this context is that a stair as a volume does not have the formal and material independence that a stair as sculpture has. The body of the stair still blends into the overall concept of the building, while a sculpture as an object seems more detached and free.

The body of the stair as a space-dividing element

In order to strengthen the corporeality and power of spatial segmentation, stairs of this category can be provided with solid constructions, thick in material strength, as well as with opaque and floor-high balustrades. In doing so, the stair especially lends itself to being an element for the separation and delimitation of various usage zones: for example, Katsutoshi Sasaki, in his multigenerational house in Okazaki, divides the lounge from the kitchen. Moreover, the thick stair wall accommodates sliding doors, permitting complete separation of the rooms (fig. 1).

In the now demolished building of the clothing store "hh style" in Tokyo, SANAA positioned the stair as a shaft leading upwards in space, and in this way divided the entrance area on one side from the high racks on the other. Though the transparent fall protection underlined the shaft's character and emphasised the independent body of the stair, the glazing provided exciting visual references across the individual zones (fig. 2).

savioz fabrizzi architectes, too, use the stair volume to structure the interior in a chalet in Val d'Hérens, Switzerland. Here, the stair stands in the middle of the building as a defining element, zoning two levels into individual functional areas. Additional partition walls can therefore largely be dispensed with. Due to the material selected, the body of the stair makes for a strong contrast. The rough concrete clearly distinguishes itself from the remaining, entirely wood-clad walls (fig. 3).

Embaixada arquitectura take the volumetric appearance of the stair even further: the volume of the double-flight stair in the

1 The stair acts as a hybrid wall section which does not inhibit the material concept of the space. Multigenerational house, Okazaki (JP) 2013, Katsutoshi Sasaki + Associates
2 hh style, Tokyo (JP) 2000, SANAA
3 The stair as a volume of concrete structures the interior. Chalet, Val d'Hérens (CH) 2013, savioz fabrizzi architectes
4 House on the Moor, Krumbach (AT) 2013, Bernardo Bader
5 Casa dos Cubos, Tomar (PT) 2007, Embaixada arquitectura
  a The volume of the stair develops into the upper floor.
  b The stair as a volume divides the space.

4

Casa dos Cubos in Tomar develops sculpturally and freely in the two-storey air space towards the upper floor. Its material being distinct from the surrounding walls, the stair and the upper volume form an independent "box in a box". As a result, the spatial division not only has a vertical impact but also a horizontal one (fig. 5).

The example of the residential building in Krumbach by Bernardo Bader shows how it is possible to architecturally elaborate different usage areas on two levels through the structuring function of the stair. The ground floor has been designed in grey exposed concrete, the interior of the stairwell, however, in silver fir, making it seem strongly introverted. On the upper floor, the wood accentuating the interior of the stairwell is continued as a surface on the walls. The stair thus deliberately serves the purpose of functionally and vertically separating the more private upper floor and the more public ground floor, forming a subtle threshold due to the change of material between the two zones. In the process, the space-defining elements and the material interact very closely (fig. 4).

RAAAF Architekten show an entirely different form of stair as a dividing element. They cut up one of the over 700 bunkers constructed between 1815 and 1940 at the military line of defence in the Netherlands into two parts. "Bunker 599" recedes in its appearance in favour of the one-metre wide axis leading from the path through the landscape to the lake. The stair which leads down to this sculpture and on to the water becomes one with the generated visual axis towards the sea and thus merges with the surrounding landscape (fig. 7, p. 36).

5a

b

6a

b

The stair body as space-accompanying element
The Benedictine monk and architect Dom Hans van der Laan used a system of proportion based on his theoretical writings on architectural space as the basis for design in his plans for the abbeys Roosenberg in Waasmunster and St. Benedictusberg in Vaals. [2] The buildings seem almost abstract in their rational order, consisting of walls and rows of columns, while their fundamental clarity and regularity ensure suspenseful spaces whose impact is particularly owed to the rough, haptic surfaces. Van der Laan wanted to achieve a "nobilis simplicitas", a noble simplicity, and therefore reverted to elementary forms of design. Comparable to a fugue by Johann Sebastian Bach, the applied mathematical composition comprising simple elements allows harmony and beauty to unfold. The stairs in these two abbeys seem very corporeal, not only due to their monolithic formation. They hardly impair the prevailing spatial impact as they lie laterally against the space. The solid, sloped balustrade of St. Benedictusberg Abbey clearly distinguishes itself from the vertical order of the space-defining columns (fig. 6a). By contrast, the monolithic stair in Roosenberg Abbey only edges into the foreground from out of its niche to such an extent that the order is just sufficiently broken up to allow a sense of suspense, combined with an orientation possibility, to emerge in the spatial order. This effect is enhanced by the sophisticated lighting (fig. 6b).
In the volume typology, too, echoes of Jacob's ladder can often be found, especially when a roof window lights a stairwell. The stairs in this category, however, are more strongly interwoven with the surroundings and logically develop out of them. In the house in Ajuda by Aires Mateus, one can see how a stair leading to the light takes effect as a volume (fig. 11c). The chasm formed by the stair along a wall between two buildings creates a volumetric suspense in space. The volume of the upper floor results in a triangular banister whose tip meets the ground floor (fig. 11b). These bottlenecks are deliberately orchestrated in a suspenseful manner. A section through the building shows how much the space

7

8

9

10

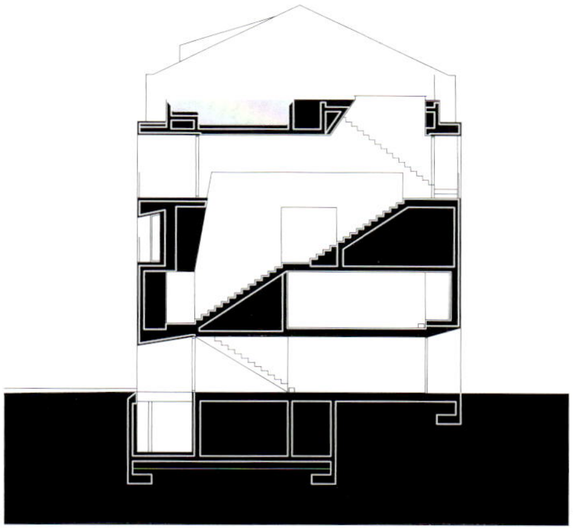
11a

11b

has been developed from a sculptural understanding using a positive-to-negative motif (fig. 11 a). The model works for the Belem Bom Sucesso project in Lisbon demonstrate this sculptural design attitude in the works of Aires Mateus (fig. 10).
As in the house in Krumbach, the design principle of having the stair articulate two different floors is reflected in the House W in Martinzell. From the ground floor, constructed in the form of a concrete base, one reaches a superimposed wooden building with a saddle roof. The architects take up this dialogue by likewise bisecting the stair, allowing the upper wooden part to freely float above the concrete bottom step, while maintaining a distance of one step between the two parts (fig. 8).

The frequently used, ceiling-high, and closed wall elements which are mostly even continued in the form of railings on the upper floor, visually and volumetrically carry forward the stair onto the upper floor.
The independence of its volume is further underlined if the stair, as in the example of the Black House by SoHo Architekten,

11c

6 Abbeys by Dom Hans van der Laan
  a St. Benedictusberg Abbey, Vaals (NL) 1968
  b Roosenberg Abbey, Waasmunster (BE) 1974
7 The stair and the path "dissect" the space. Bunker 599, Zijderveld (NL) 2013, RAAAF/ Atelier de Lyon
8 Analogy to the traditional way of construction of rural slope houses in the region: timber construction on a concrete base, House W, Martinzell (DE) 2001, Becker Architekten
9 Black House, Memmingen (DE) 2008, SoHo Architekten
10 Belem Bom Sucesso, Lisbon (PT) 2015, Aires Mateus
11 House in Ajuda (PT) 2014, Aires Mateus
  a The section shows the play with the volumes.
  b The stair as diagonal volume.
  c The stair leading to the light appears to optically narrow.

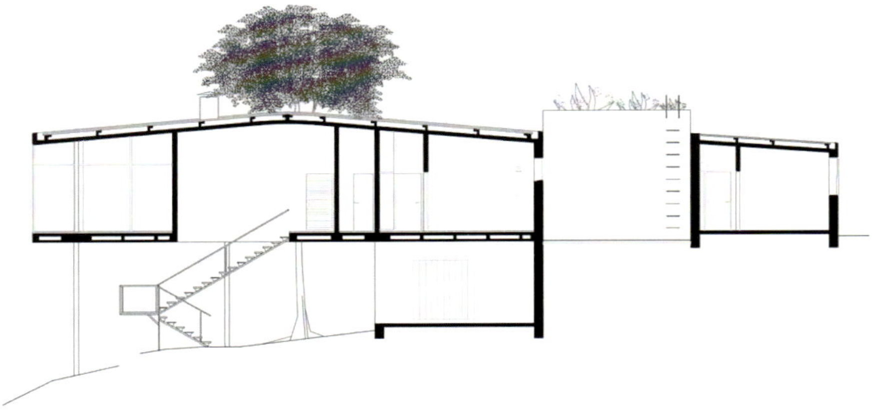

12a

b

does not rest on the floor, but seems to float (fig. 9).
All stairs in the volume category usually have in common that their design, first and foremost, requires a development in section, in order to allow articulation of the interlinkage between the usable space and the stairwell.

Continuity
While a stair as volume is about an independent body which self-assertively claims space, the objective of the incorporeal stair is to let the actual space take effect, thus appearing rather restrained in its design. The dissolved stair exclusively acts between two levels. Accompanied by highly reduced (if at all available) railings and handrails, this type of stair merely extends from the floor of the lower level to that of the upper one, and does not take shape on the floor of its destination. If one attempts to make the stair structurally as delicate as possible, it loses its above-mentioned corporeality. The diagonally positioned volume dissolves into the horizontal steps and the vertical fall protection. Thus, the surrounding space seems to continue unwaveringly, while the steps float up, delicately leading to the next level in a seemingly threshold-free manner. In most of the presented examples, the floor covering is continued on the steps, so that in the overview also all individual parts become one and the boundaries are blurred. The steps are often designed to be as thin as possible, resting on a highly reduced structure or projecting out freely.

Lina Bo Bardi, an Italian-born Brazilian architect, built a technically refined stair in 1951, which still looks modern today, underneath the actual building, the Casa de Vidro in Brazil, underlining the prevailing impression of lightness in this way. The glazed house seems to float above the tropically vegetated site on a slope. A tree within the house protrudes through another cutout in the ceiling. As such, the stair – like the tree – establishes a rootedness with the earth, and hence a kind of link to nature. Positioned in front of the narrow ground floor block, the delicate steel structure and wooden steps of the stair lead from the lower, almost untouched level to the actual residential floor of the house (fig. 12). The individual step supports are permeable, while the fall protection and handrail appear like a subdued and thus elegantly reduced line.

How extremely delicate detailing can reverse the actual spatial impression into its opposite, is demonstrated in Jesús Aparicio's sublime conversion of a former metro station into exhibition and lecture spaces in Madrid (fig. 13). The formerly barren transport facility acquires an elegance all of its own, due to the carefully detailed stair, while the strong character of the building is retained, and the space appears like one unit, despite the centrally positioned stair. The suspension, which doubles as fall protection, is worked out so fragilely that it optically recedes into the background. The stair is

13

12 Casa de Vidro, São Paulo (BR) 1951, Lina Bo Bardi
a Section, scale 1:250
b Like a tree, the stair too grows into the house from below.
13 The stair dissolves in its treads and suspension/fall protection. Documentation centre for architecture in Madrid (ES) 2016, Aparicio + Fernández-Elorza
14 "Dissolved" fall protection. Flat/office building, Tienen (BE) 2007, Office AST 77
15 The space level stands out and extends upwards. Residential building, Neusäß (DE) 2012, Manfred Lux
16 Transparency and elegance. Casalgrande Old House, Casalgrande, Venice (IT) 2011, Kengo Kuma & Associates
17 A mesh as fall protection and a folded steel stair in the Steel House, Tokyo (JP) 2007, Kengo Kuma & Associates

14

"incorporeal" as it supports the spatial impression in a restrained manner.

A narrow building in Tienen houses both the office of the Belgian architects AST 77 and a flat. Inside, a perforated black steel stair connects the office area with the residential spaces. In doing so, the stair supports the desire for transparency and openness, while still taking up the high-contrast design concept. The delicate steel cables, as well as the selected colour scheme, attempt to impair the spatial flow from one level to the next as little as possible (fig. 14).

Manfred Lux also structurally dissolves the volume of the stair in a residential building in Neusäß so that it loses its corporeality and converts itself into a layer of individual reclined steps. In the centrally positioned open stairwell, the wooden steps project out from the wall, and in terms of material, take up the wood of the floor covering. The vertical construction components, built in roughly stacked exposed concrete, stand out from them in a contrasting manner. The seemingly static material of steel as well as the required substructure in the wall are, however, not visible. A handrail or railing is deliberately dispensed with in order to support the intended impact (fig. 15).

Kengo Kuma, in two of his buildings, demonstrates how special material properties can be used for an incorporeal appearance. The Japanese architectural practice transformed an old brick house into a gallery for the tile manufacturer Casalgrande Padana. The design concept of the stair particularly emphasises the special features of a ceramic tile, thereby especially demonstrating a novel lightness, which is achieved with the aid of thin but load-bearing tiles. With its protruding, seemingly floating steps, it upends the original use of tiles, which as a rule only serve as a cover layer on a substrate. Due to technological innovations, tiles can now be manufactured to have much higher performance and in larger formats. The power of the material, which simultaneously has a thin, elegant appearance, is demonstrated here. The bottom step develops out of a ceramic fill, the raw material of the tile; a glazed transparent banister completely recedes into the background (fig. 16).

The subject of lightness is implemented in an entirely different manner in the Steel House in Tokyo. An extremely thin steel stair, stiffened by folding, is protected only by a fine, hardly visible metal fabric (fig. 17). Though in both stairs, technical aestheticisation of the applied materials is significant, they impress on account of their delicate, incorporeal appearance, which allows them to seemingly effortlessly develop up into the space. As such, their profile almost corresponds to an abstract pictogram, while their radicalness places them in strong contrast to the bulky stairs of the volume category.

15

16

17

Notes
[1] Loidl, Hans; Bernard, Stefan: Freiräume. Entwerfen als Landschaftsarchitektur. Basel 2003
[2] van der Laan, Hans: Der architectonische Raum. Leiden, New York, Cologne 1992

Furniture and Addition

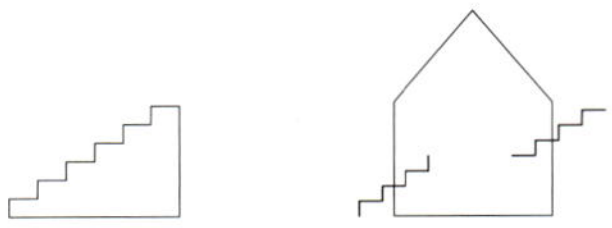

1 Japanese cupboard "kaidan tansu", stand-alone
2 House in a forest with a wooden furniture stair. "Casa in una pineta", Marina di Castagneto Carducci (IT) 2011, Massimo Fiorido Associati and sundaymorning
3 Layer House, Kobe (JP) 2003, Hiroaki Ohtani
  a Space-saving concrete louvres
  b Concrete louvres filter the light and organise the house.
4 Itami House, Itami (JP) 2012, Tato Architects
  a The stair choreographs the space.
  b The furniture is integrated as part of the stair.
  c The dining table projects into the stairwell.

1

2

Stairs in this category are distinguished by the fact that they either serve an additional function or, subsequently and complementarily, enable uses in an existing stock. The stair as a furniture item as well as stock supplement does not seem abstract and object-like as a sculpture, but is a multifaceted building element: this stair does not only serve the purpose of connecting two levels but offers further spatial, conceptual and especially functional potential. In the context of complementing an existing stock, the applied material often contrasts with the surroundings, with the result that the stair appears like an inlay inserted into the existing space.

Furniture

Parameters which constrain spatial volumes, such as confined plots, limited financial budgets, topographical particularities or minimalist spatial concepts, increasingly result in a merger and optimisation of installations into "hybrid" staircase furniture, i.e. a combination of stairs, cupboards and/or shelves, due to the intended reduction in applied resources.

Hybrid stairs in Japan

Japan in particular, due to the limited area available and the high real estate prices, is a pioneer in the tradition of these hybrid stairs. Every space is used, and there are various tools available in the market with which clothes, for example, can be pressed together to be stored in different cupboards (tansu) in a space-saving way. Kaidan tansu, so-called stair cupboards, are widespread, serving as both a storage space and a climbing aid for the roof, as they already have in traditional Japanese houses (fig. 1). Seen from the perspective of workmanship, these cupboards represent a collaborative effort between the carpenter, the painter and the smith, while the main responsibility lies with the carpenter who is, importantly, in charge of selecting the wood: for the production of furniture in Japanese interior design, this includes wood types such as paulownia (kiri), Japanese cedar (sugi), and zelkova (keyaki). The cupboards have a clear varnish finish on the outside and are complemented by wrought-iron fittings which, alongside their purely functional significance, also serve as decorative elements. Viewed historically, the tansu manifested the economic status of its user. They were, however, also used to store important documents in the drawers, and are presently still very common pieces of furniture in Japan.

Even today, due to space constraints, hybrids comprising spatial elements and furniture are widely employed in the country, since even in Japanese suburbs, land prices continue to be exorbitantly high. Near Osaka, Tato Architects have developed a residential building for a family, on a nearly 60 m² plot, with 95 m² living area on a 35 m² footprint. On such an optimised area, there is no space for storerooms. Space-defining elements therefore turn into pieces of furniture and vice-versa. In doing so, the drawer of a cabinet, for example, serves as a stair step while the stairwell is crossed by a table top. Furniture and architecture become one (fig. 4).

The Layer House by Hiroaki Ohtani also stands on a very small, 33 m² plot in Kobe, a city known for its high property prices. The limited surface area radically defines the lifestyle of a young family: individual, closed rooms and space for extra storage space are not implementable. In spite of constrained space conditions, an efficiently designed floor

3a

b

plan and the innovative layout provide high housing quality. Additionally, the walls consist of a prefabricated component system where the residents can simply pocket or "plug in" various objects in a versatile manner and as needed. The skylight admits natural light into the space, which is filtered onto the facade by concrete louvres. The motif of the louvre defines the space, due to its use on the external and internal wall. For this purpose, over 1,800 prefabricated concrete elements were threaded by hand onto taut steel rods and stacked on top of each other. They are the dominant design element and simultaneously form the load-bearing system, a space-bounding wall and an anchor point for various shelves, seating accommodation and particularly the mounts for the stairs (fig. 3).

The stair as furniture

In the "House in a pine forest" in Marina di Castagneto Carducci, Italy, the interior stair was extended into a shelf, similar to a Japanese kaidan tansu, where the risers continue as shelf panels in a close rhythm, transmitting down the occurring vertical forces (fig. 2). The shelf panels are alternately arranged at the height of the footsteps. Thanks to the change, they take up the geometry of the stair as a topic, emphasising the vertical, rising gesture of the stair. Due to the rear wall, likewise designed as a shelf while also serving as a banister, the entire installation appears very homogenous, and highly compact and cohesive. Fall protection is deliberately dispensed with.

In the Slovenian residential building by dekleva gregorič arhitekti, the area available is relatively limited. The ground floor primarily functions as a space designed

4a

b

c

5

6

7 a

b

to be open, offering many grand views of the surrounding landscape. By contrast, the upper floor is very private, only permitting views of the sky through roof windows. The stair of the building reinterprets the 'samba' stair type with offset treads, and consists of two components: on the one hand, of box-shaped steps, which can additionally be used as storage space, and on the other, of vertically lined up metal rods, which serve as mounts for the box elements and simultaneously as fall protection. Their additional function, however, is somewhat concealed: appearing completely closed in side elevation and designed simply, the additional space for books or similar items is only revealed on the rear side (fig. 5; see also "Residential building in Vrhovlje", p. 82ff.). The combination of the function of the stair and the storage area results in novel space furniture, which impresses on account of its original approach.

Amir Zinaburg, with his Square Staircase, presents a delicate steel frame that is a stair, shelf and art work in one. While the dissolved, thin tubular stair frame slightly extends the limited living area by a representative utility space, it is above all, however, an art object in an otherwise very sober space (fig. 6).

The furniture for playing and sleeping by h2o architectes in an old Paris building shows how a hybrid stair expands into an encompassing piece of furniture. It demonstrates the attempt to leave behind a tidy children's room by employing integrated storage, working and play areas. In this furniture, use as stairs equally stands alongside the other functional provisions. The compact corporeality and the colourful paint highlight the volume placed in the space. Three steps lead to a door through which the built-in furniture can be accessed. The stair on the inside then leads to the upper sleeping level (fig. 7). Due to the selected motifs of the door, the window and the stair, as well as the dual level, the furniture appears like a "house within a house".

Addition

Due to the regressive number of new buildings, construction in existing building stock is assuming an ever increasing role. It is here, in particular, that new or additional stairs are often an indispensable supplement and, for example, in the form of emergency escape routes. The need for a stair is often due to a change of use. Even if the stair may result in representing a different element, using another material or speaking a different language from the rest of the building, it must always be developed out of an engagement with the building stock in order to be successfully integrated.

The dialogue between the old and the new
Meeting the urgent need for further exhibition spaces of the Art Museum in Saxony-Anhalt, Nieto Sobejano Arquitectos designed a roof during the renovation of the Moritzburg in Halle, which they placed on top of a hitherto unused, ruinous part of the historical building stock. Suspended from the roof, additional galleries and access elements organise the space in an entirely new way. In terms of their materials and design, the installations clearly contrast with the historical building stock. This dialogue between the old and the new is conducted in a very deliberate manner: the new elements for museum use stand out against the natural stone walls due to the white paint. Likewise, the stairs purposely accentuate the stock (fig. 8). Supplemented emergency stairs and elevators in the core of the building, as well as new window mounts in the

5 Compact house, compact stair furniture. Residential building "Compact Karst House", Vrhovlje (SI) 2014, dekleva gregorič arhitekti
6 Square Staircase, Islington House, London (GB) 2015, Amir Zinaburg
7 Play and sleeping furniture, Paris (FR) 2009, h2o architectes
a The stair links several play levels.
b The piece of furniture as built-in object in an old building.
8 Building stock vs contemporary intervention: The black steel strongly contrasts with the building stock. Moritzburg, Halle (DE) 2008, Nieto Sobejano Arquitectos
9 Visitor centre Castillo de la Luz, Las Palmas Gran Canaria (ES) 2004, Nieto Sobejano Arquitectos
10 Cultural centre on the Azores (Arquipélago – Centro de Artes Contemporâneas), Ribera Grande (PT) 2014, Menos é Mais Arquitectos
a Monolithic stair
b Wooden stair

8

9

exhibition spaces, once again allow contemporary use of the historical spaces.

Addition, as the term already suggests, means sensitively handling what already exists. Even in the case of stairs that appear much more object-like, as at the visitor centre in Las Palmas, by the same Spanish architect team (fig. 9), the stair is always subject to the atmosphere of the space. Here, Nieto Sobejano place a new visitor axis through the building, with the aid of the stair and the walkways. In the historical context in particular, corroded steel as a material stands out, as its patina, intrinsic to the material, displays a temporal element, just as the building itself does.

In the art and cultural centre Arquipélago, on the island of São Miguel in the Azores, Menos é Mais Arquitectos complemented the former alcohol and tobacco factory by two further buildings, which serve as art and cultural centre, store, multifunction space and workshops. The new monolithic buildings, in their volume and external shape, are guided by the existing building stock, and blend into the surrounding buildings made of dark grey natural stone from the region due to their anthracite-coloured concrete surface. The existing buildings from the late 19th century, by contrast, were hollowed out and extensively renovated, in order that their cubature and materials allow the developmental history and the site to still remain readable. The stairs inside reflect this interplay of contrasts (old – new, raw – smooth, light – dark, etc.): in the spaces which appear cool, stairs differentiated on account of their workmanship are a clear and pleasant contrast, while seeming rather object-like as compact, unadorned volumes in the historical

10a

b

11

industrial buildings. The installations thus react to the spatial situation in a highly individual manner. There is no common language; instead, the architects use the stairs to respectively reinterpret the surroundings, employing, for example, a spiral staircase with an elegant railing made of brass or a fanned out wooden stair whose constructively clearly structured banister continues into the upper floor (fig. 10b).

David Chipperfield's stair for the renovation of the Neues Museum in Berlin, by contrast, follows the historical original by Friedrich August Stüler in form, course and volume. In its monolithic, almost seamless construction, consisting of white prefabricated concrete elements, it presents, indeed, a modern-abstract contrast, positioning itself equivalently alongside the exposed brick walls of the existing building stock, leaving the historical space around the central stair with room to unfold (fig. 11).

Markus Scherer and Walter Angonese, for the renovation of the South Tyrolean Museum of Culture and Provincial History – Tyrol Castle, demonstrate how the stair can become a recurrent theme – constructed in corroded steel, in this case – and represent a didactic path through an exhibition. Alongside the objects presented in the castle, it is also the existing building stock, the historical reference

12

11 Neues Museum Berlin (DE) 2009, David Chipperfield Architects
12 Watertower, De Weerribben-Wieden National Park, Sint Jansklooster (NL) 2014, Zecc Architecten
13 Stair, lighting and display case in the South Tyrolean Museum of Culture and Provincial History, Tyrol Castle (IT) 2003, Walter Angonese and Markus Scherer with Klaus Hellweger
14 Coal washing plant, Zeche Zollverein Essen (DE) 2010, hg merz
15 Townhouse "Black Pearl", Rotterdam (NL) 2010, Studio Rolf.fr

13

14

and the landscape context which form a part of the exhibition. The stair connects all parts with each other and, due to its space-consuming extensions, it itself becomes a presentation site. For the purpose of showing multimedia content, displays, niches with audio installations, cabinets and the like, are additionally integrated into the stair, which has been extended into an item of exhibition furniture (fig. 13).

Located in the midst of De Weerribben-Wieden National Park in the Netherlands, Zecc Architecten have transformed a former water tower into a viewing tower. The wooden steps of the new stair create an alternative route to the existing one, which consists of a narrow, steep wooden staircase nestling up against the inner wall. By contrast, the new, more comfortably walkable stair frees itself from the space in multiple ways, running through the high concrete tower in a zigzag fashion. Both stairs are usable while the new installation is an extension to allow the spatial volume to be experienced in a more dramatic manner. In this way, the new stair not only materially but also geometrically exhibits a clearly visible distance to the existing building stock. Similar to the project by Markus Scherer and Walter Angonese, the stair contains several additional functions, its seating accommodation providing space for relaxation (fig. 12).
This illustrates once again that a new stair in an existing building stock can offer added value alongside purely functional complementation.

With its artistic ambition, the stair in the coal washing plant of the former Zollverein coal mine, designed by hg merz, represents the necessary content-related link with history: red and yellow serve as a visual symbol for mining and iron ore production (fig. 14). Due to the orange-glowing strings, reminiscent of embers, as well as the additional lighting underneath the steps and in the handrail, the stair clearly contrasts with the heritage-protected building stock.

In the residential building "Black Pearl" by Studio Rolf.fr, the stair and the entire addition that provides the spaces desired by the client clearly contrast with the building stock (fig. 15). Due to the design of an indirectly lit interstice, this addition is structurally separated, its white volume also setting itself apart optically from the exposed brick walls. The actual habitable rooms are located in the gap between the existing stock and the extension.

The category of addition shows how sensitively and wisely planned stairs can allow existing buildings or surrounding spaces to have a suspenseful impact or even be set centre stage. In doing so, stairs can, by all means, self-confidently stand on their own. All the examples shown here illustrate that the new and the old enrich each other positively, and that the dialogue and the use of an effectively orchestrated break or gap as an accent, can result in a new, lively spatial impression.

Craftsmanship and detail: the stairs in Carlo Scarpa's oeuvre
In spatial-atmospheric terms, stairs are successful when their relationship to the

15

16 Fondazione Querini Stampalia, Venice (IT) 1963, Carlo Scarpa
a Access bridge over a canal
b Detail of handrail
17 'Samba' stair, Castelvecchio, Verona (IT) 1975, Carlo Scarpa
18 Stair of corroded steel strips, Castelvecchio, Verona (IT) 1975, Carlo Scarpa

16a

b

17

existing building stock has been worked out in an aesthetically coherent manner. An outstanding architect who always applied his design philosophy to the smallest detail and the design of stairs in particular is Carlo Scarpa. In general, Scarpa's conception of architecture is determined by the exchange between the place and craftsmanship in the construction of buildings. In their conception and construction, his buildings always display detailing with many variants. The position of each step is carefully conceived, and every stair has been developed from a sensitive understanding of the site.

This is demonstrated at several locations in the Palazzo Querini in Venice: the bridge, which spans the canal like a light arch (fig. 16a); the protective measures against the dreaded floods; the garden; and the pòrtego (Venetian for "portico"), the typical entrance hall. As an example, the handrail of the access stair may be mentioned here. Scarpa designed the mounts of the vertical steel struts such that he recessed the metal in the zones where the hand touches the railing, complementing it by a horizontal wooden strut (fig. 16b). As such, the handrail can be ergonomically used and has a pleasant haptic feel, with Scarpa having taken references from shipbuilding in its conception. The steps start out in stone, thus establishing a clear connection to the paving material of the square; above the water, however, a separate construction made of wood and steel is placed on top, referring to the bridges of Venice. This emphasis on the individual elements and their detailed treatment is even more evident in the garden, which Scarpa developed like a microcosm by placing the landscape with the water and the architecture in dialogue with each other. Scarpa created total works of art that impress due to the dedication to their workmanship. Every niche, every drain and every joint is well thought out. Every construction element has been coherently worked through in itself and placed in context in a sophisticated manner.

In the Castelvecchio in Verona, Carlo Scarpa was able to very intensively dwell on the historical building stock from 1957 to 1975. The various stairs demonstrate how sensitively he responded to the respective location and always attempted to find the right dialogue between the old and the new, the material and the construction. As such, the 'samba' stairs along a narrow chasm between the site and the building are ideal for overcoming a height difference (fig. 17). At another location in today's museum, a corroded steel stair, appearing as an autonomous object, contrasts with the brick-lined space (fig. 18). On the ground floor in particular, the spaces which are linked by only two or three steps are visually united by minor level differences, while also being separately perceivable. Scarpa isolated the components of individual elements and reshaped them – always in close relation to the existing building stock. Using the example of the stair, this means that doorknobs, steps, handrails etc. were separately, individually designed and detailed, applying elaborate workmanship in their implementation. On the whole, this results in a kind of collage that serves as a constant reminder of the historical context.

Epilogue

The above-mentioned stairs show the wide range of possibilities for the handling of space. All the preliminary conceptual questions on the overall design of a building always also refer to a stair: should it contrast with the existing context (location, function or programme, or the building in itself)? Are relationships between various spatial zones created that go beyond a purely access-providing role? Does the stair continue an aesthetic motif or does it transform it? Are local materials and/or regional production techniques being applied?

For all the typology, however, exceptions often confirm the rule: every stair cannot always be unambiguously categorised. Yet, stairs are such an important feature of every building that it seems necessary also to conceptually design them in a sensible manner in the design process, for it is often via a stair that the first and most direct approach to a space takes place. Stairs can take up and develop aesthetic motifs, thus not only linking spaces physically but also conceptually. What all the presented stairs have in common is that they cannot be categorised separately from the building or space but always within their context. This approach is necessary since the primary concern is the continuity of a spatial idea, which ideally is then clearly reflected in the conception, the structural details and the materialisation of the stair.

Stairs can be the heart of a building, the points where spatial openness leads to communicative meeting places. The upgrading of access zones from a purely function-oriented element to open space structures presents huge aesthetic and spatial potential.

18

1

2

As already described in the preceding section on design typology, the stair is indeed dependent on the space to be accessed, but at the same time also always defines the space. The individual design idea in the context of a building influences the type of construction of a stair.

A stair serves the purpose of overcoming level differences caused by stacking horizontal planes. In doing so, alongside the design-related demands, and viewed historically, it is the geographical and cultural context in particular that represents the resources used in house building, and hence in associated stair construction. The availability of construction materials and the development of craft skills, to begin with, form the decisive boundary conditions for these tasks. So, for example, in Ticino, the stone slabs naturally occurring in the immediate spatial environment in layered natural stone walls also constitute the principal building material for houses and stairs (fig. 1); in Norway, due to the abundance of wood, the step-like carving of logs combined with methods of solid wood construction resulted in an obvious principle of stair design (fig. 2). These two examples, albeit displaying different types of construction, represent the primeval stair type, which is intrinsic to the archaic handling of locally available material (see "Longing for the archetype", p. 29ff.): the material primarily used for the load-bearing structure of a house determines the appearance of the stair.

Until the mid-19th century, mainly wood and stone were available as construction materials, the latter in the form of natural stone or bricks made of fired or dried mud. This guided the technical parameters for stair construction, while the often highly mature craft skills were derived from the associated technical options for processing and working the building material.

Stairs first developed from purely practical items into "objets d'art" in historical buildings of a representative character. Alongside the functional criterion, the stair received an additional level of meaning. The applied materials and techniques, however, were the same as in the stairs which had been purely reduced to a functional role. Balthasar Neumann, in the mid-18th century, applied common brickwork techniques, such as arched brick constructions, in the Würzburg Residence, to construct the three-flight, dog-leg stair for the representative access to the primary reception floor (see p. 14f.). The construction is entirely plastered and decorated with ornaments. Stair steps, railings and balustrades are made of natural stone. The basic construction merely serves as a shell for accommodating secondary materials for the decoratively designed surfaces. The underlying type of construction is no longer discernible when viewing the completed stair (fig. 3).
The stairs at Goethe's house on Frauenplan in Weimar have a similar design; the wooden construction was clad, partly plastered and adorned with decoratively designed surfaces – only the step and landing coverings made of wood allow a conclusion to be drawn about the applied construction material (fig. 4).

Alongside the traditional materials of stone and wood, the Industrial Revolution resulted in the addition of iron from the mid-19th century onwards, as well as concrete or reinforced concrete, from the start of the 20th century, as materials for stair construction. The cast-iron stair represents the advent of metal materials in stair construction, enabling delicately constructed elements to be created (fig. 5). As with every new material, it takes a certain time until a unique design vocabulary which is typical for the material develops. Cast-iron constructions at first replaced wood as a material; the design vocabulary and type of construction initially corresponded to replicas of wooden structures. The new material of concrete, however, made it possible to create volumetrically and sculpturally formed structures in stair construction (fig. 6).

Design and construction based on material

The classification into construction types provokes a discussion on designing and constructing in ways that are typical for a respective material. How is this to be understood? Can limitation to preferably one material, which decisively shapes appearance, be considered typical for a material? How does one evaluate the development of hybrid constructions in this context? By applying different materials acting in combination for basic structures, new formal design possibilities emerge. In the process, the recognisability of a typology-defining material no longer has priority.
Recent technical developments of materials, means of combination and processing technology open up new design-related scopes for planners, while making unambiguous classification or reduction of built examples into four basic construction typologies based on the "classic" materials (stone, wood, steel and concrete) more difficult. It is, therefore, necessary to specify further categories.
The main criteria for defining a construction typology are the available materials which are used for the primary load-bearing structure of stairs. The attempt at this classification, for a start, covers the already mentioned "classic" materials of stone, wood, steel and concrete, and furthermore, glass and hybrid structures.

1 Projecting stone steps in Ticino
2 Worked tree trunk, Norway
3 Stairwell, Würzburg Residence (DE) 1720–1744, Balthasar Neumann
4 Stairwell, residential building on Frauenplan, Weimar (DE) 1792
5 Cast-iron stair in Prince Charles' palace [Ordenspalais], Berlin (DE) 1827–1829, Karl Friedrich Schinkel
6 Spiral stair, Itamaraty Palace, Brasilia (BR) 1970, Oscar Niemeyer

3

Stone stairs

The prototype stone stair results from the stacking of stone slabs naturally occurring in the surroundings. In the next development step, dressed stone follows, out of which steps are carved. While the stacking of stone slabs usually only permits very small spans of stair constructions, if at all, dressed stone can be used to bridge larger spans, depending on the size of the raw material, and following the processing of individual stones into arched supporting structures. The stairs in the Italian community of Salemi, designed by Álvaro Siza Vieira in 1999 for the urban regeneration in the area of a cathedral which had been destroyed by an earthquake, are a good example of constructions made of layered stone. The substructure consists of quarry stone, and the block steps on top are made of precisely cut natural stone of the Pietra bianca di Trapani type (fig. 8, p. 50).
In the residential buildng in Morcote, brick – as an artificially produced substitute for stone – is laid on top of a concrete sub-stair. Here, the substructure of concrete represents the "modern" variant, while traditional stone stairs made of bricks were normally supported by walled vaults (fig. 9, p. 50).

4

5

The characteristic tectonics of stone stairs results from the material-based property of predominantly being able to accommodate compressive stresses for vertical forces or vaulting. Stone, being a heavy building material with a high bulk density, is used in stairs for a solid, monolithic effect and does not develop the elegance of material-reduced stairs made of other materials. An exception are stairs consisting of stone slabs embedded into and projecting out from a solid wall, forming self-supporting treads. These centuries-old stairs create the impression of high-tech audacity (fig. 7, p. 50).

6

7

Wooden stairs
Wooden stairs developed, on the one hand, from the prototype of the sloping tree trunk worked into a step-like shape, and on the other, from ladders, which were originally made of grown round bars with a small diameter. Until the beginning of the 20th century, the anisotropic material of wood, in component design and dimensions, was subject to available beam dimensions, which derived directly from grown tree trunks (fig. 2, p. 48). Rod-shaped, aligned constructions of closed and open string stairs are derived from them. In Central Europe, the wooden stair is well-developed due to extensive timber resources. Already in the 19th century, these construction techniques were presented in textbooks on stair construction for the carpentry and joinery profession, almost in a catalogue-like manner (fig. 10).

In spite of the highly developed stair construction culture, it was the craft-based, holistic simplicity which dominated wooden staircases. Though the construction elements were adorned with embellishments and decoration or had handcrafted surfaces, depending on the period, the simple basic structure remained recognisable. Later, the application of industrially manufactured wooden composites became predominant. Rod-shaped, aligned beams of glued laminated timber or solid structural timber replaced the beams originally obtained from grown tree trunks. In addition, undirected slab-shaped materials, such as wooden fibre boards or laminated wood panels for surface-filling applications, became available. The construction of the wooden stair was largely reduced to a few elements. These stairs give the impression of an intuitively

8

9

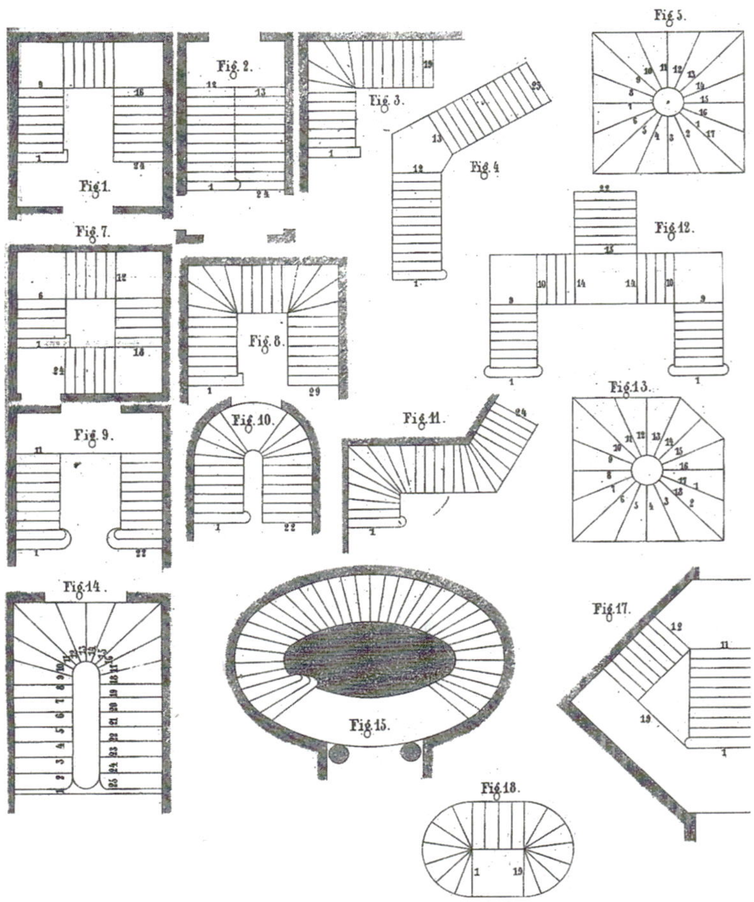

10

7 Stair in Abhaneri (IN)
8 Urban regeneration in Salemi (IT) 2000, Álvaro Siza Vieira
9 Residential building in Morcote (CH) 2008, Markus Wespi + Jérôme de Meuron Architekten
10 Plate 1 from W. H. Behse: "Treppenwerk für Architekten, Zimmerleute und Tischler sowie für Baugewerk- und Gewerbeschulen" [Stairs for architects, carpenters, and joiners as well as for craft and trade schools] from the year 1873
11 Single-family home in Ghent (BE) 2010. Dierendonckblancke Architecten
12 Emergency stair in the USA
13 Art Nouveau stair, Hôtel Tassel, Brussels (BE) 1892, Victor Horta

11

comprehensible method, giving laypersons, too, a sense of constructional understanding, and hence of safety.

The example of the stair in the residential building in Ghent by Dierendonckblancke Architecten shows a minimalist closed string stair with mortised solid wooden steps, which rests on timber beam landings suspended from above on steel rods (fig. 11). The basic geometric configuration does not include a well hole. Ascending and descending inner closed strings only have a few millimetres of interstitial space, through which a tensile structure runs for fall protection.

Steel stairs
Steel stairs display an industrial character. They recall stair towers, emergency staircases, or ship stairs. Initially, they didn't have a representational character, thus being adorned and constructed in a technically reduced manner. Familiar images of buildings from large cities in the USA, displaying external emergency staircases, demonstrate, however, that these stairs decisively shape the architecture due to their large dimensions. For this reason, decorative elements were developed for staircase components which went beyond pure functionality (fig. 12).
The Jugendstil introduced modern cast-iron constructions into architecture. The stairs received style-forming floral ornaments and were integrated as objects into the buildings (fig. 13).

Steel was the new material of the early 20th century, with assigned attributes such as "high-performance, slender, and profiled". The "Neues Bauen" ["New Objectivity"] helped achieve the breakthrough for steel stairs. The propagated development of a simple design vocabulary followed the principle of constructional economy. The motif of the ship stair, with its reduced material use, became definitive. Analogous to the above-described construction types of wooden stairs as closed or open string constructions, simple structures with transparent load-bearing behaviour of construction elements were created.
By making full use of the properties of the material, stairs could be designed to be highly transparent and almost dematerialised.
Due to the further development of processing technologies in steel construction, two trends manifested themselves in architecture with respect to stair construction:

Incorporeal, dematerialised and almost floating stairs
The steel spiral staircase in the house in Imabari by Toru Murakami Architect & Associates is a newel stair that almost seems to dissolve in space thanks to the minimised use of material (fig. 14, p. 52). As a result, this stair completely subordinates itself to the unobstructed space, though newel stairs usually appear object-like, due to their basic geometric shape, and normally rather attract attention. The impression of dematerialisation achieved here is only attainable by steel construction: by the skilful combination of profile steel, cables and steel rods, resulting in a high-performance load-bearing system, making full use of the respective load-bearing capacity.

Corporeal folded stair of flat steel
The application of flat steel, which is used in steel stair construction in the form of struts, folded or bent as load-bearing material and in a surface-bearing manner, has strongly increased in recent years, due to the digitally controlled processing machines available today. In contrast to the steel stairs described above, these constructions do not require

12

13

14

15

16

17

profile steel as the load-bearing structure, making origami-like forms with high aesthetic appeal possible in the first place.

The stair in Skara Cathedral by AIX Architekter is a folded stair where every third riser projects as cantilever and is structurally fixed to the parallel concrete wall, resulting in a seemingly floating folded structure, with carefully planned detailing and implementation (fig. 15).

In the connecting stair on the upper floor of the Juilliard School in New York by the architects Diller Scofidio + Renfro/FXFOWLE, flat steel plates are also used as the load-bearing structure. The U-shaped cross section of the stair uses the sideward flat steel railings as closed strings, which are connected with each other by welded-on tread plates and include open risers (fig. 16).

Concrete stairs
Reinforced concrete is the defining construction material of the 20th century. By combining the two components concrete and steel, constructions with high structural performance were developed which, due to the plasticity and malleability of reinforced concrete, made great aesthetic freedom in design possible. Owing to the numerous available techniques for designing concrete surfaces – thanks to the variability of concrete, on the one hand, by using colouring and additive substances, and on the other, the diverse modification possibilities with respect to the surface finish, as in formwork, for example – there are almost no design-related limits for planners (fig. 17).

Contrary to these aesthetic possibilities marked by a high degree of individuality, the concrete stair also developed as an element in industrialised building. Straight-flight stairs with simple geometries in the form of prefabricated reinforced concrete components represent an economically unrivalled building product. These components are often applied in situations where aesthetic appeal plays a subordinate role, such as in emergency stairs, in commercial building, etc.
The architect Peter Böhm, however, proves with reference to the example of the Lanxess Arena (Kölnarena until 2008), that these formally extremely reduced components can, by all means, have high aesthetic appeal when integrated into a design concept (fig. 18).

Glass stairs
Technological advancement in glass materials allows glass to become a load-bearing material, taking into account specific constraints. The entrance stair in the subterranean Apple Store in New York demonstrates the aesthetic possibilities which are exhausted to the fullest in this example (fig. 19). At first glance, both the staircase and the glass cube protruding from the square and enveloping the staircase seem to be constructed only of glass. The glass panes are employed as two-dimensional load-bearing elements, but must be structurally connected with each other using steel connectors. These construction elements or building components, however, visually recede into the background to the extent that they don't compete with the dominance of the glass. Nevertheless, the structure is a hybrid construction of glass and steel.

CAD and CAM
The entry of digital planning and manufacturing tools into the production process enabled individualised planning and construction procedures, which had been impossible or uneconomical before. Freely developed stair forms are defined by the sculptural design as well as the appearance of surfaces. To begin with, the

14 Residential building in Imabari (JP) 1999, Toru Murakami Architect & Associates
15 Skara Cathedral (SE) 2000, AIX Architekter
16 Juilliard School in New York (US) 2009, Diller Scofidio + Renfro / FXFOWLE
17 Spiral stair, Neues Museum, Nuremberg (DE) 1999, Staab Architekten
18 Lanxess Arena, Cologne (DE) 1998, Peter Böhm
19 Apple Store on Fifth Avenue, New York (US) 2006/2011, Bohlin Cywinski Jackson
20 Armani flagship store on Fifth Avenue, New York (US) 2009, Doriana and Massimiliano Fuksas

18

19

materials of the load-bearing construction do not play a role in form finding.
The spiral staircase developed for the Armani showroom in New York, with its sculptural appearance, could initially be categorised as a free-form concrete stair (fig. 20). However, the construction drawing of this stair displays an inner framework of steel tubes, which is encased in a fibre cement cladding that follows the sculptural design. The inner steel tube framework serves as a load-bearing structure and defines the rough structure, which is covered by the detailed cladding, defining the final shape. The principle is similar to car body construction in the automotive sector, where, as a rule, a relatively inelegant supporting frame (usually of metal) provides the structure; the body shell, placed over it, is form-giving and manufactured from different materials, such as steel sheet, aluminium sheet or fibre-reinforced plastic. This shape subsequently receives a freely selectable surface coating.

The latter examples bring us back to the beginnings of the symbolic stairs, as illustrated in the example of the Würzburg Residence (fig. 3, p. 49). This object-like stair, like the stair in the Armani showroom, was built using the respective technical means available when it was created. Here too, however, the materials of the exposed surfaces are form-defining, while encasing a structural framework.
In summary, it can be said that the constructional resources available to stair construction can be employed in both a form-defining and an ancillary manner, i.e. without an aesthetic appeal of their own. The planner's design determines how the technological means are applied.

20

Project examples

Jacob's ladder and Sculpture

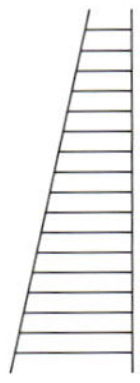

Stepped house in Brugg (CH)
Ken Architekten, Zurich

This Jacob's ladder provides access to the flats in the stepped house, accompanied by light and in an uninterrupted manner.

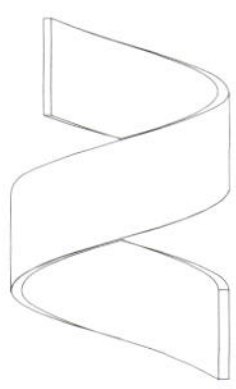

Winery in Bargino (IT)
Archea Associati, Florence

The sculptural stair of the winery distinguishes itself in a markedly formal manner from the building, and thus becomes an object displaying a pronounced uniqueness due to its bold design.

Stage and Landscape

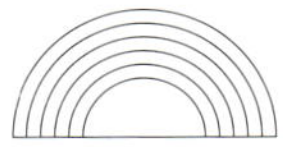

Store conversion in New York (US)
OMA/AMO, New York/Rotterdam

Inside the store, the stair acts as a stage: for positioning the mannequins, on the one hand, and as a catwalk for the shoppers, on the other.

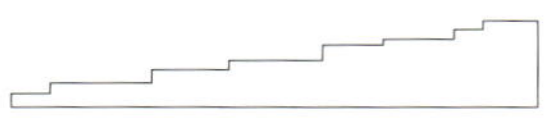

City library in Seinäjoki (FI)
JKMM Arkkitehdit, Helsinki

With the colourful accentuation by the seat cushions, the stair here is the continuation of the reading landscape.

Aesthetics of technology vs Longing for the archetype

Gallery and bar in Kyoto (JP)
Florian Busch Architects, Tokyo

The folded steel stair is reduced and elegant. The aesthetics of technology require precise detailing and technical understanding.

School building in St. Peter (CH)
Conradin Clavuot, Chur

Log construction is one of the traditional building techniques in Grisons. This archaic stair transforms the context into a modern, contemporary design vocabulary.

Volume vs Continuity

Church and community centre in Cologne (DE)
Sauerbruch Hutton, Berlin

In the nave, the stair leading to the pulpit is articulated as a volume, and thus divides the surrounding space.

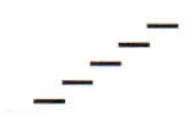

Hotel in Obanazawa (JP)
Kengo Kuma & Associates, Tokyo

The delicate stair subtly continues the space onto the upper level without ruining the spatial impression. The stair seems incorporeal and blends into the holistic spatial concept.

Furniture and Addition

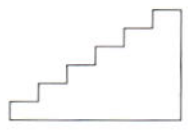

Residential building in Vrhovlje (SI)
dekleva gregorič arhitekti, Ljubljana

The piece of furniture is simultaneously a stair, and, thanks to this hybridity, creates spaciousness even in a small flat's floor plan.

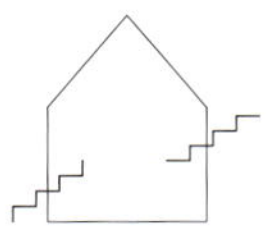

Exhibition and event centre, Franzensfeste (IT)
Markus Scherer, Meran
Walter Dietl, Schlanders

Distinguishing itself formally and in terms of material from the context, while being constructed in such a restrained manner that respect for the building stock predominates, the stair avoids appearing object-like.

Stepped house in Brugg

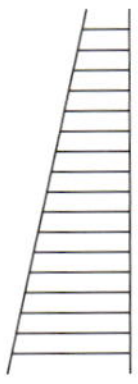

Architects: Ken Architekten, Zurich
Contributors: Jürg Kaiser, Lorenz Peter, Martin Schwager, Gian Andri Mohr, Friederike Wisler, Charles Wülser
Structural engineers: Heyer Kaufmann Partner, Baden
Planning / completion: 2008 / 2013

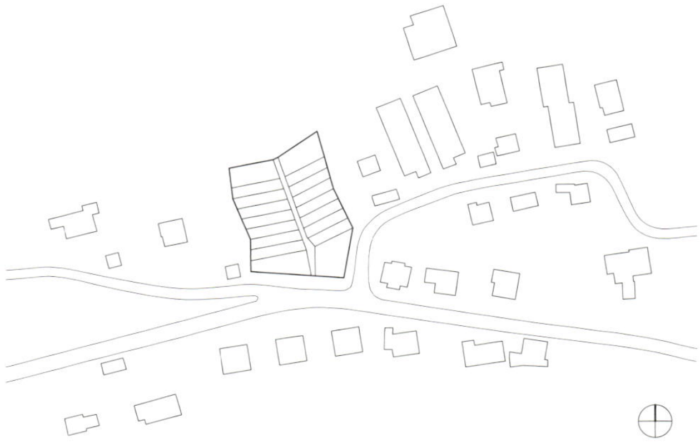

Site plan
Scale 1:4,000

Located on a south-facing slope on the outskirts of the small Swiss town of Brugg, this stepped house holds its ground in the midst of a heterogeneous housing development. The circumferential wall of varnished exposed concrete condenses the 16 freehold flats into a self-confident, large-scale form. With its irregular bends, it responds to the topography of the slope. The surfaces of the immediate surroundings, a lawn and asphalt, directly adjoin the building.

On the south-eastern corner, the asphalt flows up to the entrance hall. From here, a Jacob's ladder-shaped stair, as well as an inclined elevator, provide access to the eight residential levels. In addition, the end of the characteristic stair grants access to a common space and playground on the topmost platform of the building. Simple but robust materials, such as the prefabricated, exposed concrete steps, as well as a colourful, warm sun-yellow coat of paint define the stairwell. It is lit by a glass door at the end of the stair and by sideward windows, which rhythmise the space in a suspenseful manner. Similar openings perforate the circumferential walls in an irregular pattern, lighting or ventilating the parking garage, as well as the bathroom and cellar spaces. The stair and the elevator form the central spine of the complex, which is clearly discernible externally in the form of a concrete ribbon. On both sides of this, the flats are arranged in spatial layers running parallel to the slope, directed towards spacious roof terraces along the entire breadth. Every flat has two access options: an elevator entrance in the rear spatial layer, as well as an entrance from the stair, directly at the facade. From here, the residential area extends along the wholly glazed terrace front up to the external wall.

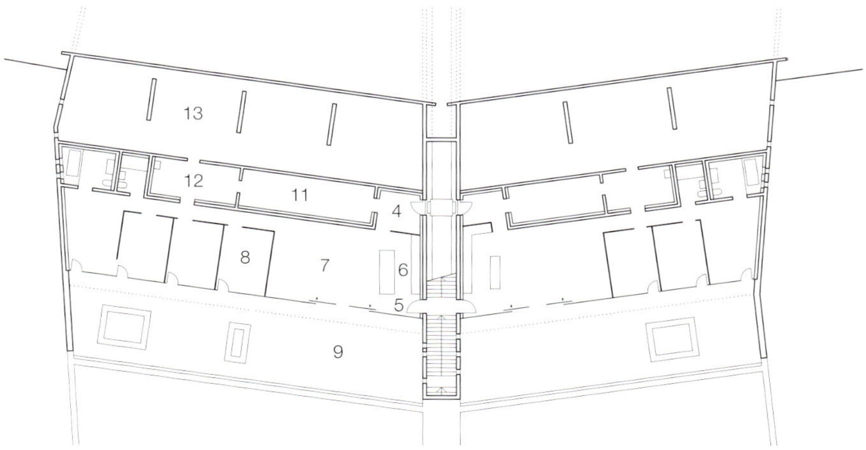

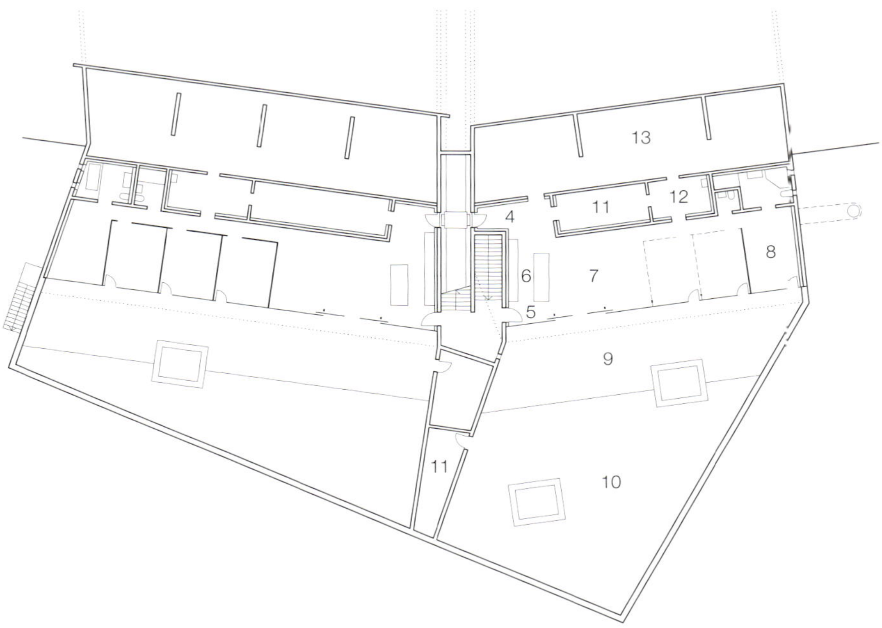

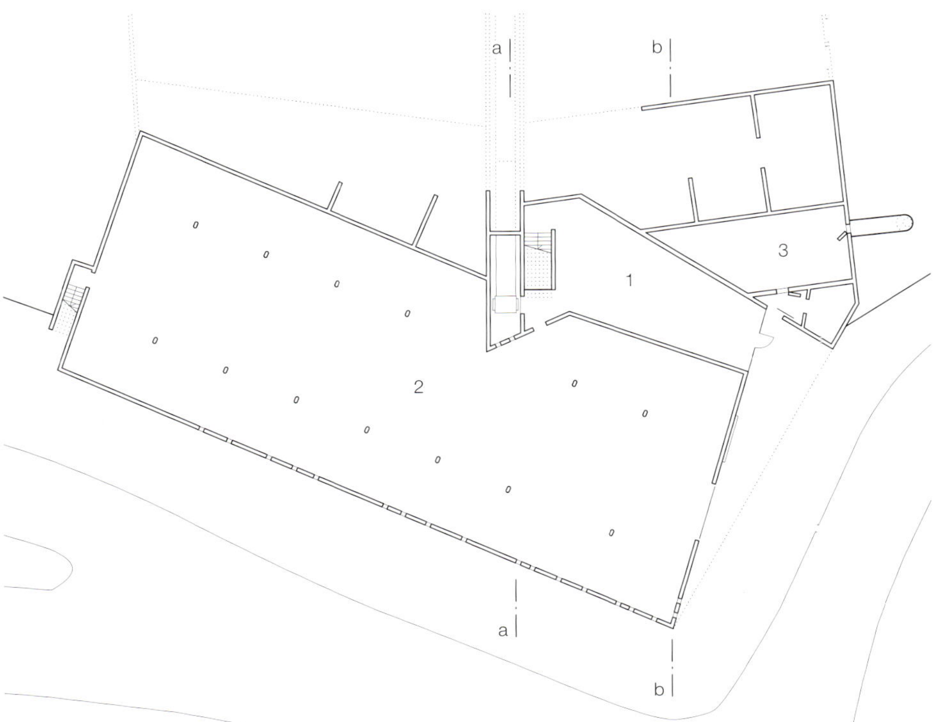

5th floor
1st floor
Ground floor
Scale 1:500

1 Entrance hall
2 Car park
3 Shelter
4 Entrance to the flat (from the inclined lift)
5 Access (from staircase)
6 Kitchen
7 Living / dining room
8 Room
9 Roof terrace
10 Roof garden
11 Storeroom (unheated)
12 Laundry (unheated)
13 Cellar / building services

Sections Scale 1:500

1 Entrance hall
2 Car park
3 Shelter
4 Roof terrace
5 Living / dining room
6 Storeroom (unheated)
7 Cellar / building services
8 Playground / community terrace

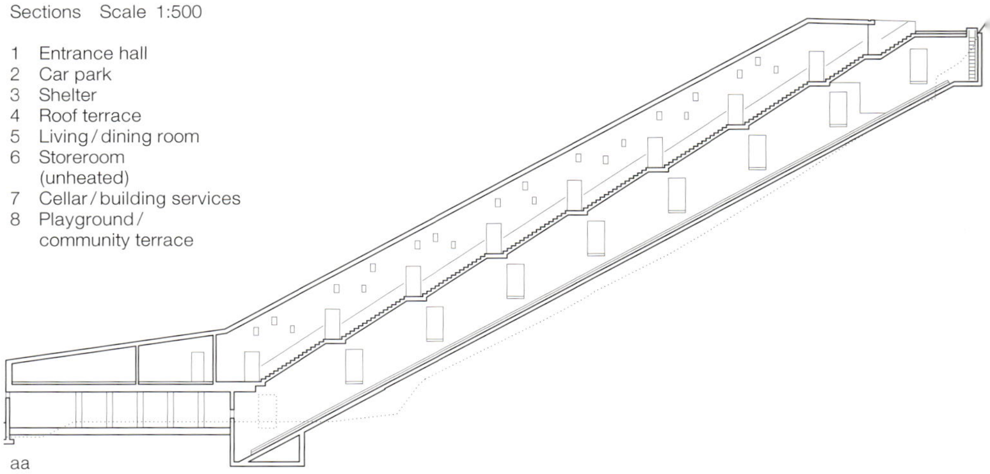

aa

Section stair Scale 1:50

9 Stairwell ceiling:
Sealant liquid plastic coloured 50 mm
Ceiling reinforced concrete 300 mm
Thermal insulation 40 mm
Wooden battens 40 mm
Acoustic panel wood-wool slab 25 mm

10 Stair landing:
Cover PVC 9 mm
Rubber pellet mat 8 mm
Cement screed 30 mm
Reinforced concrete 250 mm
Thermal insulation wood-wool 50 mm

11 Stair flight prefabricated reinforced concrete element

12 Outside stair landing:
Floor coating plastic, water-permeable, sound-insulating,
Cover layer of colourful rubber and gravel granulate coloured 8 mm
Sealant liquid plastic 5 mm
Reinforced concrete on a gradient 100–170 mm
Reinforced concrete 250 mm
Thermal insulation wood-wool 50 mm

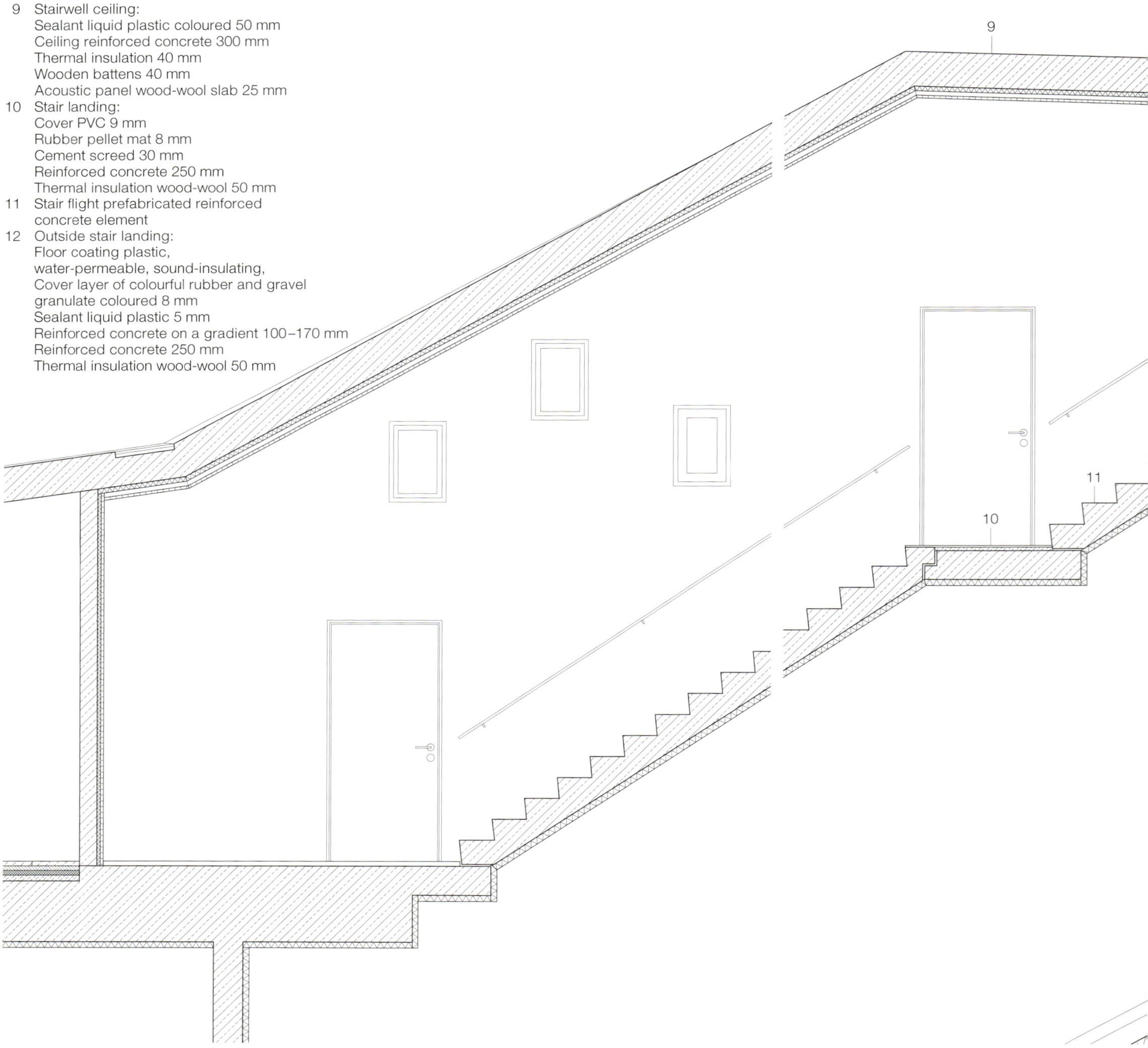

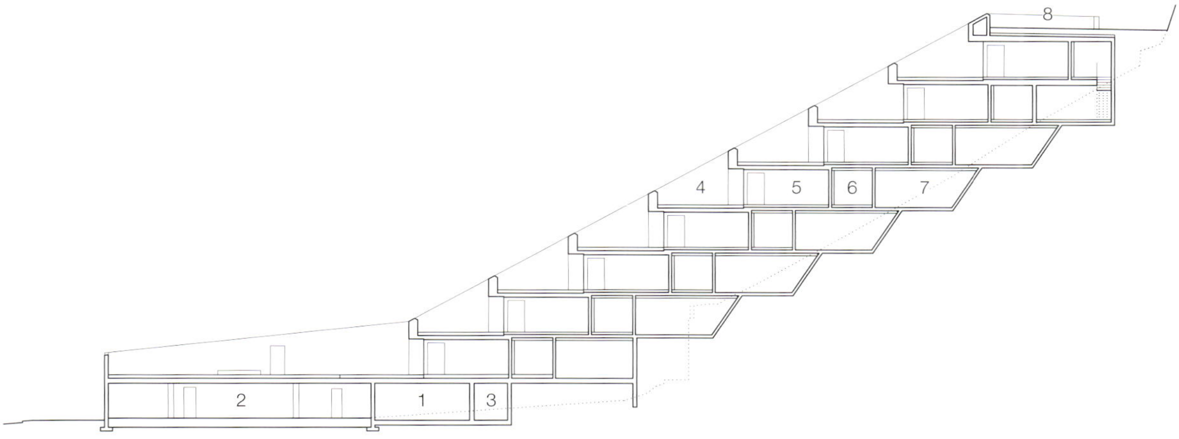

bb

Winery in Bargino

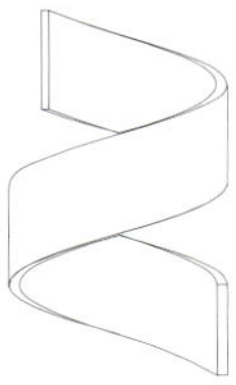

Architects:	Archea Associati, Florence-Laura Andreini, Marco Casamonti, Silvia Fabi, Giovanni Polazzi
Contributors:	Francesco Giordani
Structural engineer:	AEI Progetti, Florence
Planning/completion:	2004/2012

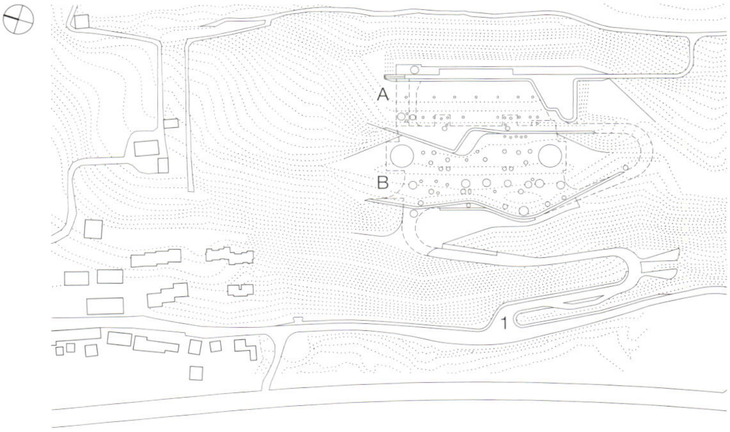

Located south of Florence, the Antinori winery seems to merge with the landscape. The almost 40,000 m² building complex, which is both the production site and head office, is almost completely concealed in the hill. All that remains visible are two facade ribbons between vine-planted roof surfaces, a sculptural stair made of corroded steel, and supporting walls of reddish brown exposed concrete. The heart of the wine-making process is comprised by the lower level, with its wine press, stainless steel fermentation tanks and vaulted cellar, where the barrique barrels are stored. Above this, the recessed topmost part of the building accommodates the delivery area and the filling funnel for the grapes, as well as the bottling plant and storehouse. On the downhill side, three levels with administrative and visitors' areas are adjoined, including a shop, a museum, a lecture room, a tasting facility and a restaurant. Circular, partly glazed openings allow daylight to enter the subterranean areas, creating suspenseful visual relationships. A distinctive, spiral-shaped circular stair is placed in front of the facade, leading visitors from the underground car park to the main entrance, and on to the roof terrace and the restaurant. With its varying radii, the stair winds itself around the "central" column four times, and has a total length of 100 m. The construction is a box girder with complex geometry, made from 35 parts that were welded together on site. The 17 m high steel stair, weighing 105 t, is fixed to the column only at the bottom, the roof terrace and at three points. As such, and in spite of its mass, it seems light and sweeping – a sculptural outside staircase, inviting users to slowly walk up the 118 steps to enjoy the far-reaching view of the hilly Tuscan landscape.

Site plan
Scale 1:7,500
Section
Floor plans
Building part B
Scale 1:1,500

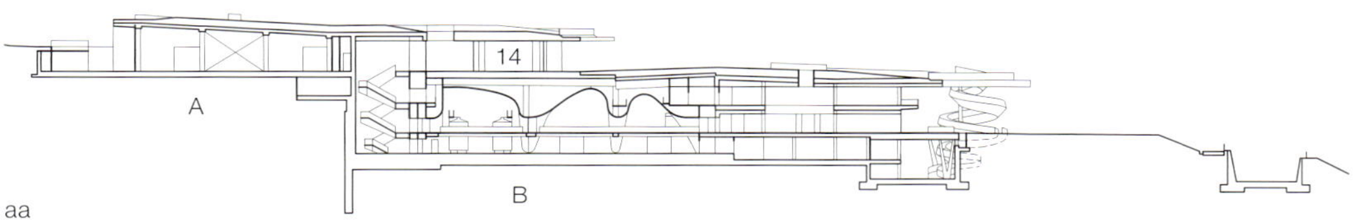

aa

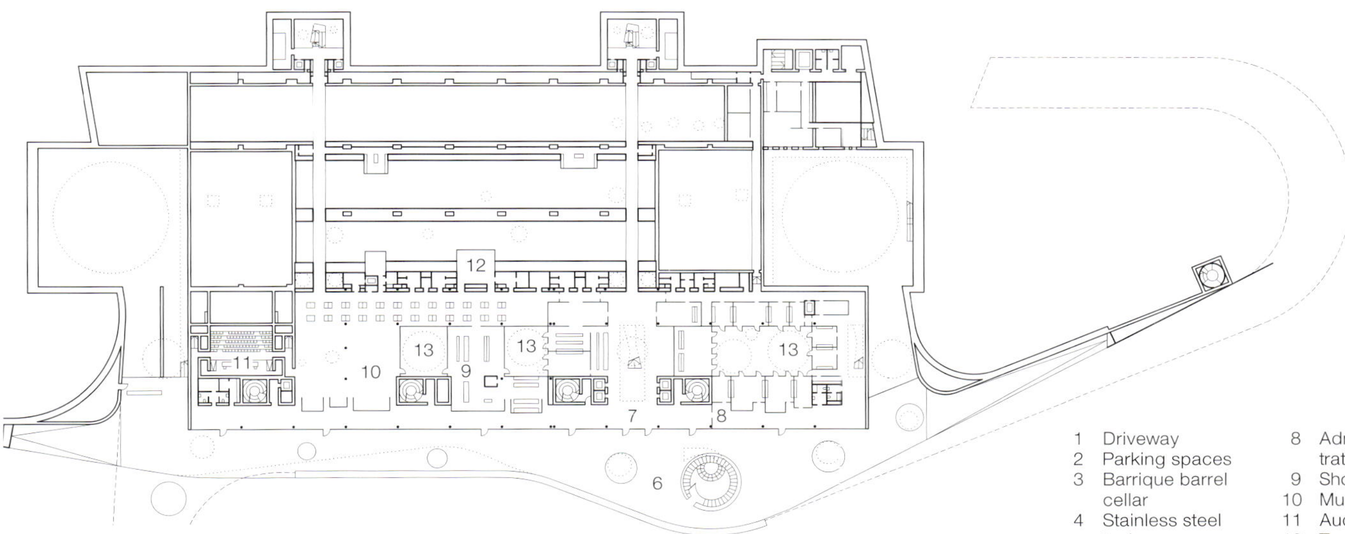

Visitor area level

1 Driveway
2 Parking spaces
3 Barrique barrel cellar
4 Stainless steel tanks
5 Wine press
6 Terrace
7 Reception
8 Adminis-tration
9 Shop
10 Museum
11 Auditorium
12 Tasting facility
13 Courtyard
14 Restaurant

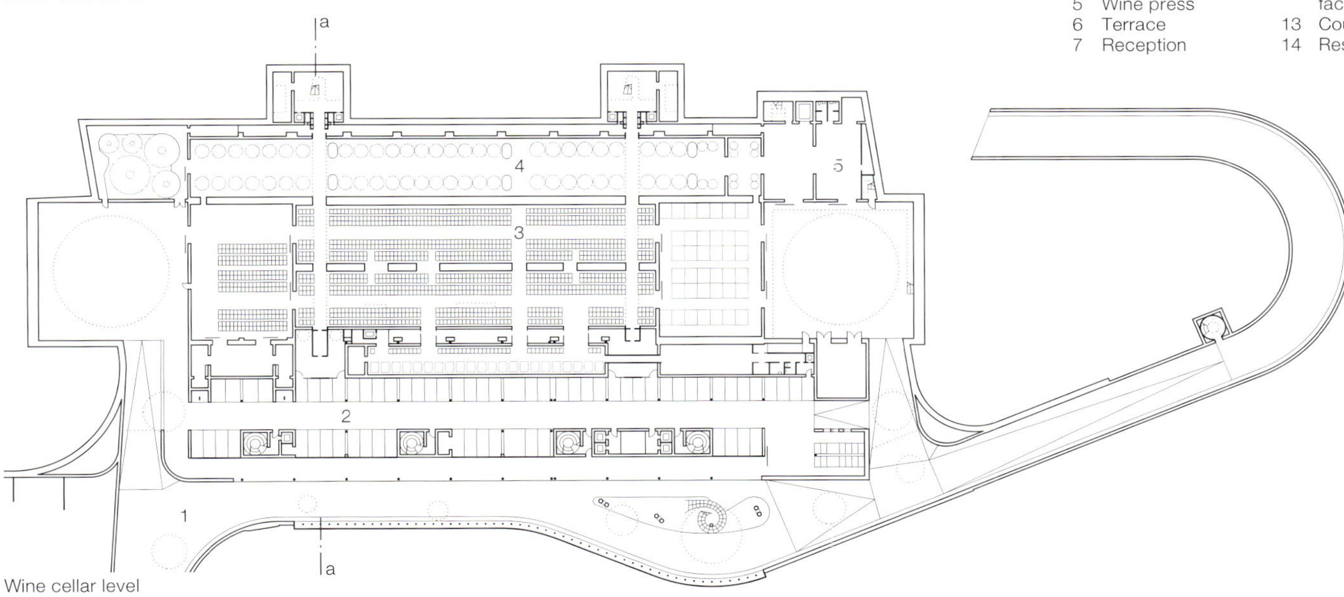

Wine cellar level

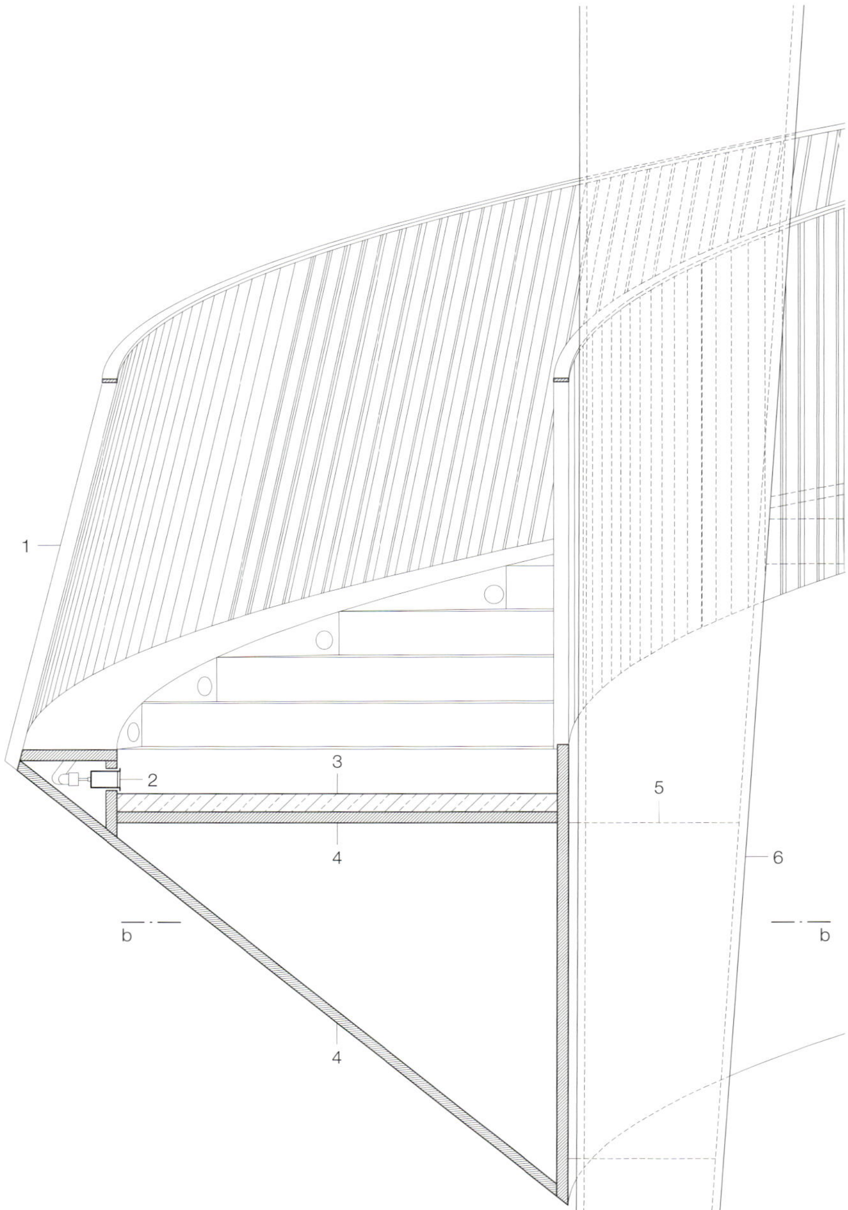

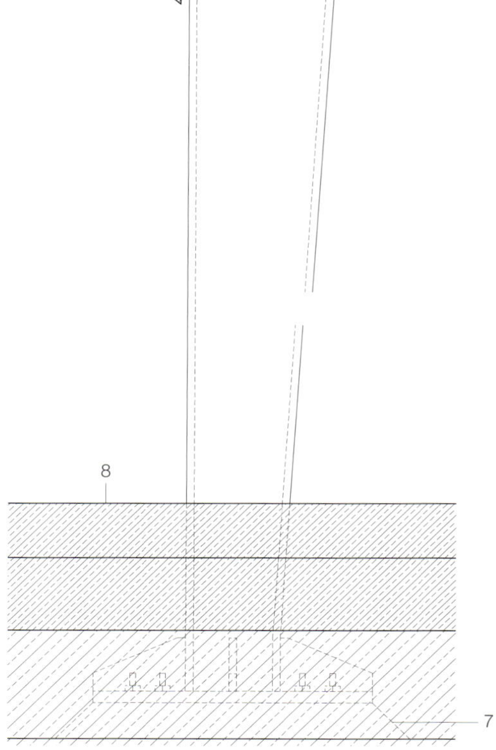

Spiral stair:
Vertical section • Horizontal section with connection to column
Scale 1:20

All steel parts: corroded steel
1 Banister flat steel ⏥ 40/10 mm
2 Lamp
3 Step covering in-situ concrete 60 mm, reinforced with glass fibre and wire mesh, surface brushed
4 Box girder steel sheet 30 mm, welded
5 Beam / connection to column
Flat steel ⏥ 35 mm
6 Column steel profile ∅ 250/20–600/10 mm
7 Column mount reinforced concrete
8 Floor construction:
Concrete screed coloured 150 mm, reinforced with glass fibre and wire mesh
Concrete screed 200 mm reinforced with glass fibre and wire mesh
Reinforced concrete 300 mm

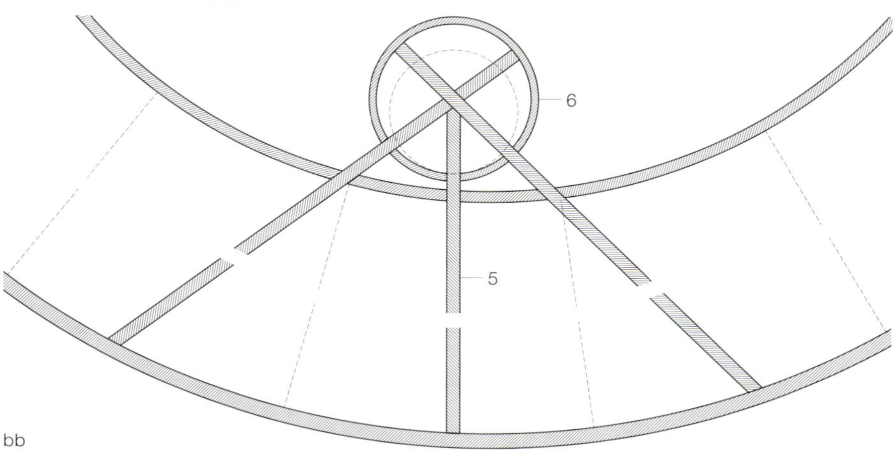

bb

Store conversion in New York

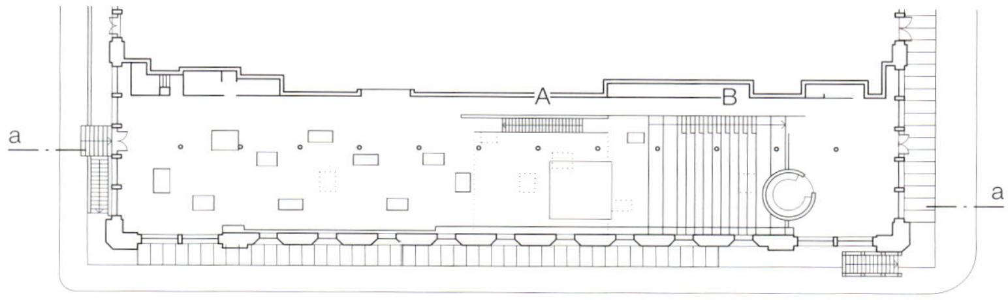

Architects: OMA/AMO, New York/Rotterdam
Rem Koolhaas, Dan Wood, Ole Scheeren, Markus Schaefer

Planning/completion: 2000/2001

Floor plan Scale 1:750

The Prada Store in SoHo is the first of three large stores, prior to those in Los Angeles and San Francisco, where Rem Koolhaas has realised new sales ideas for the fashion company from Milan. The prestigious object is not a store in the conventional sense, but an adventure space, a shopping experiment, as well as a private and public space at the same time. At night, the commercial clothing store turns into a place for culture, an auditorium with a capacity of 200, for film screenings, lectures, or performances. The focus of all these cultural activities is a large, wave-like wooden stair, which swings down from the entrance level and also serves as seating accommodation. Since the visitors represent an important part of the overall setting, the boundaries between spectators and performers blur during the events. The stair represents a stage for both participating parties in equal measure. The view, both from and onto the stage, is similarly highly significant. During regular sales operations, the steps turn into a stage for shoes or handbags. On the opposite side, the wave again splashes upwards in the form of a smooth wooden surface. A platform can be folded out from this surface. Via a narrow stair on the side, visitors can access further sales areas in the rear part of the store. Clothes and accessories are exhibited in differently sized cages of expanded metal, hanging freely in the space; digitally controlled, they run on tracks in the ceiling and can change their position; and for events, the cages are collected. The lower turning point of the wave provides access to additional sales rooms, a cosmetics section, as well as changing rooms in the basement.

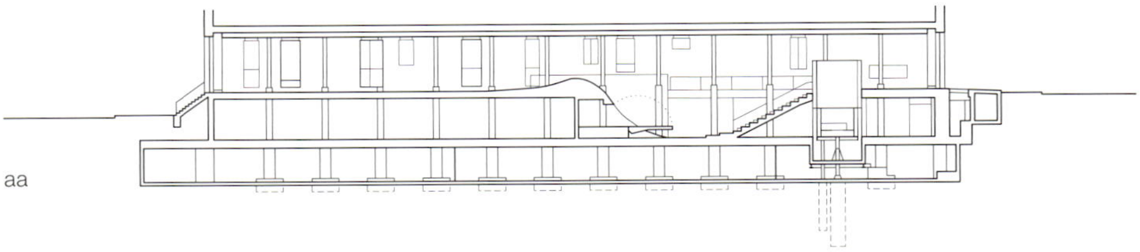

Section
Scale 1:750
Detail sections
Scale 1:10

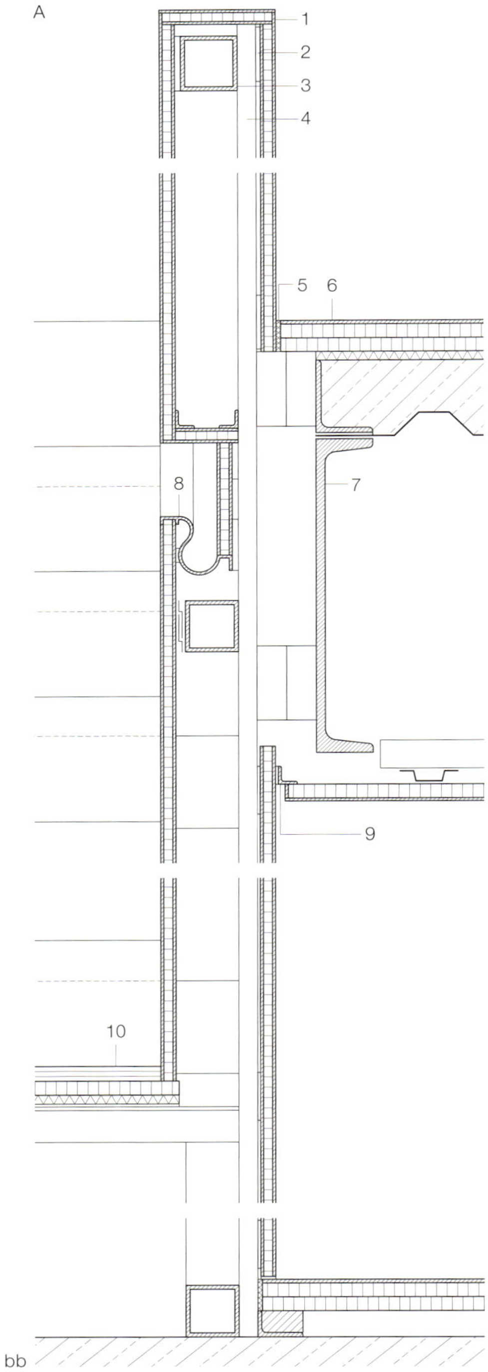

1 Aluminium sheet on plywood panel 20 mm glued
2 Spacer disc
3 Frame of aluminium tubes ⌀ 76/76 mm
4 Aluminium rod ⌀ 25/25 mm
5 EPDM 6 mm
6 Floor construction:
Aluminium sheet glued on plywood panel 20 mm, two-ply soft fibreboard 12 mm
7 Steel beam of bridge structure
8 Handrail extruded aluminium sheath
9 Aluminium angle ∟ 25/25 mm
10 Tropical wood zebrawood 18 mm
11 Plywood panel 20 mm
12 Soft fibreboard 12 mm
13 Equalising pad
14 Inserting strips zinc 3/6 mm
15 Steel profile 220 mm
16 Steel angle ∟ 40/60 mm
17 Laminated safety glass of 2× toughened safety glass 10 mm
18 EPDM 6 mm
19 Aluminium sheet on plywood panel 20 mm glued
20 Plywood panel 20 mm
21 Soft fibreboard 12 mm
22 Glass mount aluminium profile
23 Equalising pad
24 Steel angle ∟ 100/75/8 mm
25 Reinforced concrete ceiling on trapezoidal sheet
26 Ceiling construction of steel profiles
27 Handrail extruded aluminium sheath 50/30 mm
28 Stainless steel tube ⌀ 20/20 mm
29 Tropical wood zebrawood 18 mm
30 Plywood panel 20 mm
31 Soft fibreboard 12 mm
32 Steel sheet 5 mm
33 Cantilever beam steel profile 320 mm
34 Steel angle ∟ 40/60 mm
35 Suspended ceiling, aluminium polished

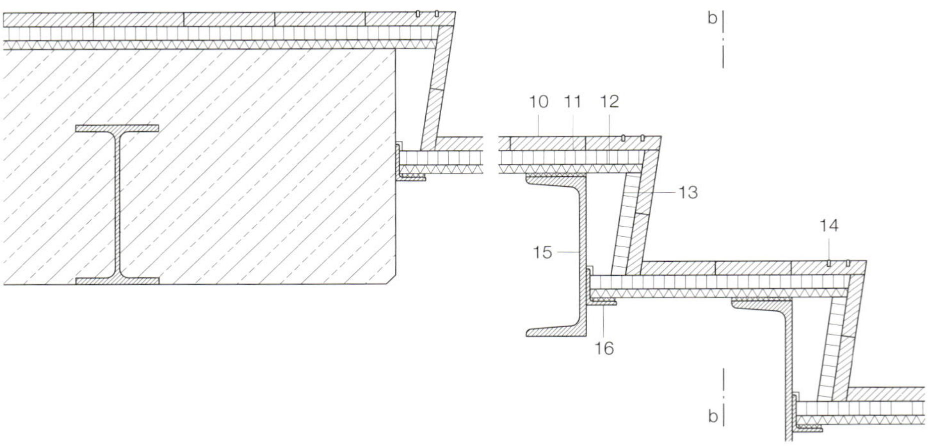

B

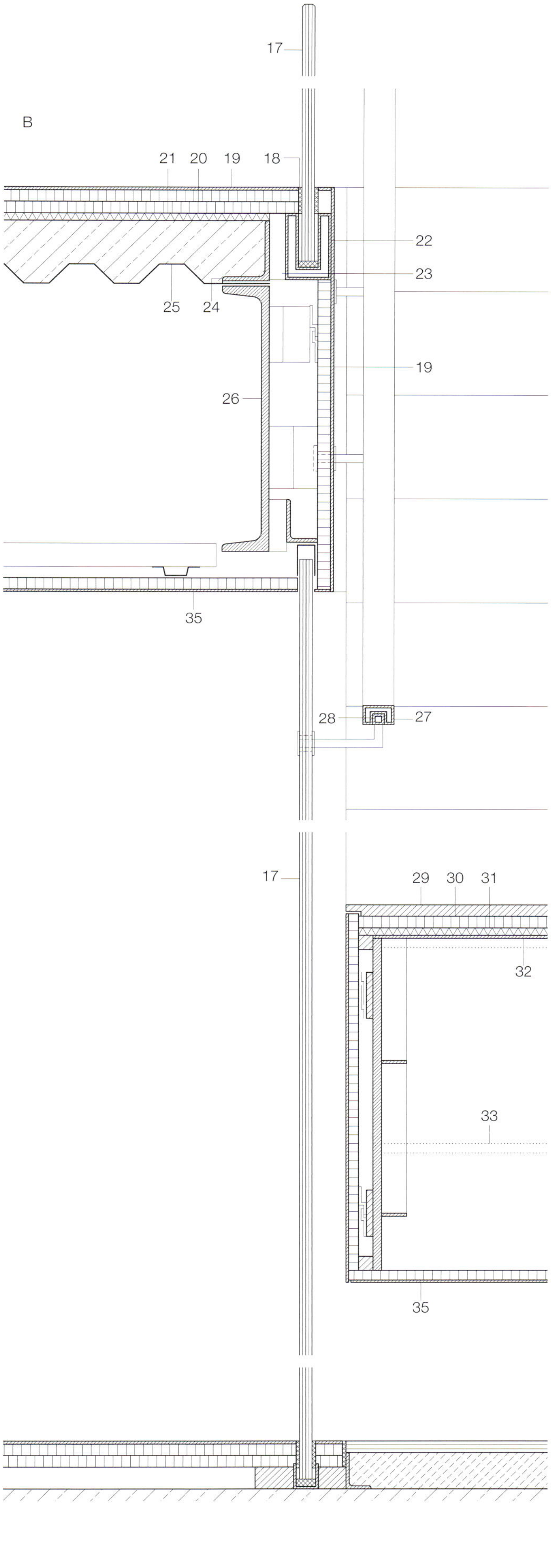
17
21 20 19 18
22
23
25 24
19
26
35
28 27
17
29 30 31
32
33
35

cc

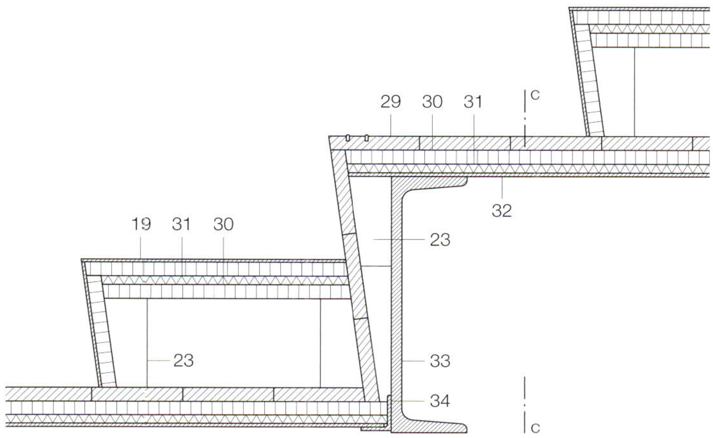
29 30 31
c
32
19 31 30
23
23
33
34
c

City library in Seinäjoki

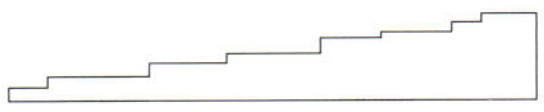

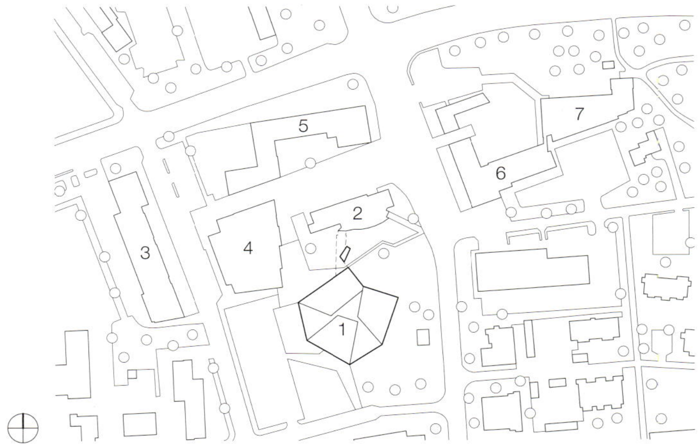

Architects:	JKMM Arkkitehdit, Helsinki Asmo Jaaksi, Teemu Kurkela, Samuli Miettinen, Juha Mäki-Jyllilä
Contributors:	Aaro Martikainen, Päivi Meuronen, Teemu Toivio
Structural engineer:	Eero Pekkari, Ramboll Finland, Espoo
Planning/ completion:	2008/2012

The small town of Seinäjoki in western Finland has gained a certain popularity owing to its city centre designed by Alvar Aalto. The church, the town hall, the library, the community centre, the district administration and the theatre form a harmonic ensemble of predominantly white, copper-clad buildings. After more than 40 years, due to population growth on the one hand and new developments in the media sector on the other, the city library no longer met current requirements. The new building complements the functions of the old building, and is connected to it by a tunnel. In its scale and materials, the new library refers to the existing building stock, while self-confidently speaking a contemporary architectural language. On the outside, the building is divided into three parts, which blend into a single whole inside. Though the individual areas are clearly differentiated from each other due to their floor plan geometry, the main spaces seamlessly merge into each other, permitting diverse visual relationships. The diversely sloping in-situ concrete ceilings, with their exposed framework structure, lend the spaces a sculptural character, and simultaneously conceal the long-span wooden support structure of the roof. Conceptually, the library is not supposed to be just a repository of media, but also a meeting place and lounge for interacting with media. The heart of the building is undoubtedly the "reading landscape", a free-standing staircase with colourful seat cushions. This creates a spacious link between the main level and the basement, which houses the youth section and the intersection with the Aalto library. In addition,

Site plan Scale 1:5,000
Sections • Floor plans Scale 1:1,000

1 New library

Neighbouring building to Alvar Aalto:
2 Old library (1965)
3 Official building (1968)
4 Local theatre (1987)
5 Town hall (1962)
6 Community centre (1966)
7 Church (1960)
8 Intersection with old library
9 Games
10 Books for young people
11 Music, films
12 Seating niches
13 Reading steps
14 Exhibition
15 Information / service
16 Stacks
17 Café
18 Newspapers
19 Foyer
20 Multipurpose hall
21 Administration
22 Distribution
23 Mobile library store
24 Play area
25 Children's books
26 Reading room
27 Books
28 Conference room
29 Staff café

it invites users to linger and read on the seat cushions, which are in various shades of green. The cushions are placed on the stair, bridging two steps each and thus ensuring a pleasant seat height and seat depth. As such, they can also be used as seats for spectators at events. In order not to undermine the impact of the free-standing stair, it is accompanied by only one handrail on each side; apart from that, its appearance is reduced to the homogeneous white treads and the colourful seat cushions.

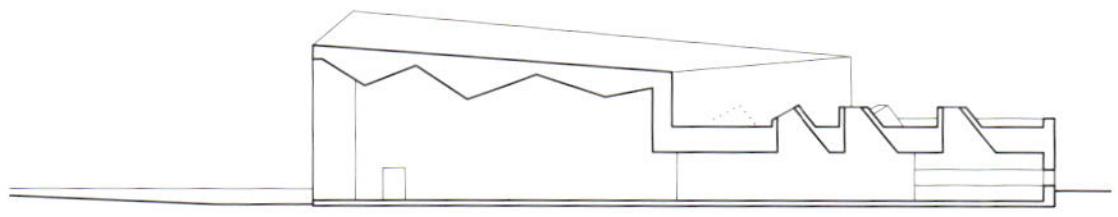

aa

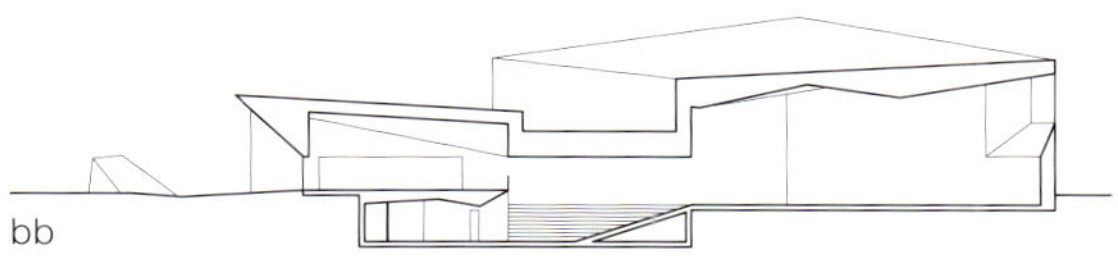

bb

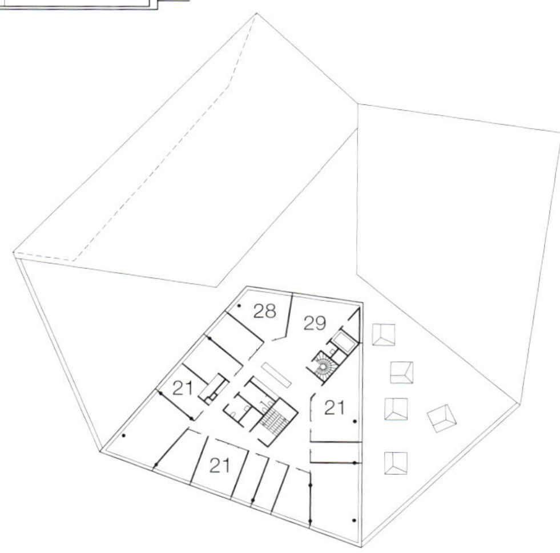

Upper floor

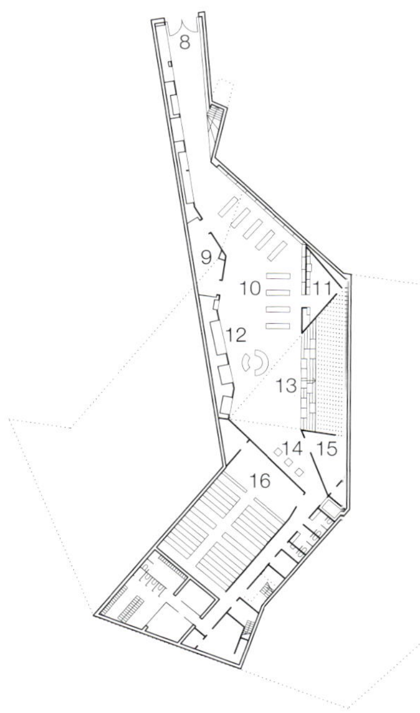

Basement

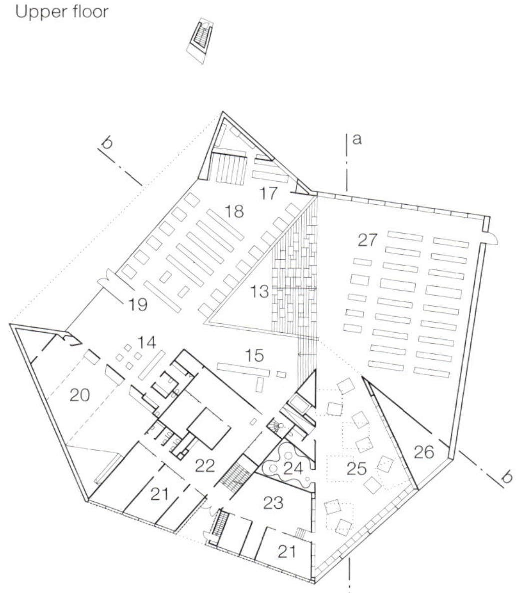

Ground floor

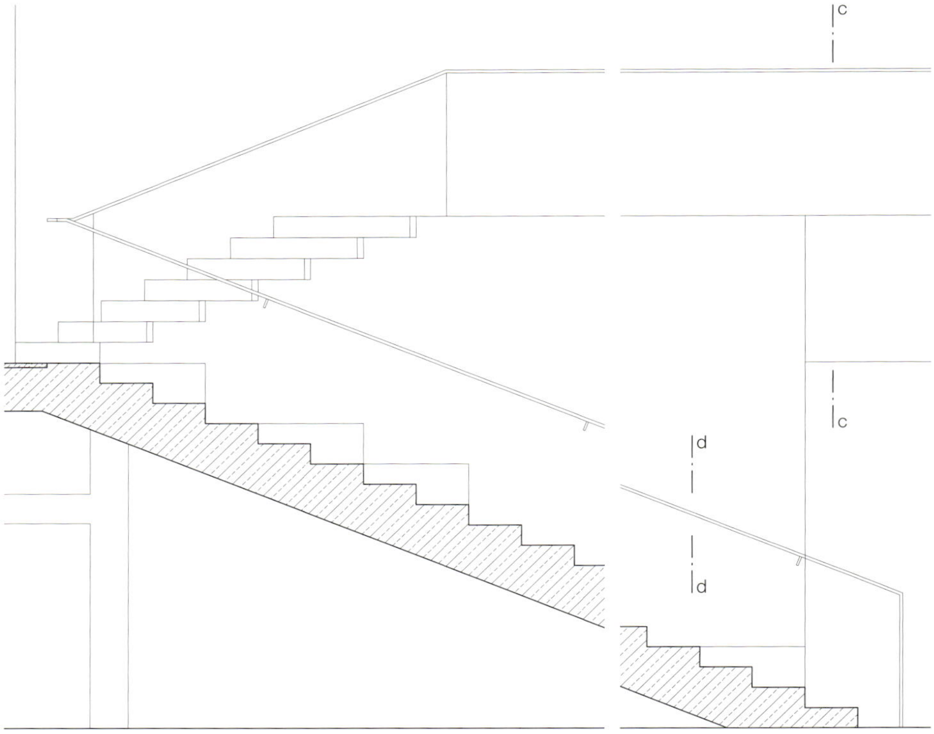

Vertical section stair
Scale 1:50
Details banister
Scale 1:5

1 Handrail flat steel 50/20 mm
2 Steel rod Ø 8 mm, mounted in reinforced concrete wall
3 Steel profile grooved 5 mm, embedded in reinforced concrete wall, painted on room-facing side
4 Handrail steel tube ▱ 50/30/2.5 mm, welded on steel profile
5 Laminated safety glass 8 + 8 mm, mounted in aluminium profile
6 Carpeted floor 6 mm
Reinforced concrete
Thermal insulation 20 mm
Acoustic panel 10 mm
7 Flat steel grooved 3 mm
8 Acoustic panel 10 mm
Flat steel grooved 5 mm

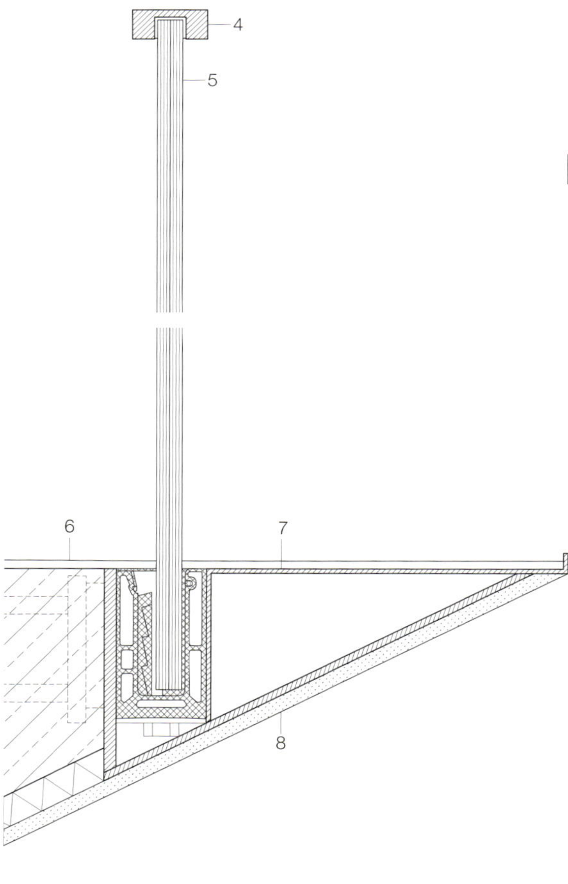

cc

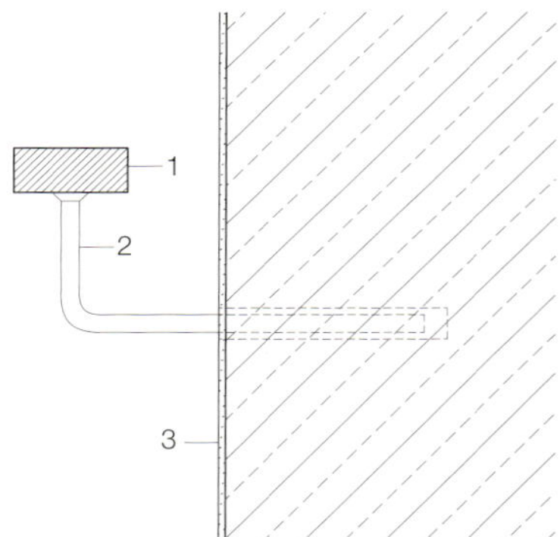

dd

Gallery and bar in Kyoto

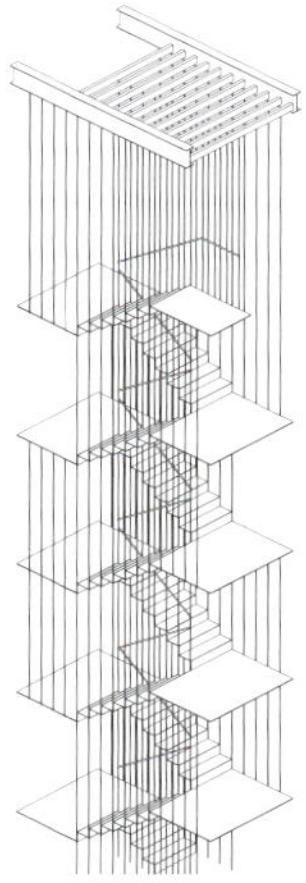

Architects:	Florian Busch Architects, Tokyo
Contributors:	Sachiko Miyazaki, Suguru Takahashi (Project head)
Structural engineer:	OAK Masato Araya, Tomonori Kawata, Tokyo
Planning / completion:	2014/2015

On the outskirts of the famous entertainment quarter Pontocho in the centre of Kyoto stands K8, a small building with a bar and a gallery – a continuous interior extending over eight levels. The building shell, a homogeneous yet constantly changing surface, creates an ambiguity that is often found in the architecture of Kyoto. Several hundred wooden louvres create a sense of movement, as if the building were continuously reacting to its surroundings. The stair, which dominates the entire interior, develops into a vertical meeting place here, owing to enlargements in the landings. It embodies the concept of the whole building: an almost stoic reduction, right up to the "absence" of details. This is made possible by the application of black steel, but also by employing numerous refined technical solutions with an aesthetic all their own, and which ultimately decisively shape the image of the stair. The access space becomes a meeting place or a visitors to the bar, lending the narrow plot a surprising spaciousness.

Axonometric drawing stair
Floor plan • Section
Scale 1:200

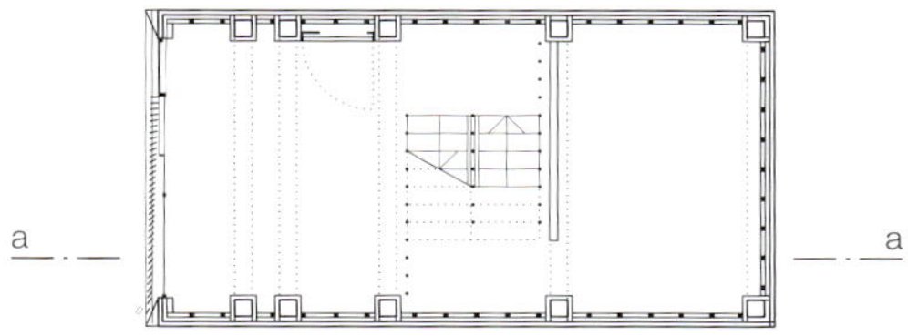

1st floor

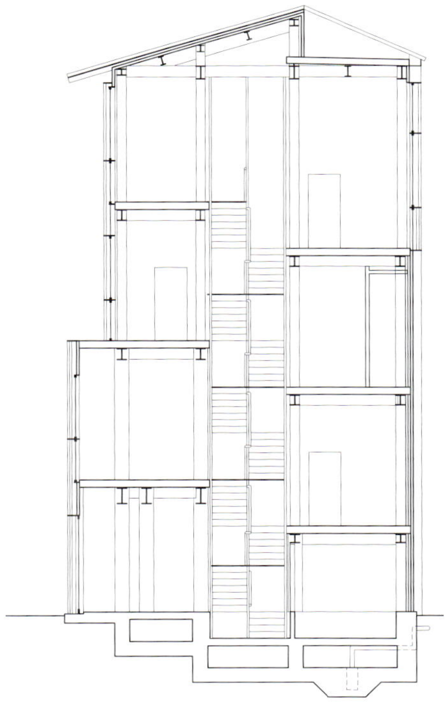

aa

Vertical sections stair Scale 1:20

1 Sealing sodium silicate
Screed 35 mm, smoothed
Reinforced composite concrete slab 160 mm
2 Black steel profile ▭ 200/9 mm, PU coated
3 Black steel profile L 120/120/9 mm, PU coated
4 Steel profile IPE 250
Fire safety cladding mineral wool 30 mm
5 Landing black steel panel 16 mm, PU coated
6 Tread and riser black steel profile
▭ 400/9 mm, PU coated, welded together
7 Steel rods Ø 10.8 mm,
on M12, welded to riser
8 Handrail steel tube Ø 21 mm, PU coated
9 Steel profile ▭ 184/100/9 mm
10 Steel profile IPE 300, fire safety cladding
mineral wool 30 mm

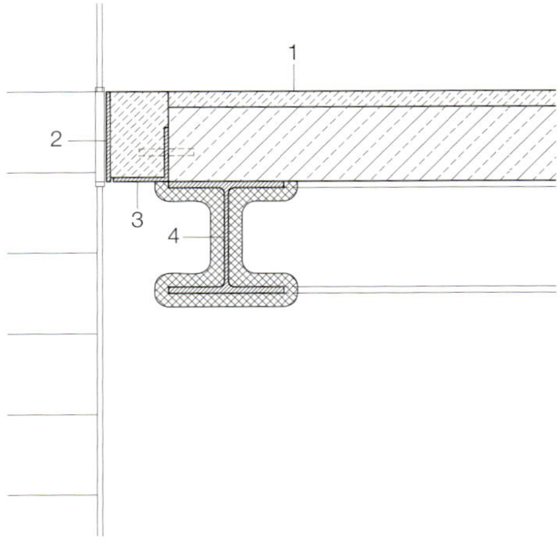

School building in St. Peter

Architects:	Conradin Clavuot, Chur
Contributors:	Claudia Clavuot-Merz, Norbert Mathis, Alex Jörg, Paula Deplazes
Structural engineer:	Jürg Conzett, Chur
Planning / completion:	1996 / 1998

In the Schanfigg, a high valley near Chur, the traditional rural way of construction has been continuously preserved ever since the 16th century, both in terms of the settlement structure and the types of log construction. One of the design-defining factors of the complex was to further develop the building stock, consisting of the existing community hall and the new multipurpose hall, the recreational area with a nursery, and the school building. The log building, virtually the prototype of modular construction, has been translated into a contemporary design vocabulary. The horizontal, 11.5 × 20.0 cm thick, shaved and otherwise untreated wooden beams have retained a residual moisture of approximately 12 % despite a long storage period. This dries up over time, leading to shrinkage of the beams, especially laterally towards the annual rings, while longitudinal shrinkage can be ignored. In order to give the movable system, which partly comprises large log walls (up to 36 m long and 7.50 m high), a high static load capacity, it is fixed to an immovable system by means of a dynamic connection: the horizontal logs can move down along vertical mullion with screwed-on dovetail profiles; the internal walls consist of double log walls. The stairwell is particularly impressive. With its stacked wooden steps, banisters, and balustrades, it reflects the materiality of the surrounding walls. The archaic treads, corresponding to the dimension of the log beams, join together at every step. They are held in place by the banister in the form of a solid closed string on the space-facing side and the accompanying wall, and are attached to it invisibly.

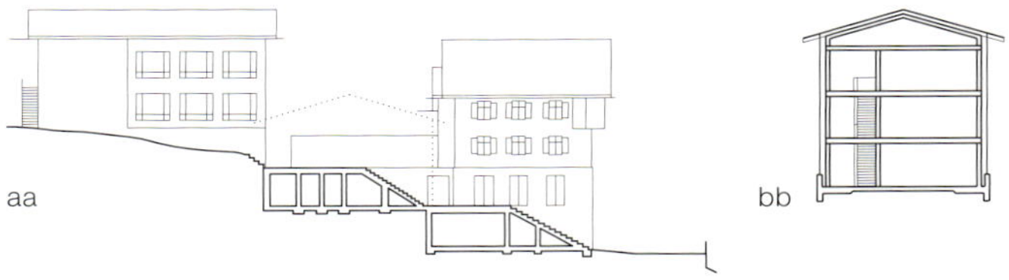

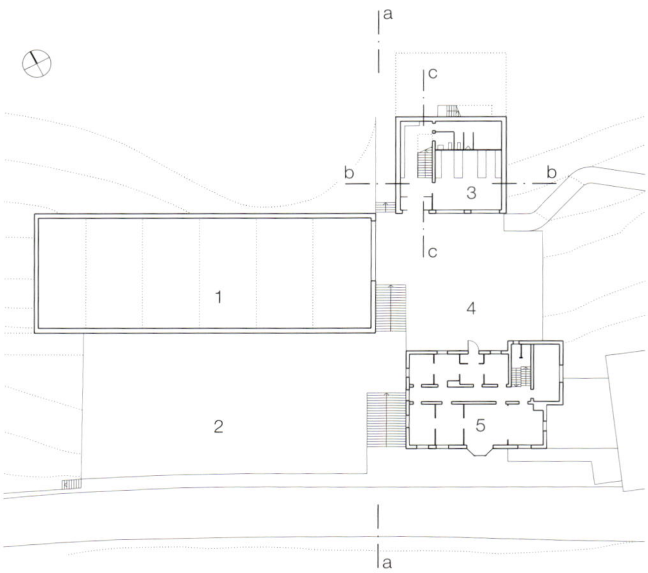

Sections
Floor plan
2nd floor
Scale 1:800

1 Multipurpose hall
2 All-weather area
3 School building
4 Recreational area
5 Community hall (building stock)

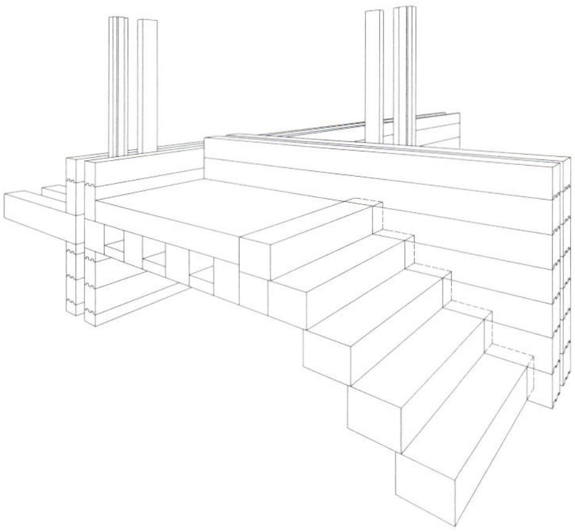

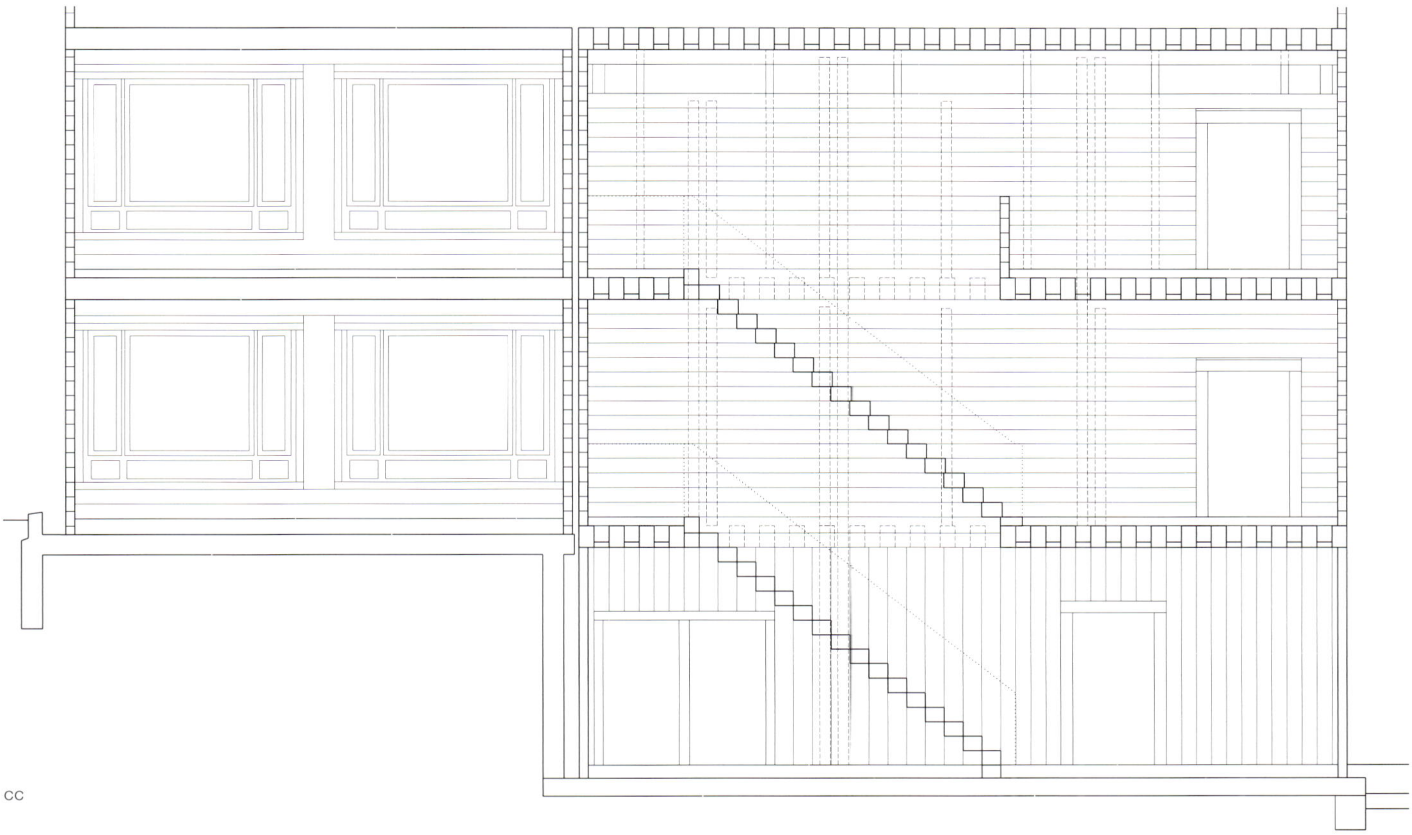

cc

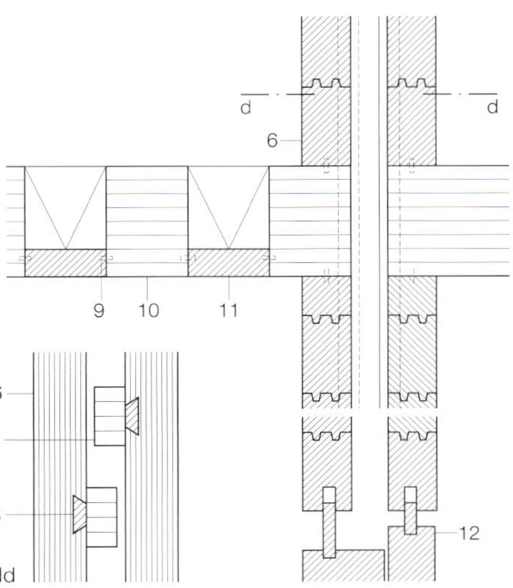

dd

Section cc Scale 1:100
Interior wall detail Scale 1:20
Stair detail Scale 1:20

6 Flat-lying log 115/200 mm
7 Mullion glued laminated timber 70/140 mm
8 Hardwood dovetail, glued on and screwed
9 Hardwood dowel
10 Beam glued laminated timber 200/280 mm
11 Plank 60/200 mm
12 Door frame of square timber elements
13 Log in the area of the stair opening 155/200 mm
14 Wooden guide element 45/50 mm, screwed and glued on log
15 Tread 220/250 mm
16 Connecting dowel Ø 20 mm, between step and log
17 Standing log interior wall 115 mm
18 Connection anchor system between wood and reinforced concrete Ø 12 mm,
19 Threshold larch wood 115/50 mm
20 Mortar layer 20 mm

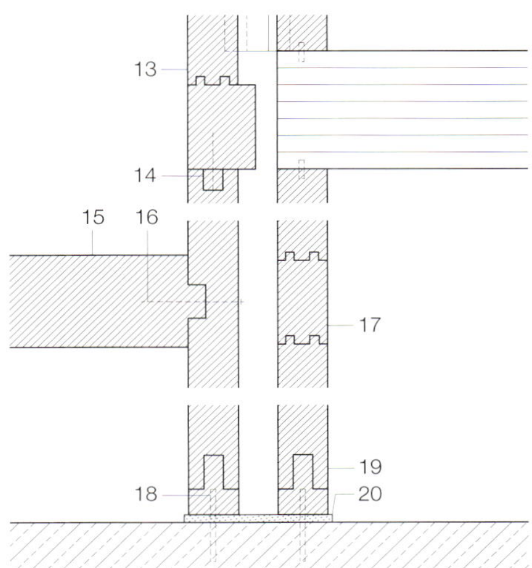

Church and community centre in Cologne

Architects:	Sauerbruch Hutton, Berlin Louisa Hutton, Matthias Sauerbruch, Juan Lucas Young
Project heads:	Jürgen Bartenschlag, Vera Hartmann
Structural engineers:	Horz + Ladewig, Cologne
Planning / completion:	2009/2013

Located on a plot in Cologne-Stammheim, the new building of the Protestant Immanuel Church nestles in an old stock of trees. Owing to the use of diagonal wooden planking for cladding the facades of the individual building parts, the building project gently blends into its surroundings. A low foyer under the gallery provides access to the church building, with visitors subsequently experiencing the nave's full height of 11 m. The prefabricated timber panels and columns are unclad, while the brushed and white waxed surfaces expose the grain of the wood; the floor covering consists of a light polished screed. The rib structure, with columns of 7.5 × 30 cm, together with the infilled panels, results in a stiffened supporting structure, which includes the roof and the wall sections.
The gallery is accessed by a single-flight stair, which is designed as a volume, owing to its closed, head-high strings, and thus optically separates the actual foyer from an access corridor for ancillary rooms. To avoid a too massive appearance of the stair, it is only supported by the floor and ceiling, and is otherwise freely load-bearing. The saw tooth-shaped underside of the stair reveals the individual steps. In this way, the stair takes up the form of the stepped beams rising above the foyer, which serve as seating benches for the gallery. The architects break up the altogether minimalist design by using a ceiling-high screen, comprising 3,800 colourful wooden louvres in 27 different colours, which rises behind the altar, floating like a curtain in front of the organ. An opening built into the screen facilitates easy conversion of the furniture of the altar area. The spaces can thus be flexibly used by the community.

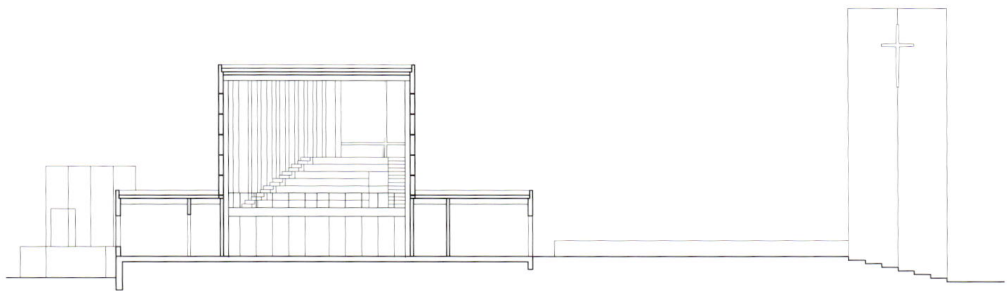

aa

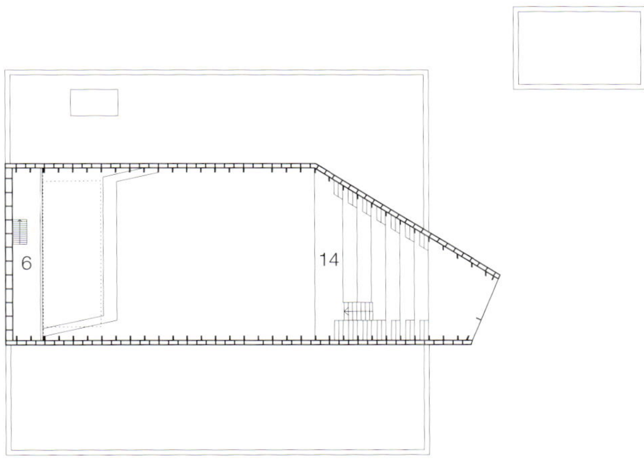

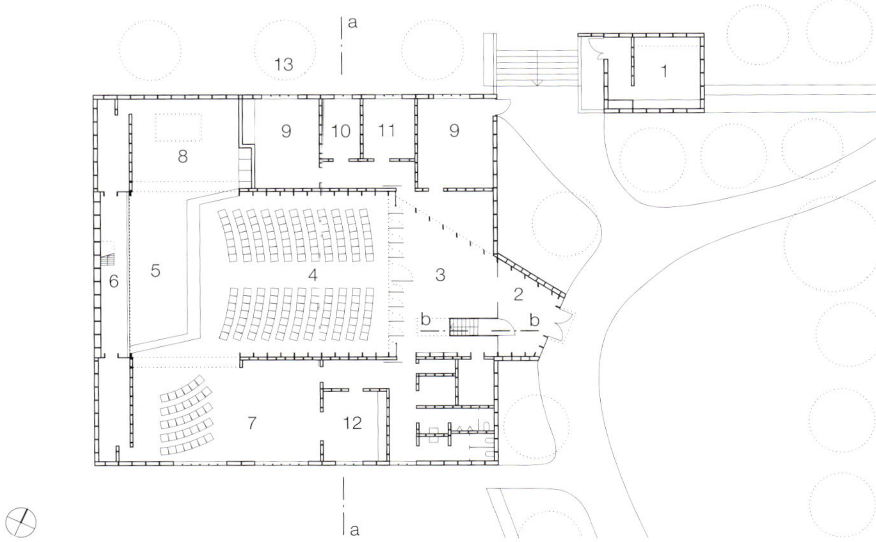

Section • Floor plans
Scale 1:500
1 Oratory
2 Vestibule
3 Foyer
4 Nave
5 Altar
6 Organ
7 Multipurpose room
8 Band rehearsal room
9 Multipurpose room of the community
10 Sexton's room
11 Sacristy
12 Kitchen
13 Columbarium
14 Gallery

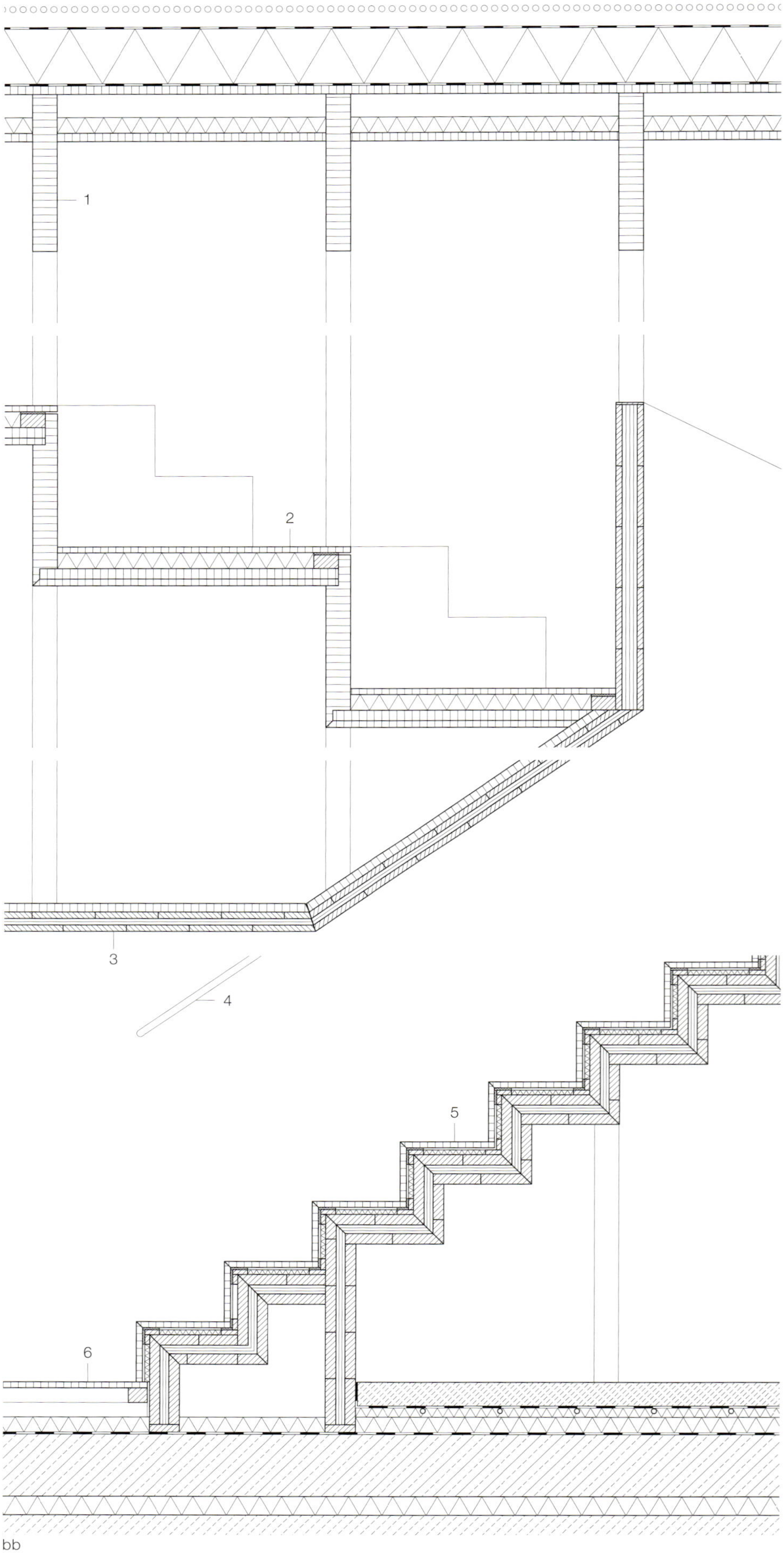

Vertical section nave
Scale 1:20

1 Beam laminated veneer lumber 75/500 mm
2 Three-layer panel spruce white waxed 19 mm
Substructure square timber 80/40 mm
in between: impact sound insulation 50 mm
laminated veneer lumber panel 33 mm
laminated veneer lumber 21 mm
3 Cross laminated timber 63 mm
Three-layer panel spruce white waxed 27 mm
4 Banister round steel ∅ 20 mm
5 Laminated veneer lumber panel spruce
white waxed 27 mm
Impact sound insulation 20 mm
Cross laminated timber 93 mm
6 Laminated veneer lumber panel spruce
white waxed 27 mm
Substructure square timber 50/60 mm
Air space 40 mm
Thermal insulation hard foam 40 mm
Sealant
Floor slab reinforced concrete 200 mm
Thermal insulation XPS 60 mm
Blinding layer

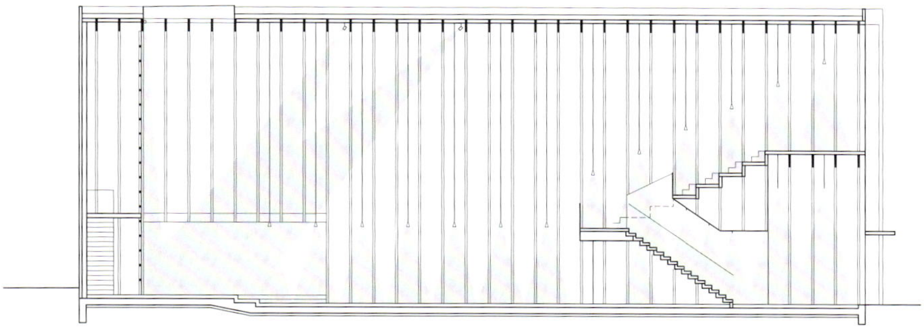

Section with lighting Scale 1:300

Hotel in Obanazawa

Architects:	Kengo Kuma & Associates, Tokyo
Contributors:	Makoto Shirahama
Structural engineer:	K. Nakata & Associates, Tokyo
Planning/ completion:	2005/2006

Located in the snowy north of the Japan's main island of Honshu, Obanazawa is known for its hot springs. Traditional Japanese hostels are strung along the Ginzan River. The existing building of the 100-year-old hotel "Ginzan Onsen Fujiya" was largely dismantled and reconstructed using both new and old components. Towards the outside, the facades, with their clear structure of enlarged window openings and uniform wooden louvres, reflect a modern interpretation of the Japanese guesthouse.
Inside, a spacious two-storey foyer has been included in the building structure. Japanese handmade paper adorns many wall surfaces. Panels of sliced bamboo canes zone the entrance and access areas, together with the nearly transparent wall elements made of etched glass. The seemingly floating, single-flight stair, suspended from steel rods and leading to the second floor, is so minimalist that it almost seems disembodied. Sparingly distributed, plainly designed pieces of furniture in the foyer and the guestrooms, moreover, contribute to the creation of "modern" contemplative spaces in the traditional building shell.

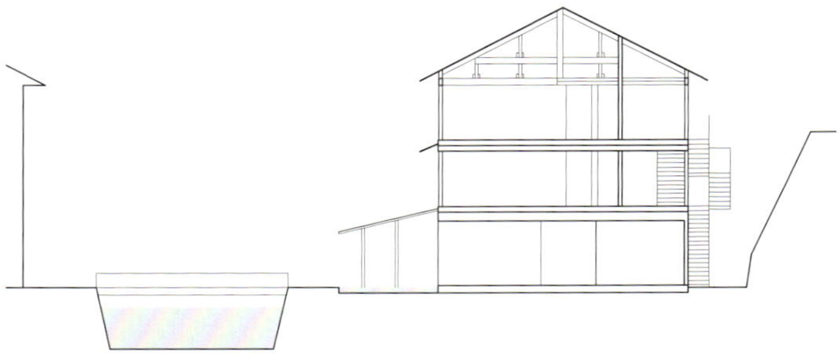

aa

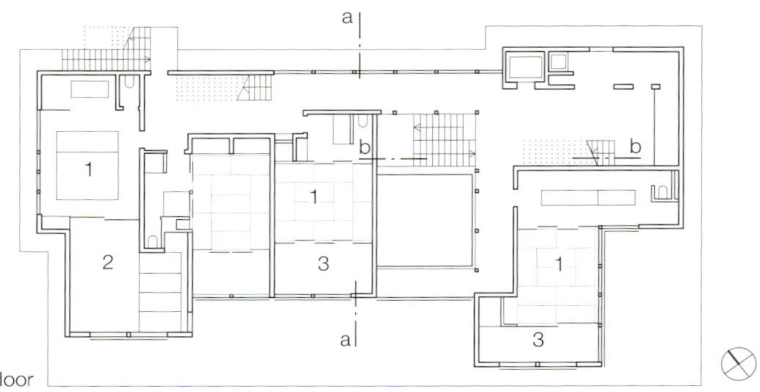

1st floor

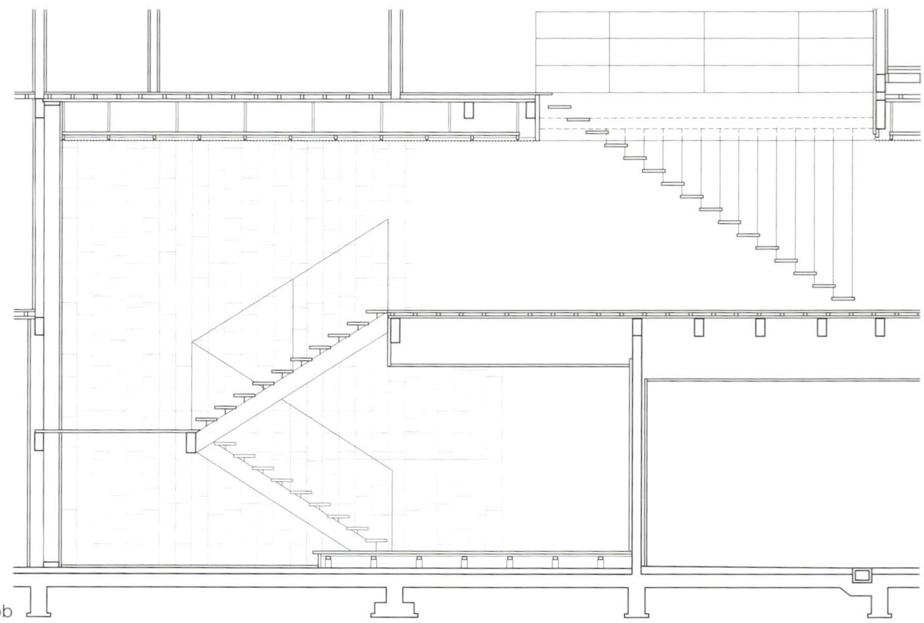

bb

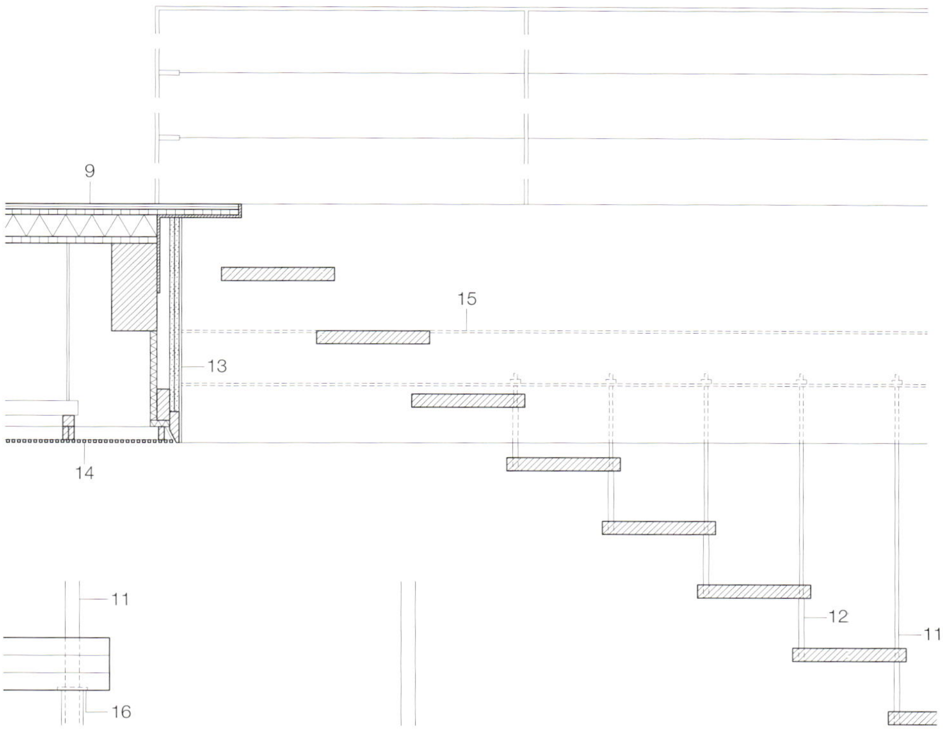

Section • Floor plan Scale 1:400
Section stairwell Scale 1:100
Section stair Scale 1:20
Details stair Scale 1:5

1 Guestroom
2 Dining area
3 Loggia
4 Japanese paper glued, aluminium hydroxide paper, plasterboard 2× 12.5 mm, Multilayer panel 9 mm
5 Japanese paper glued
6 Acrylic glass translucent
7 Steel sheet bent 1.6 mm
8 Illumination unit, magnetically mounted
9 Parquet elm 15 mm, multilayer panel 12 mm, insulation 60 mm, multilayer panel 18 mm
10 Tread elm 36 mm
11 Steel rod treated with phosphoric acid ∅ 9 mm
12 Steel sheath treated with phosphoric acid ∅ 14/2 mm
13 Japanese paper glued, aluminium hydroxide paper, plasterboard 2× 12.5 mm
14 Suspended ceiling: Cladding bamboo rods on elm frame
15 Suspension stair steel profile C 75/150 mm
16 Washer treated with phosphoric acid 2 mm
17 Nut welded to washer

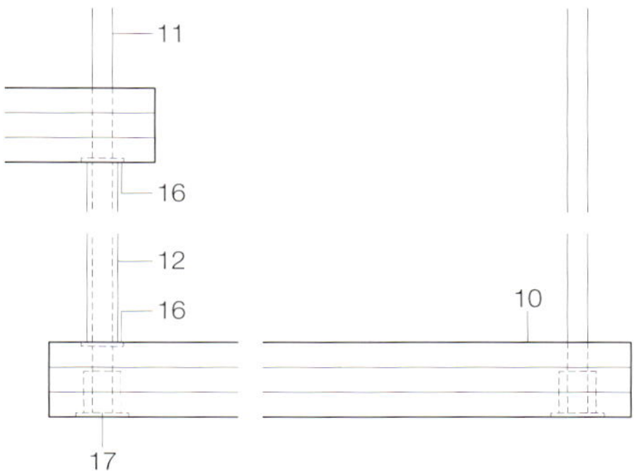

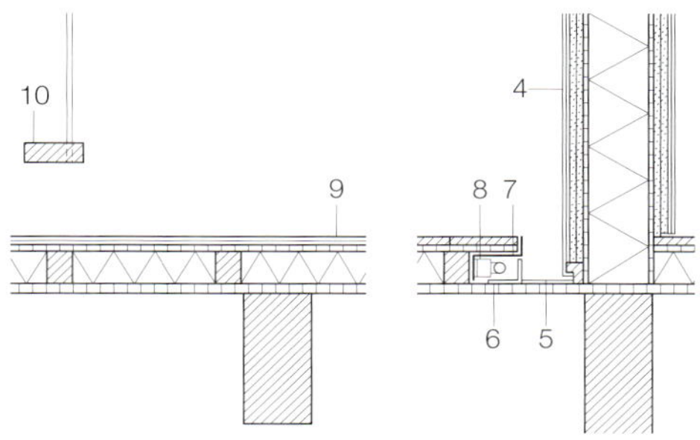

Residential building in Vrhovlje

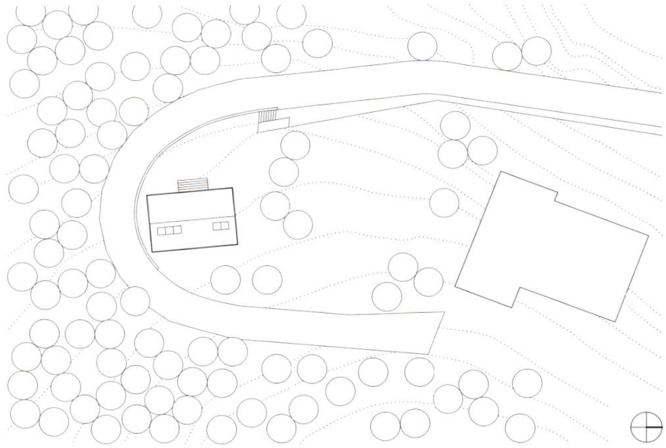

Architects:	dekleva gregorič arhitekti, Ljubljana
Contributors:	Aljoša Dekleva, Tina Gregorič, Lea Kovič, Vid Zabel
Structural engineer:	Luka Pavlovčič, Ljubljana
Planning/ completion:	2011/2014

The Venetians used the trees around Trieste to build their city on wooden poles, leaving behind a barren landscape with limestone soil. The traditional houses of the karst region mainly consist of this stone; their closed cubature, with sloping roofs and almost windowless facades, protects the residents from the elements. This single-family home, which the architects call “Compact Karst House”, takes up this tradition and reinterprets it. Deviating from the original and manually highly elaborate construction method, they selected a hybrid supporting structure of brickwork, with a sloping roof of reinforced concrete. However, in order to lend the structure a monolithic, stone-like character, the facade received an external layer of stone and concrete, creating a structure that comes alive. The living areas themselves are housed in two wooden cubes, which stand freely in the external shell and are connected by a bridge. It is to this bridge that the single-flight stair leads from the ground floor. The box-shaped wooden steps of the stair, suspended from steel rods, can be used as shelves on the rear side, thereby serving both as furniture and access. To save space, the access-providing furniture takes up the motif of a so-called samba stair. Every step is divided into two sections staggered in height, permitting comfortable use of the stair despite the high gradient. All installations, including the walls and floors between the levels, consist of multi-layered spruce wood. Large openings on the ground floor of the house provide views of the landscape, while skylights in the two bedrooms offer glimpses of the sky.

Site plan
Scale 1:1,000
Sections
Floor plans
Scale 1:200

1 Entrance
2 Fireplace
3 Bathroom
4 Kitchen / dining room
5 Built-in cupboard
6 Children's bedroom
7 Play bridge
8 Air space
9 Bedroom

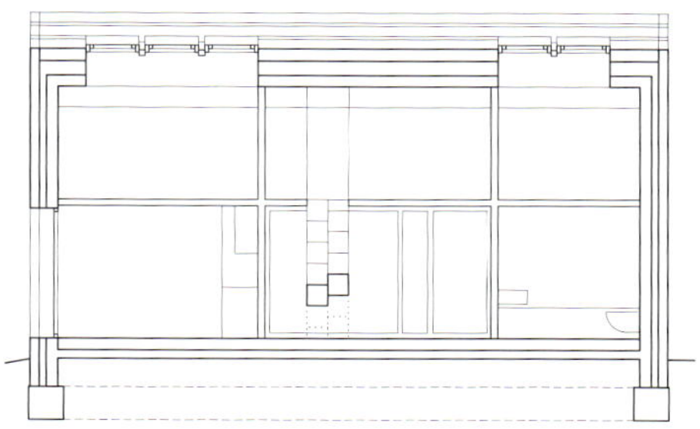

aa

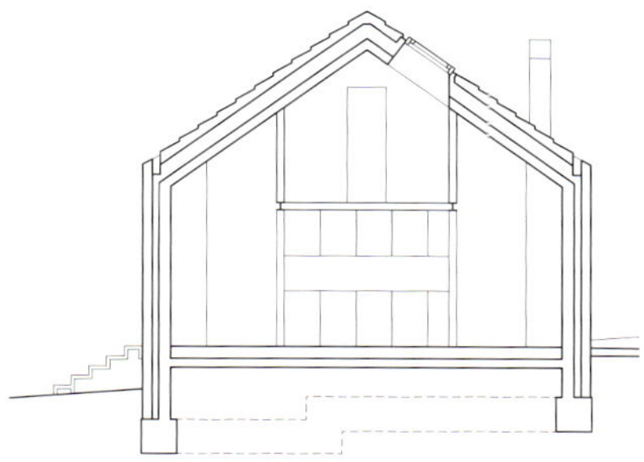

bb

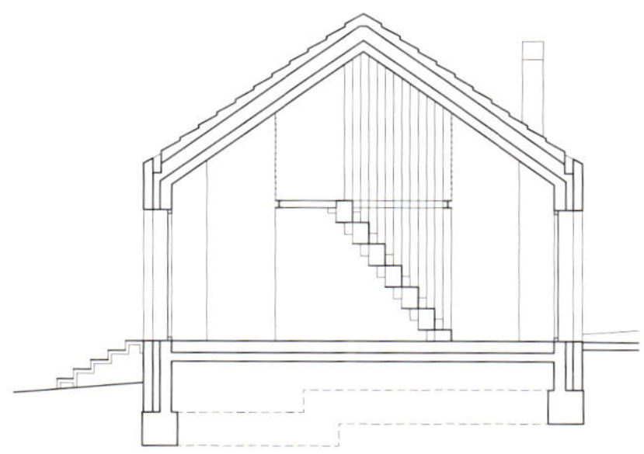

cc

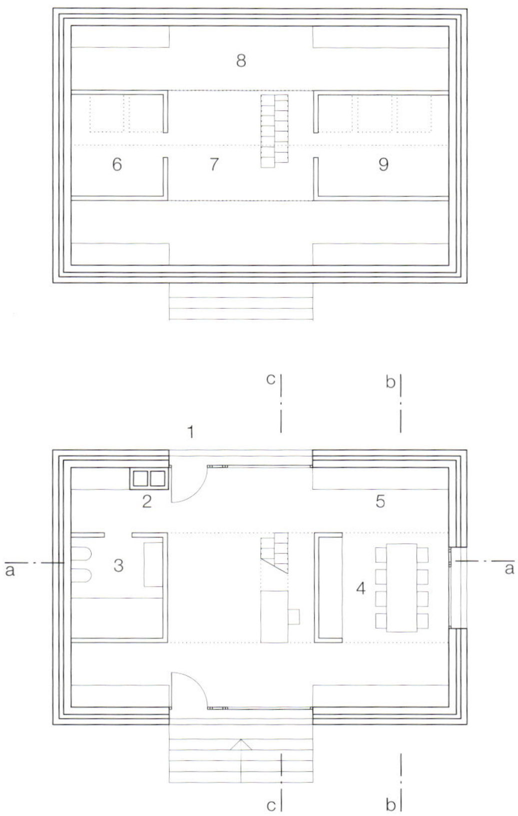

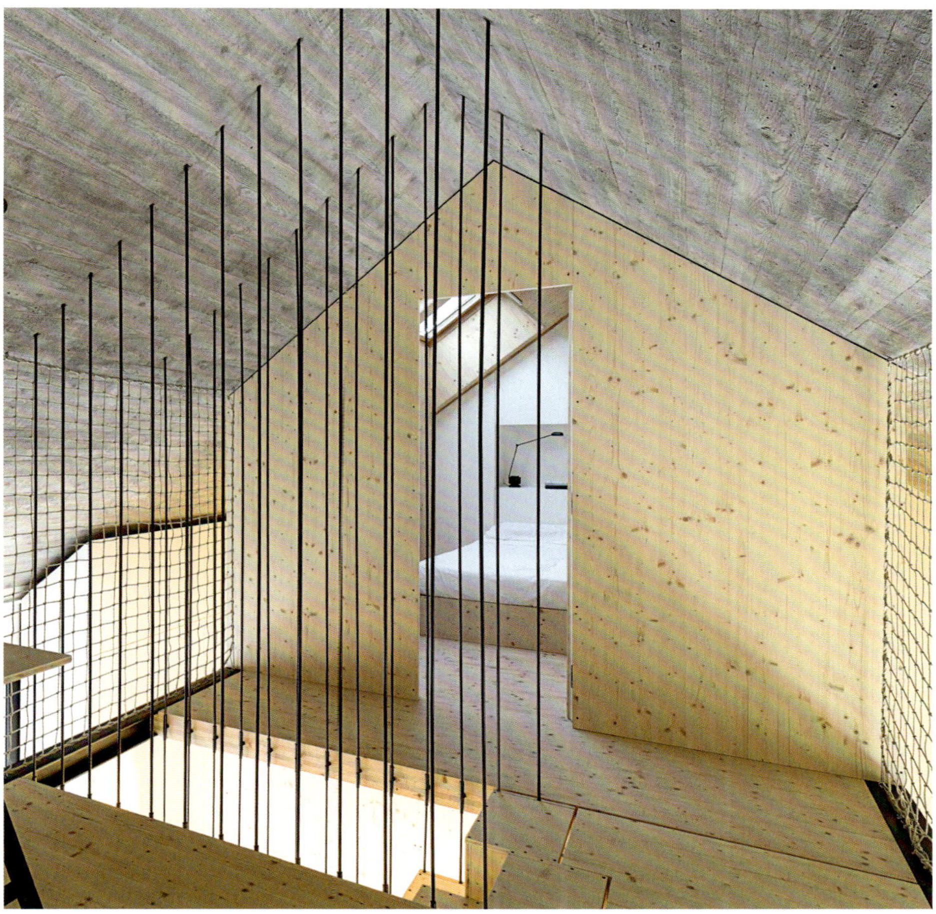

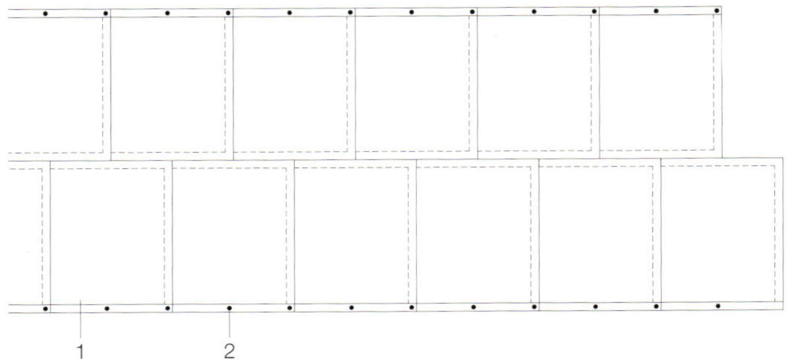

dd

Detail sections stair/shelf
Scale 1:20

1 Stair gradient 189/280 mm
Three-layer panel spruce 19 mm
2 Steel rod black ∅ 10 mm
3 Steel profile ⌶ 120 mm
4 Sheath with thread
5 Screed smoothed 20 mm
Screed reinforced 60 mm
Underfloor heating in
thermal insulation 30 mm, PE foil
Thermal insulation EPS 70 mm
Polymer bitumen sealant
Reinforced concrete 150 mm

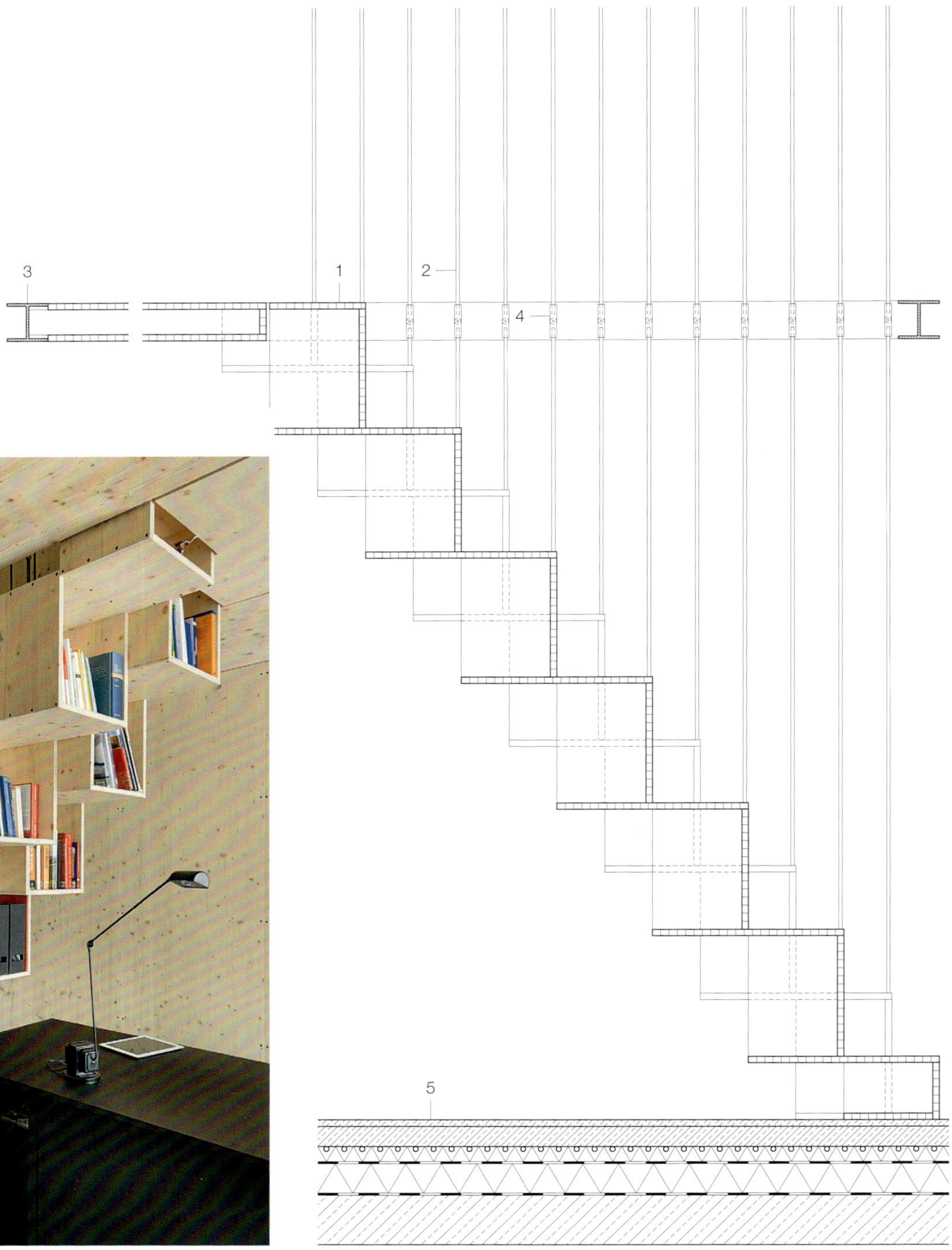

Exhibition and event centre, Franzensfeste

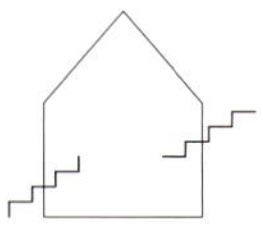

Architects:	Markus Scherer, Meran Walter Dietl, Schlanders
Contributors:	Heike Kirnbauer, Elena Mezzanotte
Structural engineer:	Baubüro Klaus Plattner, Bolzano
Planning/ completion:	2005/2009

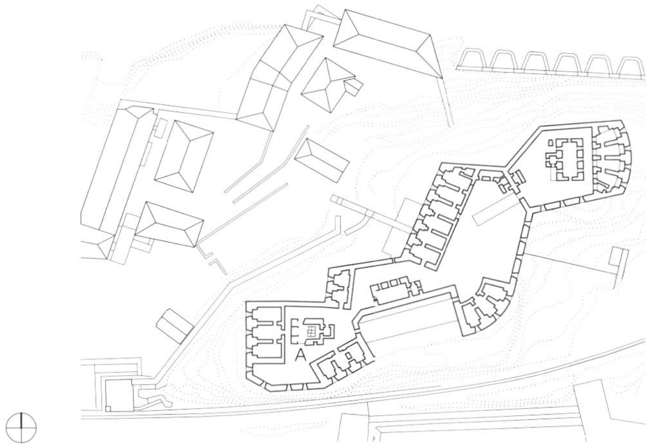

Site plan middle fortress
Scale 1:3,000

Franzensfeste Fortress, dating from 1838 and located at one of the narrowest points in the Eisack valley near Brixen, is the size of a small town at 20 hectares. It consists of three parts: the upper, the middle, and the lower fortress level. Following its acquisition by the state of South Tyrol, the cultural monument was to become a meeting place and a site for cultural exchange. The focus of the revitalisation of the former defensive fortification was on conserving the existing building stock, and especially the fortress character, to a large extent, and to utilise them by means of specific minimalist interventions. The walls, consisting of large granite blocks, were renovated, the roofs were sealed and the windows repaired. Closed-off wall sections were reopened and later additions removed. A small number of carefully selected elements create new routes within the complex, enabling their use as an exhibition space. A new 22 m long vertical shaft, dug right through the rock, provides a link from the lower to the middle fortress. Inside it, the new black reinforced concrete stair sculpturally winds up, terminating – in conjunction with the elevator tower – in the former powder magazine, which now houses the arrival building. Owing to the use of reinforced concrete for the load-bearing elements and of steel in the area of the balustrades, the stair clearly distinguishes itself in its materiality from the rock walls and the stonework of the existing buildings. The gentle restoration of the vaults, consisting of exposed brickwork; the plastered wall surfaces, partly adorned with paintings; as well as the unambiguous readability of the new interventions, create a successful dialogue between the historical building stock and contemporary architecture.

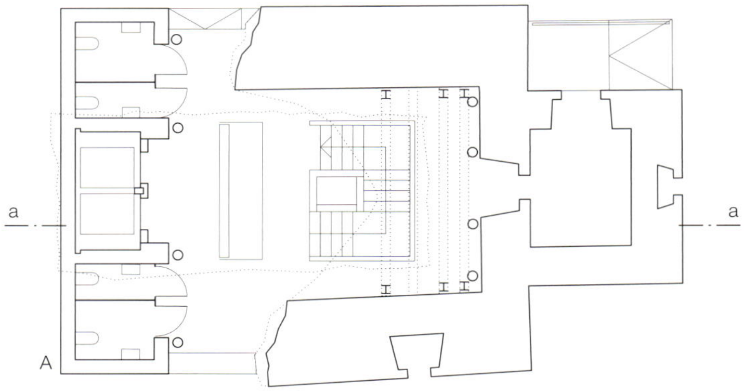

aa

Floor plan • Section
Scale 1:100
Isometric drawing stair without scale
Detail sections stair
Scale 1:10

1 Handrail flat steel ▭ 50/10 mm
2 Steel tube ◻ 20/20 mm
3 Cover strip flat steel ▭ 20/3 mm
4 Banister infill expanded metal
5 Baluster flat steel ▭ 40/20 mm
6 Steel profile L 40/40/5 mm, welded to baluster
7 Reinforcement strip flat steel ▭ 40/20 mm
8 Steel angle 120/40/3 mm
9 Connecting angle steel 20/20/3 mm
10 Grating 50 mm
Steel profile U 120
11 Stair landing reinforced concrete 175 mm
12 Head plate steel on steel profile U 120
13 Cladding expanded metal

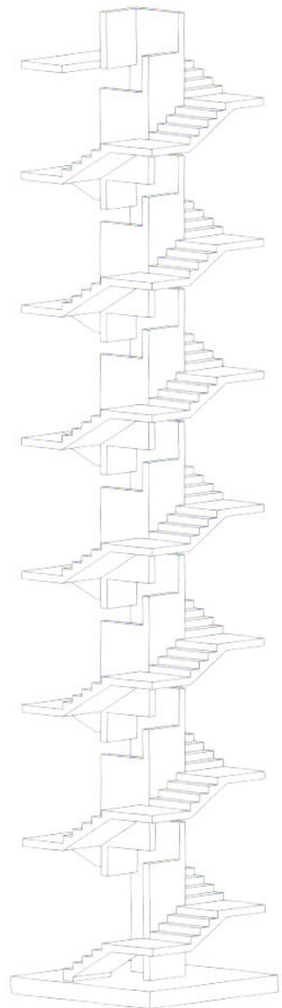

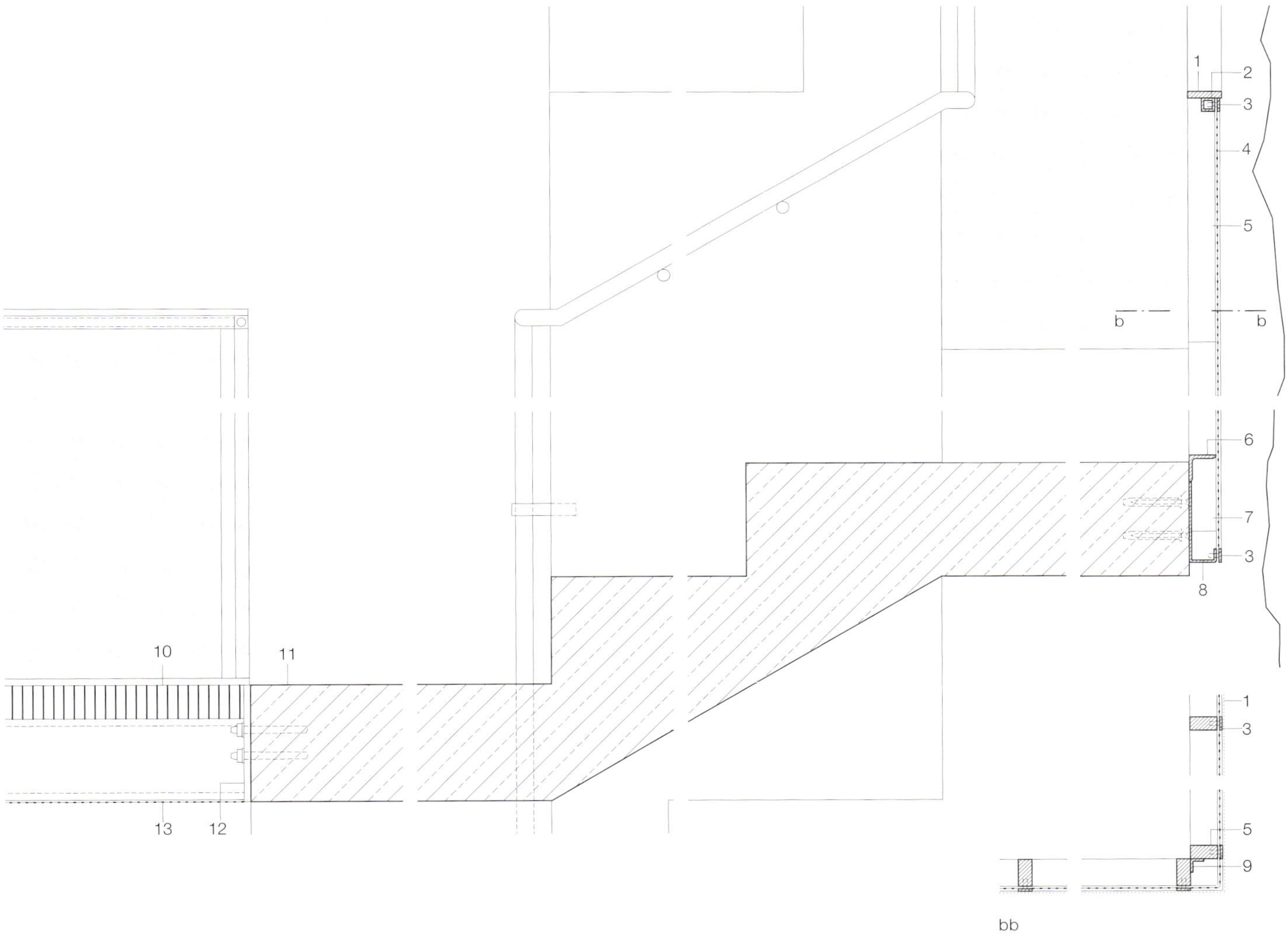

Typology		Project	Materials	Form	Construction
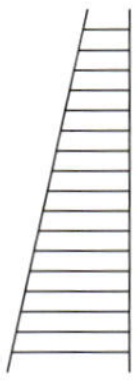	 1	Ken Architekten Stepped residential building Brugg (CH) 2013 DETAIL 11/2014	Reinforced concrete	Single-flight cascading stair with intermediate landings	Prefabricated concrete element
	 2	Vittorio Magnago Lampugnani Office building Basel (CH) 2008 DETAIL 4/2010	Solid wood (European walnut) on OSB panel, reinforced concrete	Single-flight cascading stair with intermediate landings	Floor-wise, longitudinal-span solid construction of in-situ concrete, clad all around in composite wood panels
	 3	Aires Mateus Residential building Estrela (PT) 2016	Microcement coating on screed, reinforced concrete	Single-flight stair with intermediate landings	Cross-span in-situ concrete construction embedded in the concrete walls flanking the stair
	 4	Wespi/de Meuron Stone house Brione s. Minusio (IT) 2005	Reinforced concrete	Single-flight stair with intermediate landings	In-situ concrete stair concreted against ground soil, embedded into the flanking concrete walls
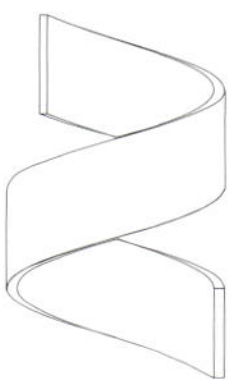	 5	Archea Associati Antinori Winery Bargino (IT) 2012 DETAIL 4/2014	Corten steel, in-situ concrete, reinforced with glass fibre and wire mesh, flat steel	Spiral stair	Box girder comprising several individual components welded together on site, attached to the newel and roof/bottom Support: concrete column and steel profile
	 6	Steven Holl Department of Philosophy New York University New York (US) 2007	Steel, perforated steel	Multi-flight stair	Closed string stair of white coated steel with folded treads and risers of steel sheet with surface-wide walkable covering
	 7	Massimiliano Fuksas Armani store New York (US) 2009 DETAIL 4/2012	Rolled steel sections and sheets, steel tube, glass fibre reinforced concrete Banister: aluminium mesh, steel tube, glass fibre reinforced concrete	Spiral stair	Prefabricated, inlying steel structure with white coated concrete cladding, steel tube strings
	 8	ARX Portugal Market hall Abrantes (PT) 2015	Concrete, white	Spiral stair	Floor-wise, longitudinal-span reinforced concrete construction of in-situ concrete with flanking concrete banisters as string-like girders

Typology		Project	Materials	Form	Construction
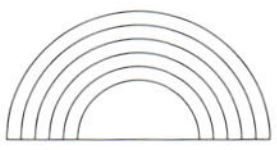	 1	OMA Prada store New York (US) 2001 DETAIL 4/2002	Tropical zebrawood on plywood panel and steel profiles	Single-flight stair	Cross-span steel girders under each step with mounted composite wood panel cladding following the stair line
	 2	Diller Scofidio + Renfro/FXFOWLE Juilliard School New York (US) 2009 DETAIL 4/2010	Steel sheet step, bent and coated, side wall coated steel plate	Single-flight stair	Welded steel, supported at the top and bottom on steel building block, veneered
	 3	Vector Architects Seashore Chapel Qinhuangdao (CN) 2015	Reinforced concrete, white	Single-flight stair	Exposed reinforced concrete construction of in-situ concrete
	 4	Rojkind Arquitectos Síclo Mexico City (MX) 2015	Concrete	Single-flight stair	Solid reinforced concrete construction with smooth formwork surfaces of in-situ concrete
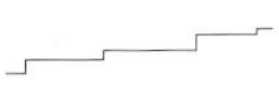	 5	JKMM Library Seinäjoki (FI) 2012 DETAIL 6/2013	Concrete, seat cushions	Single-flight stair	Reinforced steel construction with smooth formwork surfaces of in-situ concrete topped by seat cushions
	 6	Yamazaki Kentaro Nursery Sakura (JP) 2014 DETAIL 7+8/2016	Timber floor boards (Japanese cedar) on plywood panel	Single-flight stair	Shell of reinforced concrete with composite wood panel construction on shims
	 7	Vector Architects Library Beidaihe (CN) 2015 DETAIL 4/2016	Bamboo, laminated on battens, screed, reinforced concrete	Single-flight stair	Shell of reinforced concrete and mounted composite wood panels with laminated bamboo surface
	 8	Foreign Office Architects (FOA) International Passenger Terminal Yokohama (JP) 2002 DETAIL 11/2004	Untreated Ipé hardwood, folded plate of steel, reinforced concrete	Single-flight stair terminating on the grounds	Wooden deck, partly as stepped form, on sealed reinforced concrete ceiling

Project examples
Matrix

Typology		Project	Materials	Form	Construction
	1 	Florian Busch Residential building Kyoto (JP) 2015	Steel	Two-flight stair	Steel construction, suspended on round steel profiles
	2 	AIX Arkitekter Cathedral Skara (SE) 2000 DETAIL 4/2002	Steel, rubber covering	Single-flight stair	Welding plate in concrete wall (every 3rd riser), welded steel plates, steel frame, railing attached to the wall via the handrail
	3 	Bohlin Cywinski Jackson Apple Store New York (US) 2006/2011	Glass	Spiral stair	Point-mounted glass treads with string-like glass balustrades on both sides
	4 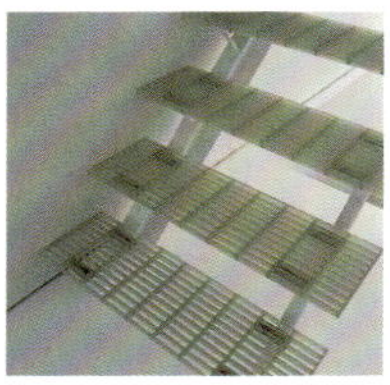	Kengo Kuma & Associates Plastic House Tokyo (JP) 2002 DETAIL 12/2002	Glass fibre reinforced plastic, steel	Single-flight stair	Steel tube and U-shaped steel profile with steel sheet bracing projecting from the wall and resting on steel tube
	5 	Conradin Clavuot School building St. Peter (CH) 1998 DETAIL 1/2000	Solid wood	Single-flight stair	Support on the wall with tenon joint and additional metal screw, and supplementary screw-based attachment to the rope railing
	6 	Studio Mumbai Belavali House Mumbai (IN) 2012	Tinted and smoothed cement slurry, tropical wood	Single-flight stair with curved bottom end	Treads and risers of tropical wood, mounted in the wall and the closed string
	7 	Roger Boltshauser, Martin Rauch Mudhouse Rauch Schlins (AT) 2008	Steps of in-situ concrete with stones sieved from the soil and bound by trass lime	Spiral stair	Projecting in-situ concrete steps clamped into the flanking rammed earth wall
	8 	Buchner Bründler Architekten Summer residence Linescio (CH) 2008 DETAIL 6/2014	Solid concrete	Single-flight stair	Monolithic planked formwork in-situ concrete as exposed concrete construction

Typology		Project	Materials	Form	Construction
	 1	Sauerbruch Hutton Church Cologne (DE) 2013 DETAIL 10/2014	Laminated veneer wood panel spruce/three-layer panel; square timber	Single-flight stair	Folded cross-laminated timber construction defining the stair geometry, reinforced by laminated veneer wood panels as exposed surface of white waxed spruce
	 2	zanderroth architekten Housing complex Berlin (DE) 2010 DETAIL 5/2012	Concrete, white plaster	Two-flight stair	Flights of prefabricated concrete elements with balustrades of white coated engineered panels
	 3	savioz fabrizzi architectes Chalet Val d'Hérens (CH) 2013	Exposed concrete	Bent (near quarter-turn) stair	Exposed, smooth-panel formwork in-situ concrete produced in combination with the flanking concrete walls
	 4	SoHo Architektur Schwarzes Haus Memmingen (DE) 2008	Solid wood	Single-flight stair	String-like walls of composite wood panels suspended from the above-lying concrete ceiling, combined with open treads of the same material
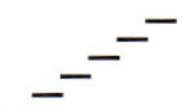	 5	Kengo Kuma & Associates Fujiya Onsen Obanazawa (JP) 2008 DETAIL 4/2008	Solid wood steps (elm); steel rods	Single-flight stair	Solid wood steps suspended from steel rods
	 6	TNA Weekend house Karuizawa (JP) 2006 DETAIL 10/2007	Veneered birch press board, steel	Multi-flight stair	Veneered birch press board, fixed on the side by steel profile, closed string of flat steel
	 7	Aparicio + Fernández-Elorza Exhibition space Madrid (ES) 2016	Steel	Single-flight stair	Round steel rods as both-sided suspended construction above flat steel panel, attached to the ceiling and fixed to the floor, with attached steps of flat steel
	 8	Manfred Lux Residental building Neusäß (DE) 2012 DETAIL 7+8/2015	Solid wood steps (oak) on steel mounts	Bent stair	Steel brackets projecting step-wise from the flanking exposed concrete wall with mounted solid wooden treads

Typology		Project	Materials	Form	Construction
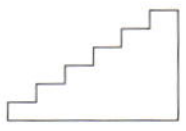	 1	dekleva gregorič arhitekti Residential building Vrhovlje (SI) 2014 DETAIL 7+8/2015	Three-layer spruce, steel rods	Single-flight samba stair	Stair geometry of three-layer wood panels, stacked as shelf boxes and suspended on steel rods from the ceiling above
	 2	Aires Mateus Residential building Alcobaca (PT) 2011	Plasterboard, white coating, reinforced concrete, natural stone steps	Single-flight stair	Solid reinforced concrete construction embedded into the flanking sidewalls, white filler
	 3	Walter Angonese and Markus Scherer with Klaus Hellweger Tyrol Castle Meran (IT) 2003	Corroded steel	Multi-flight stair	Steel construction surfaces of corroded steel panels
	 4	Massimo Fiorido Associati Residential building Marina di Castagneto Carducci (IT) 2008	Teak	Single-flight stair	Composite wood panels with teakwood surface, folded over the course of the stair geometry, with underlying shelving
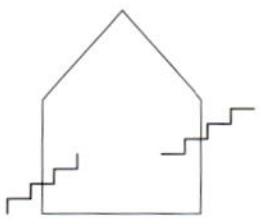	 5	Markus Scherer, Walter Dietl Fortress Franzensfeste (IT) 2009	Reinforced concrete stair, black, railing filling expanded metal flat steel	Multi-flight stair	Box girder of welded steel panels, comprising a base plate and string-shaped, closed, load-bearing banister on both sides, partly suspended on tension rods
	 6	Studio Rolf.fr Black Pearl Residence Rotterdam (NL) 2008	Wood, opaque white coat of paint	Single-flight stair	Wooden open string stair clad in wooden slats, opaque coat of paint
	 7	Nieto Sobejano Visitor centre Las Palmas Gran Canaria (ES) 2004 DETAIL 5/2014	Corroded steel	Single-flight stair	Box girder of corroded steel panels, comprising a base plate and string-shaped, closed, load-bearing banister on both sides
	 8	Carlo Scarpa Castelvecchio Verona (IT) 1975	Corroded steel	Single-flight stair	Corroded steel straps suspended from the ceiling, perpendicularly bent and extended up to the flanking wall as treads

1 Kaze-no-Oka Crematorium, Nakatsu (JP) 1997, Fumihiko Maki

Stairs allow the users of a building to overcome height differences between different levels in a building by means of ascending in a step-by-step manner. Apart from having an aesthetic purpose, they primarily serve functional criteria. Ideally, the user of a staircase doesn't consciously become aware of it during its daily use. This requires a geometric design adapted to the human body. Moreover, further aspects need to be considered for usability. The planning of a staircase follows criteria which are illustrated in greater detail below.

In Germany, building legislation stipulates that staircases form a part of the state building codes. These define the minimum requirements with respect to stairs lying in the path of emergency escape routes. The complete normative delineation of stairs is described in greater detail in the section "Regulatory framework/standardisation" (p. 109f.)".

Detailed and authoritatively defined requirements for the planning and construction of stairs are specified in DIN 18065 Stairs in buildings [1]. This standard, ranked as a generally recognised code of practice, contains the bulk of the normative requirements that must be met when planning and constructing stairs. It specifies terms, measurement rules and main dimensions for staircase construction. The associated specifications are presented in a more detailed manner in the following sections.

The contents of nationally binding legal regulations in Germany are also relevant internationally. The terminology introduced therewith can be adopted without restriction. The requirements for measurement rules and main dimensions, however, display national differences. These are sometimes clearly noticeable when using staircases in various countries. In the Netherlands, for example, the legal requirements for staircase widths, rise heights and tread depths were significantly different from those in Germany as late as the 1990s [2]. Stairs in the Netherlands are correspondingly steep, so that transportation of bulky and heavy objects within residential units and down staircases is, in part, only possible by moving backwards, similarly to descending a ladder. In the meanwhile, due to relevant legislation from 2012, the legal requirements in the Netherlands have approached the normative requirements in Germany. In Austria, ÖNorm B 5371 2010-09-01 regulates the profile of requirements for staircases similarly to DIN 18065, while in Switzerland, it is various laws and regulations that do so. A content-related comparison in these four countries, however, results in principally much the same requirements.

Stair types

Stairs are differentiated according to their basic forms. Their designations refer to these basic distinguishing features, i.e. stairs with straight and/or spiralled flights. Free-form staircases are not discussed in depth in this section.

The type and form of a staircase determines the spatial impact of the stair and the stairwell. The type of use, the routing in a building, and the gauging of the space surrounding the staircase directly depend on the shape of the staircase. Straight flights of stairs permit comfortable walking. Combined with a shallow gradient, they often serve representative purposes (fig. 3, p. 96).

As part of emergency escape routes, straight flights of stairs constitute safely passable and efficient staircase types.

2

3

Spiral staircases as well as combined spiralling and straight types of stairs are often used in spatially confined conditions as space-saving staircases. Spiral staircases are especially suitable in multilevel air spaces due to their sculptural effect (fig. 6 and p. 52, fig. 17) on the one hand, and the fact that, in combination with a continuous motion sequence and the constantly changing position of the user on the staircase, they provide a good overview of the surrounding space.

Stair parts

Depending on the type of staircase, stairs consist of various parts which are assigned different functions. The following explanations are guided by DIN 18065, section 3, "Terminology".

Flight of stairs / Tread line

A flight of stairs is an uninterrupted sequence of at least three risers between two levels. If the height difference between two levels is less than three risers, one speaks of equalising steps. Equalising steps are not permissible as part of emergency escape routes.

A tread line is a construction line which indicates the usual path of a staircase user and lies within the walkable area. Individual steps divide the stair tread line into regular tread widths.

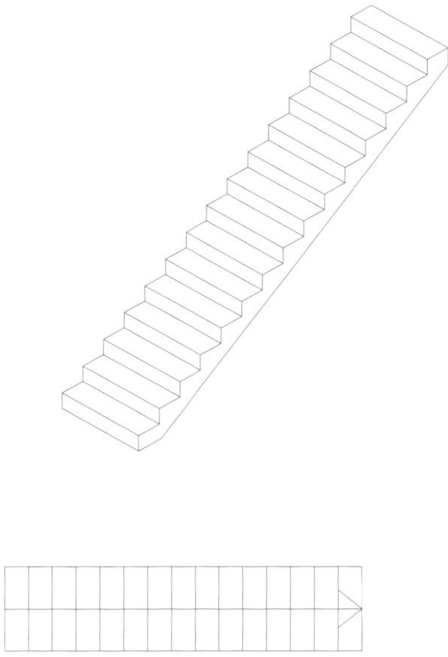

Single-flight straight stair

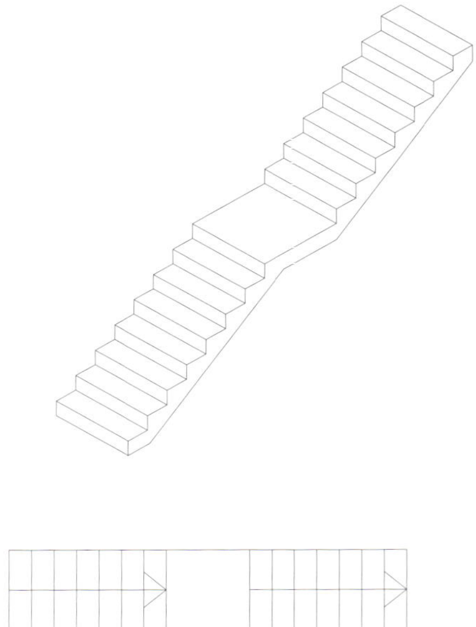

Two-flight straight stair with intermediate landing

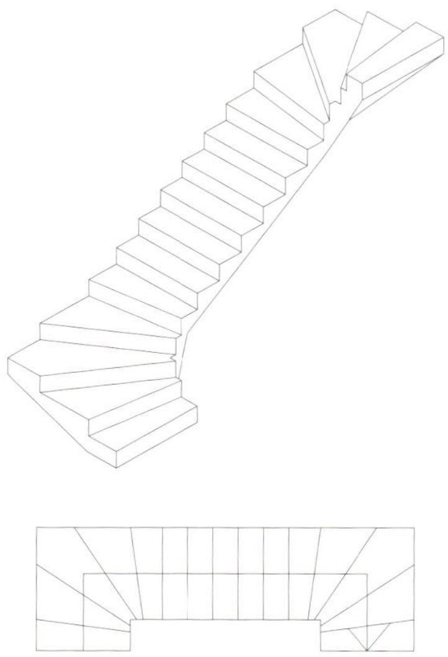

7 Single-flight double quarter-turn stair

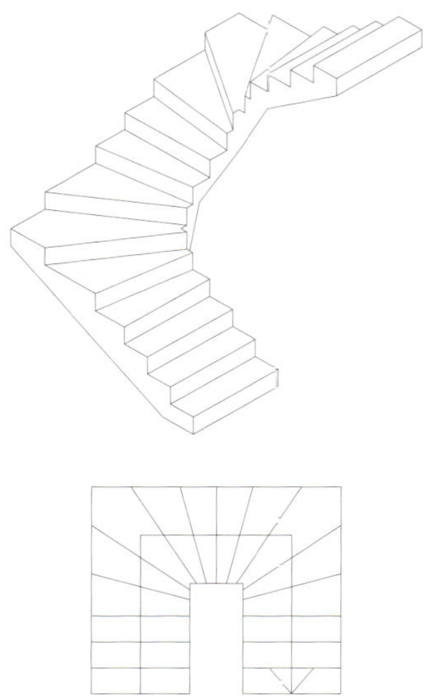

Single-flight half-spiral stair

2 Steep, single-flight stair in a confined stairwell, residential building, Tokyo (JP) 2015, Makoto Takei + Chie Nabeshima
3 Shallow, single-flight stair in a spacious stairwell, Museum Georg Schäfer, Schweinfurt (DE) 2000, Volker Staab Architekten
4 Two-flight dog-leg stair with intermediate landing
5 Single-flight half-spiral stair, housing complex in Bucharest (RO) 2014, ADN Birou de Arhitectură
6 Newel stair, State Archive in Liestal (CH) 2007, EM2N
7 Stair types

4 

5 

6 

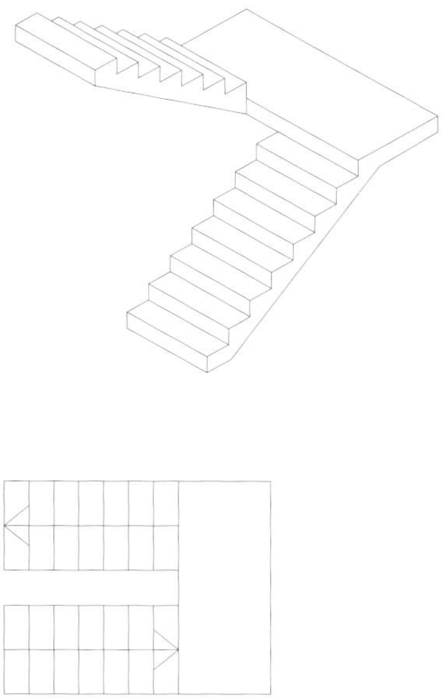

Two-flight dog-leg stair
with intermediate landing

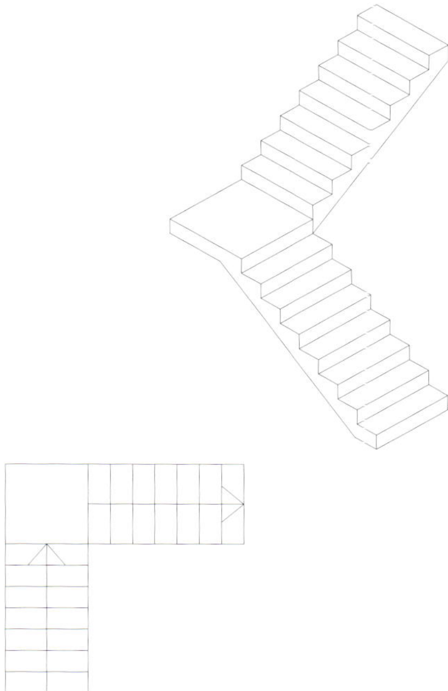

Two-flight bent stair
with intermediate landing

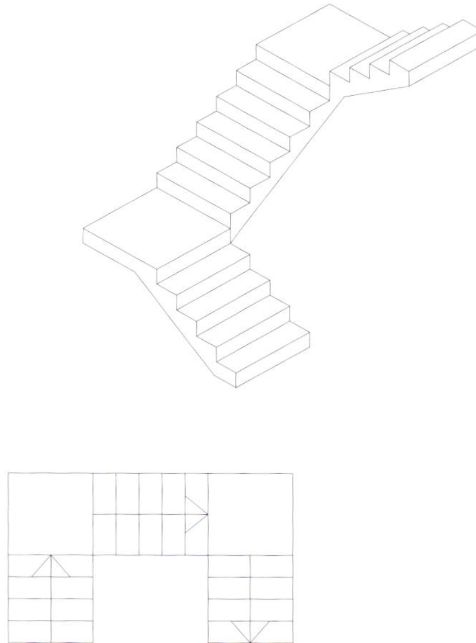

Three-flight double-bend stair
with intermediate landings

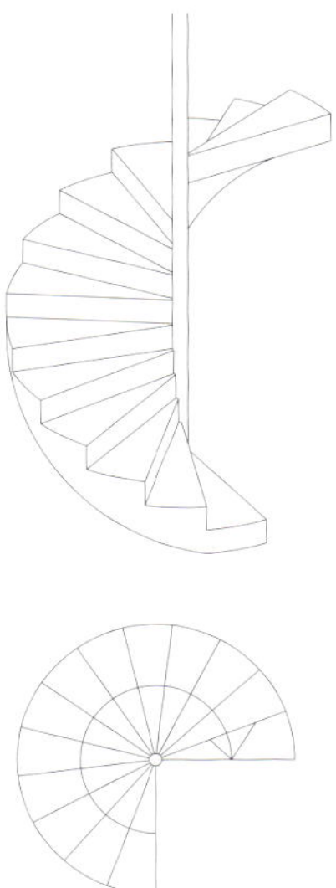

Stair with newel
(newel stair)

Stair with well hole
(spiral stair)

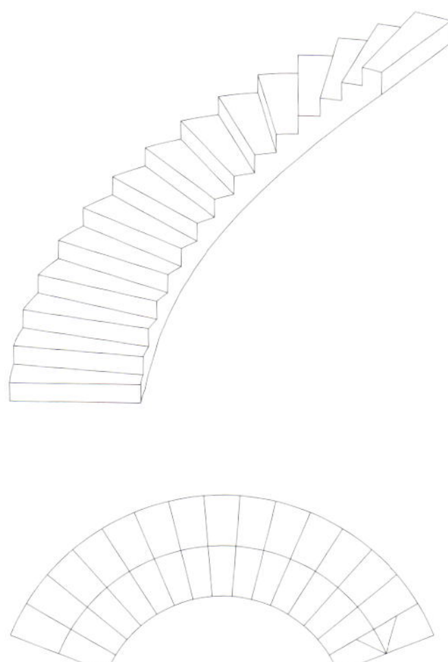

Arched stair

8

9

8 Open stair, residential bu lding in Amsterdam (NL) 2013, meesvisser
9 Closed stair, residential building in Berlin (DE) 2010, zanderroth architekten
10 Stair parts
11 Steps of a closed and open stair
12 Bad Aibling Town Hall (DE) 2012, Behnisch Architekten
13 Gradient of ramps, stairs, ladders with example rises (r) and tread widths (t) in cm
14 Minimum and maximum dimensions for treads and risers as per DIN 18065
15 Minimum dimensions of the usable flight width
16 Banister height

Landing / Intermediate landing
The landing of a staircase is located at the start or end of a flight of stairs, forming a stairhead, and is often a part of the ceiling. The intermediate landing interrupts two flights of stairs and is positioned between ceilings in order to comply with the maximum permissible number of steps in a flight of stairs. In multi-flight staircases, it serves as turning landing for a change in direction.

Steps
Consisting of a riser and a tread, a step is usually walked in a single footstep in a flight of stairs. In the process, the uppermost step of a flight of stairs is the exit step while the lowermost one is the bottom step. The bottom step is neither different in shape nor in material from the other steps. It is on the same level as the exit landing and can be designed, in its shape and materials, like the landing and the other steps.

The step tread is the horizontal part of a step, while the riser is the vertical part.

Well hole, stairwell
The well hole is the enclosed void space between the flights of stairs, the staircase landings, including the banister, when viewed from the top.

The stairwell is the opening in the respective ceiling to accommodate a stair coming in from a lower level.

Banister, handrail
Fall protection along flights of stairs and landings is provided by the banister. The handrail of the staircase, a grip-secure component, is a walking aid for staircase users. It is mounted on banisters, spindles, or on walls running along a staircase.

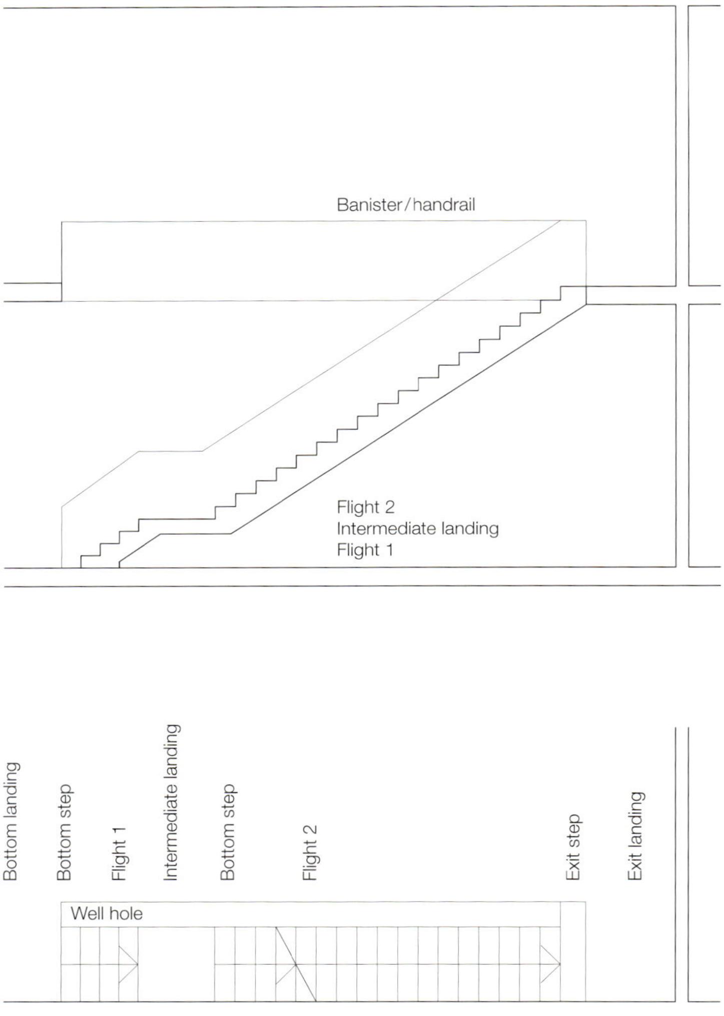

10

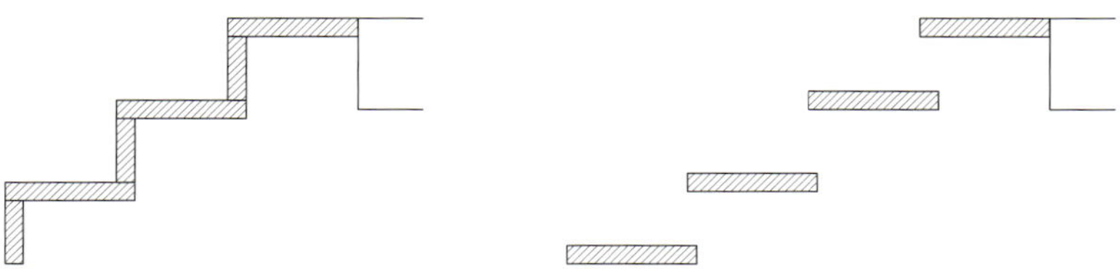
11

12

String, stringer, base plate, newel
A string encloses a flight of stairs laterally, forming a load-bearing component for accommodating steps. A stair's stringer supports the steps as a load-bearing girder. In cases where a two-dimensional, sloping component supports the steps on its upper side, one speaks of a base plate. A newel is the load-bearing core in the centre of a spiral staircase (see "Types of construction", p. 104ff.). All these construction parts of a staircase must be designed in accordance with the selected building material and the overall design of the stair.

Open or closed stairs
While an open staircase contains, as its name already suggests, openings between the treads, a closed staircase contains risers in their place. The type of implementation depends on the material and structure.

Dimensioning basics
The general principles for the dimensioning and construction of stairs in Germany are laid down in the state building codes as well as in special regulations for buildings with specific uses, such as the Arbeitsstättenrichtlinie [Ordinance on workplaces] or the Versammlungsstättenverordnung [Ordinance on places of assembly]. The supplementary DIN 18065, section 4ff., "Measurement rules", as well as basic ergonomic principles are used to further differentiate and specify the requirements. When planning and constructing stairs, these rules must be applied with great care and precision. The permissible tolerances, as described in DIN 18065, section 7, specify a low margin in this respect and represent maximum deviations. Other design-related deviations resulting from specific material properties or production and assembly-related

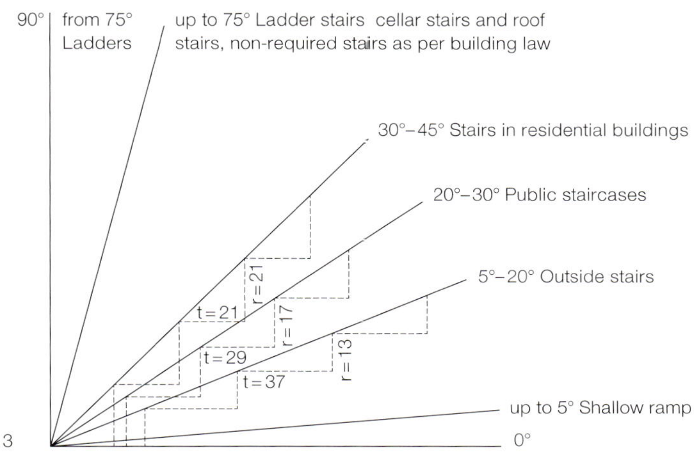

13

As per DIN 18065	Rise r max. [mm]	Tread t min. [mm]
Required stairs	190	260
In residential buildings with no more than two flats; stairs leading to habitable spaces	200	230
In residential buildings with no more than two flats; stairs not leading to habitable spaces	210	210
In all other buildings	190	260
Non-required stairs in all buildings	210	210

14

Required stairs	Width
In residential buildings with no more than two flats and within flats	> 80 cm
In all other buildings (BayBO) [Bavarian Building Code]	> 100 cm
In high-rise buildings (HochhVO) [Ordinance on high-rises]	> 125 cm
In places of assembly: for every 150 persons depending on the emergency escape route, but max. 250 cm/flight; configuration as per the seating in the space (VStättVO) [Ordinance on places of assembly]	100 cm
In sales outlets (VkVO) [Ordinance on sales outlets]	> 200 cm < 250 cm
Non-required stairs	> 50 cm

15

Banister heights (DIN 18065)	Height
Residential buildings, fall height up to 12 m	> 90 cm
Workplaces, fall height up to 12 m	> 100 cm
Fall height over 12 m	> 110 cm

16

20

21

determined use of a stair. It is therefore recommended that a clearance height of at least 2.10 m be specified when planning stairs in buildings.
As per DIN 18065, the usable landing depth must correspond to at least the required usable flight width. Additionally, the landing depth is specified to have at least 3 or 2.5 goings, according to Item 6.3.4. "Going for landings", Table 1. Moreover, for intermediate landings in the run of single-flight stairs, it is useful to likewise consider the tread line rule, with 2r + t = tread line, when planning landing depth. As such, landing depth should be t + (2r + t) • x (fig. 19b, p. 101). In doing so, it is possible to avoid a short and disturbing intermediate step in a flowing movement sequence when walking the full extent of the entire staircase, including an intermediate landing.

The profile of the stairwell at right angles to the direction of movement includes further dimensional definitions alongside that of the clearance height and width, as per DIN 18065. The usable flight width is permitted to have clearance restrictions in the lower lateral area, for example due to stair strings, as shown in fig. 20. As such, laterally up to 10 cm and heightwise up to 15 cm are permissible (fig. 22). This rule has generous margins – the risk of stepping on this area and correspondingly incurring negative consequences when walking on a stair is very high for persons who are dependent on using the handrail. Especially small children or elderly persons have a high safety need, and may place the foot facing the handrail very close to the lateral stair edge, as seen in orthogonal projection. It is, therefore, recommended that the permissible dimensions are only fully utilised once this aspect has been taken into consideration.

The lateral banister spacing of at least 5 cm is appropriate and plausible for round or angular handrails with small dimensions. DIN 18065 does not regulate the geometric shape of handrails with respect to grip safety. Only the grip width is restricted to between 2.5 and 6 cm. In this respect, DIN 18040 "Construction of Accessible Buildings" makes further demands where compliance also seems useful in areas with other planning requirements.

Lateral step margins often include a gap for aesthetic reasons to show a floating or deliberately detached step (figs. 21, 23). This lateral gap between the step edge and the stairwell wall is stipulated to be a maximum of 6 cm, a measure which at first glance seems appropriate. Nevertheless, planning should also take the expected user group into account. For users with small feet and correspondingly small treads, 6 cm is much more than half the shoe width. This presents the risk of twisting one's ankle when the foot is directly placed at the lateral step edge.

With spiral stairs, the tread line (see p. 96) can be freely selected within the

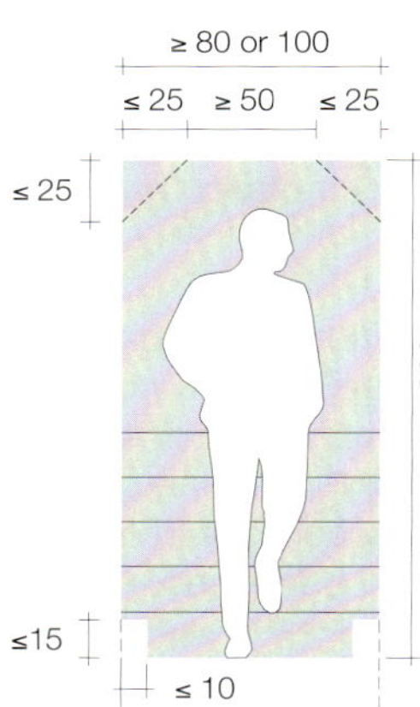

22

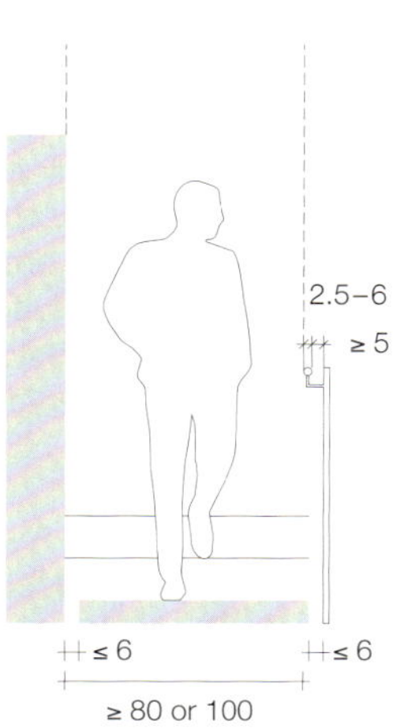

23

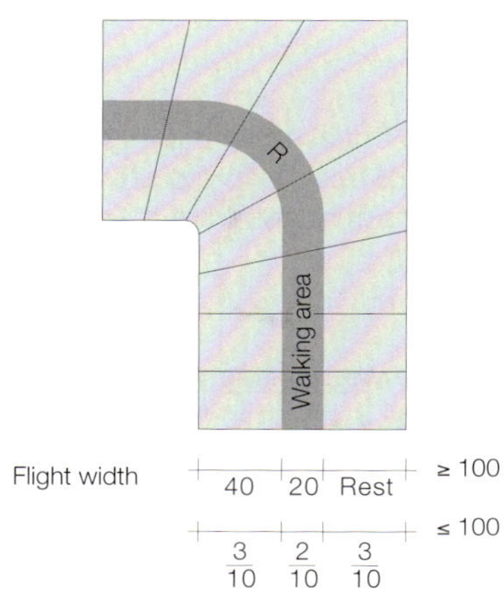

24

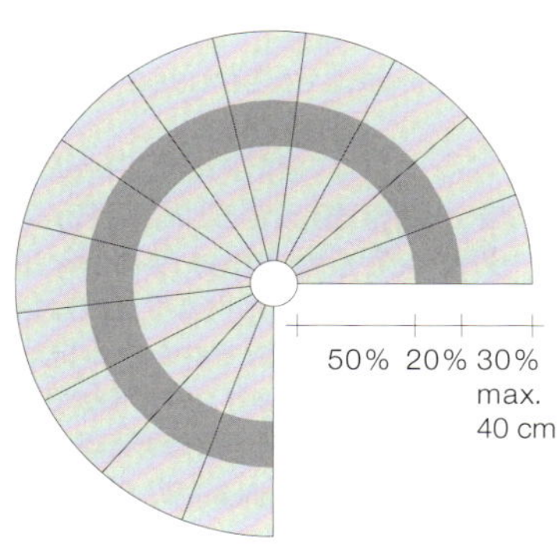

25

12

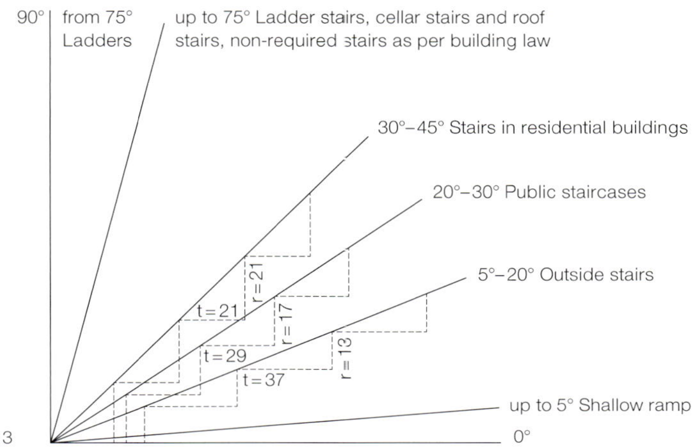

13

String, stringer, base plate, newel
A string encloses a flight of stairs laterally, forming a load-bearing component for accommodating steps. A stair's stringer supports the steps as a load-bearing girder. In cases where a two-dimensional, sloping component supports the steps on its upper side, one speaks of a base plate. A newel is the load-bearing core in the centre of a spiral staircase (see "Types of construction", p. 104ff.). All these construction parts of a staircase must be designed in accordance with the selected building material and the overall design of the stair.

Open or closed stairs
While an open staircase contains, as its name already suggests, openings between the treads, a closed staircase contains risers in their place. The type of implementation depends on the material and structure.

Dimensioning basics
The general principles for the dimensioning and construction of stairs in Germany are laid down in the state building codes as well as in special regulations for buildings with specific uses, such as the Arbeitsstättenrichtlinie [Ordinance on workplaces] or the Versammlungsstättenverordnung [Ordinance on places of assembly]. The supplementary DIN 18065, section 4ff., "Measurement rules", as well as basic ergonomic principles are used to further differentiate and specify the requirements. When planning and constructing stairs, these rules must be applied with great care and precision. The permissible tolerances, as described in DIN 18065, section 7, specify a low margin in this respect and represent maximum deviations. Other design-related deviations resulting from specific material properties or production and assembly-related

As per DIN 18065	Rise r max. [mm]	Tread t min. [mm]
Required stairs	190	260
In residential buildings with no more than two flats; stairs leading to habitable spaces	200	230
In residential buildings with no more than two flats; stairs not leading to habitable spaces	210	210
In all other buildings	190	260
Non-required stairs in all buildings	210	210

14

Required stairs	Width
In residential buildings with no more than two flats and within flats	> 80 cm
In all other buildings (BayBO) [Bavarian Building Code]	> 100 cm
In high-rise buildings (HochhVO) [Ordinance on high-rises]	> 125 cm
In places of assembly: for every 150 persons depending on the emergency escape route, but max. 250 cm/flight; configuration as per the seating in the space (VStättVO) [Ordinance on places of assembly]	100 cm
In sales outlets (VkVO) [Ordinance on sales outlets]	> 200 cm < 250 cm
Non-required stairs	> 50 cm

15

Banister heights (DIN 18065)	Height
Residential buildings, fall height up to 12 m	> 90 cm
Workplaces, fall height up to 12 m	> 100 cm
Fall height over 12 m	> 110 cm

16

17 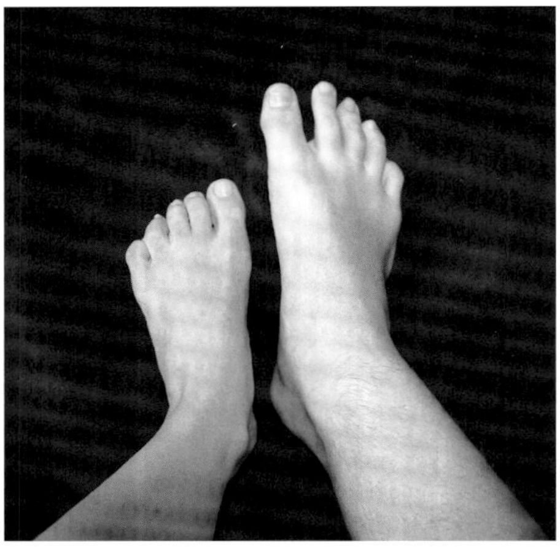

reasons, must lie within the designated tolerances in the constructed output.

Until the 2000-01 edition, DIN 18065 demanded specification of treads, risers, and gradients in centimetres. Since the 2011-06 edition (current edition 2015-03), these measurements must be specified in millimetres. This tight dimensioning without much room for manoeuvre proves the enormous importance of staircase geometry for its usability, both in terms of standard frequency of use and its great significance as a construction element that is a part of emergency escape routes.

The section "Regulatory framework/ standardisation" (p. 109f.) refers in detail to the legally binding nature of laws, standards and ordinances with respect to the planning and construction of stairs.

Terminology
The use of standardised terms, as described below and analogous to DIN 18065, is a prerequisite for the precise naming and planning-based implementation of the measurement rules, which are described in the section that follows.

- Rise r and tread t
  The dimension r denotes the stair rise in mm and in terms of the difference between two step edges lying on top of each other in elevation. The dimension t denotes the stair tread in mm and in terms of the difference between two leading step edges lying on top of each other in plan view, measured within the run of the tread line, as defined by planning.

- Gradient r/t
  The ratio of the rise r to the tread t in mm denotes the gradient or rise/run ratio and defines the pitch or inclination of a staircase.

- Nosing n
  The nosing n is the distance which the leading edge of a step projects beyond the tread width of the step beneath.

- Clearance height of a stair
  The dimension of the clearance height of a stair over the course of stair gradients is measured vertically to the undersides of the above-lying construction components, as measured from an imaginary line connecting the leading step edges (pitch line). The measurement correspondingly proceeds above the horizontal surfaces of the landings.

- Rise
  In open risers, the rise is the distance between the top of a tread to the underside of the tread of the above-lying step.

- Side clearance
  The finished dimension between the treads of a flight of stairs, a landing, or a handrail, and bounding elements, such as walls or banisters, is called side clearance.

- Tread length
  The tread length of a stair is the tread line from the leading edge of the bottom step to the leading edge of the exit step, as measured on a floor plan.

- (Usable) Flight width
  The flight width denotes the constructional width in terms of a floor plan dimension. If a flight of stairs adjoins bounding elements such as walls, it is measured up to the surface of the wall of the shell construction.
  The usable flight width, by contrast, denotes the finished dimension in ready-to-use condition. It is measured horizontally between bounding surfaces, parts and/or inner handrail edges or their projections.

- Usable landing depth
  Just like the usable flight width, the usable landing depth is a finished dimension, as measured at handrail height.

- Banister height
  The banister height is measured as a vertical finished dimension from the leading edge of a tread or the surface of a landing to the upper edge of the banister.

Measurement rules
To ensure the usability of a staircase, there are various measurement rules which particularly take into account physiological aspects. In order to be generally valid, these measurement rules adapted to the body must cover a wide range of different body sizes.

- Tread line rule: 2r + t = tread line
  The starting point for the calculation of the tread line is the average stride length of human beings. DIN 18065 mandatorily specifies this under Item 6.1.2 as lying between 590 und 650 mm. The ideal measure is specified as 630 mm.

- Safety rule: t + r = 460 mm
  This rule ensures that the tread widths of a step are sufficiently large.

- Comfort rule: t - r = 120 mm
  The difference between the tread minus the rise results in the steepness of the stair gradient. The comfort rule defines the ideal measure requiring the least effort when walking on the stair.

18

A gradient r/t of 170/290 mm corresponds exactly to all three of the above measurement rules.
The safety rule and the comfort rule, however, are recommendations only and are not subject to binding specification in any of the federal states in Germany.

Application
The basics of dimensioning and designing a stair in a building, for application in planning processes, are discussed in greater detail below. The main dimensions given in figs. 14–16 are minimum requirements within the framework of binding normative requirements based on DIN 18065. In many planning processes, the minimum requirement very often already represents the maximum planning-related possibility for the utilisation of spatial resources. Compliance with the specified minimum requirements with respect to usability and physiological perception in particular does not meet the requirements of daily use in each case.

Fig. 19a shows a clearance height of, for example, at least 2.00 m. Since average body sizes of human beings are continuously growing, there is an increasing number of staircase users who make contact with adjoining construction parts, at least with the tips of the hair, when descending in a slightly forward-bent posture on a stair with a clearance height of 2.00 m. Already persons with a body height of more than 185 cm notice this contact and perceive it as unpleasant. This results in an insecurity on the part of users in the usually subconsciously

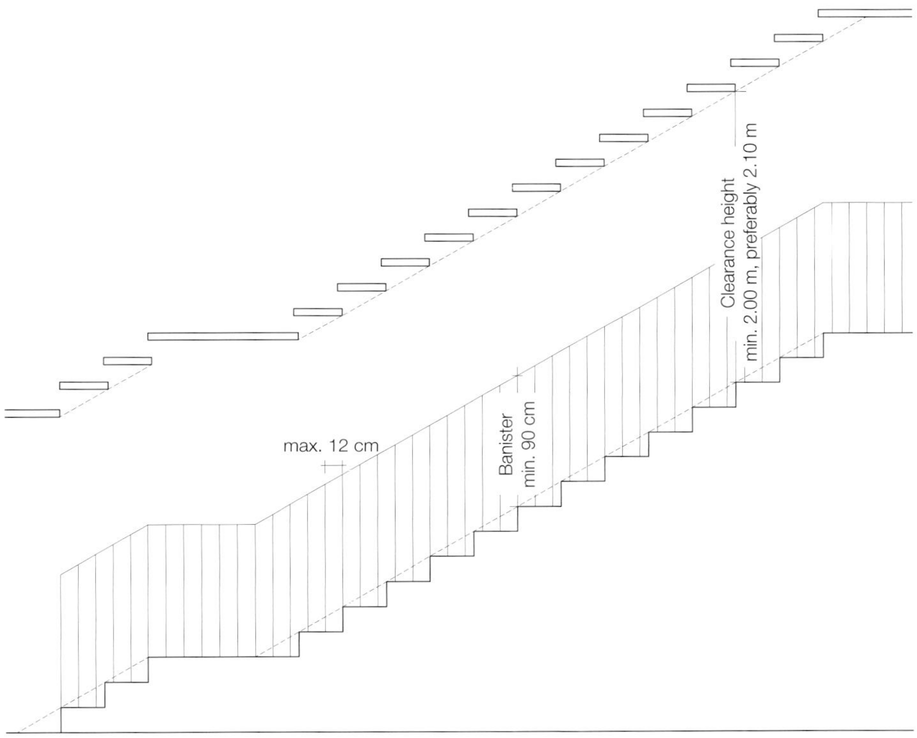

19a

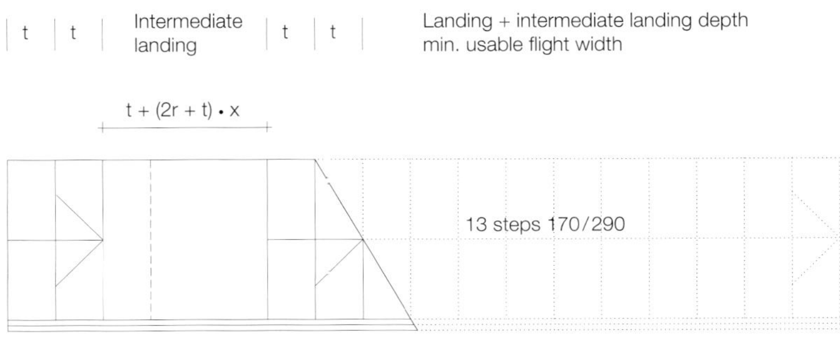

Intermediate landing after max. 18 steps

b

17 Different foot sizes
18 Museum in Nuremberg (DE) 2000, Volker Staab
19 Graphic depiction of measures

20

21

determined use of a stair. It is therefore recommended that a clearance height of at least 2.10 m be specified when planning stairs in buildings.
As per DIN 18065, the usable landing depth must correspond to at least the required usable flight width. Additionally, the landing depth is specified to have at least 3 or 2.5 goings, according to Item 6.3.4. "Going for landings", Table 1. Moreover, for intermediate landings in the run of single-flight stairs, it is useful to likewise consider the tread line rule, with 2r + t = tread line, when planning landing depth. As such, landing depth should be t + (2r + t) • x (fig. 19b, p. 101). In doing so, it is possible to avoid a short and disturbing intermediate step in a flowing movement sequence when walking the full extent of the entire staircase, including an intermediate landing.

The profile of the stairwell at right angles to the direction of movement includes further dimensional definitions alongside that of the clearance height and width, as per DIN 18065. The usable flight width is permitted to have clearance restrictions in the lower lateral area, for example due to stair strings, as shown in fig. 20. As such, laterally up to 10 cm and heightwise up to 15 cm are permissible (fig. 22). This rule has generous margins – the risk of stepping on this area and correspondingly incurring negative consequences when walking on a stair is very high for persons who are dependent on using the handrail. Especially small children or elderly persons have a high safety need, and may place the foot facing the handrail very close to the lateral stair edge, as seen in orthogonal projection. It is, therefore, recommended that the permissible dimensions are only fully utilised once this aspect has been taken into consideration.

The lateral banister spacing of at least 5 cm is appropriate and plausible for round or angular handrails with small dimensions. DIN 18065 does not regulate the geometric shape of handrails with respect to grip safety. Only the grip width is restricted to between 2.5 and 6 cm.
In this respect, DIN 18040 "Construction of Accessible Buildings" makes further demands where compliance also seems useful in areas with other planning requirements.

Lateral step margins often include a gap for aesthetic reasons to show a floating or deliberately detached step (figs. 21, 23). This lateral gap between the step edge and the stairwell wall is stipulated to be a maximum of 6 cm, a measure which at first glance seems appropriate. Nevertheless, planning should also take the expected user group into account. For users with small feet and correspondingly small treads, 6 cm is much more than half the shoe width. This presents the risk of twisting one's ankle when the foot is directly placed at the lateral step edge.

With spiral stairs, the tread line (see p. 96) can be freely selected within the

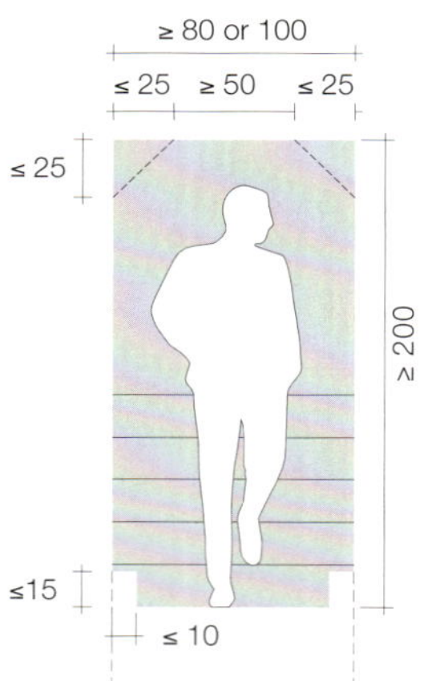

22

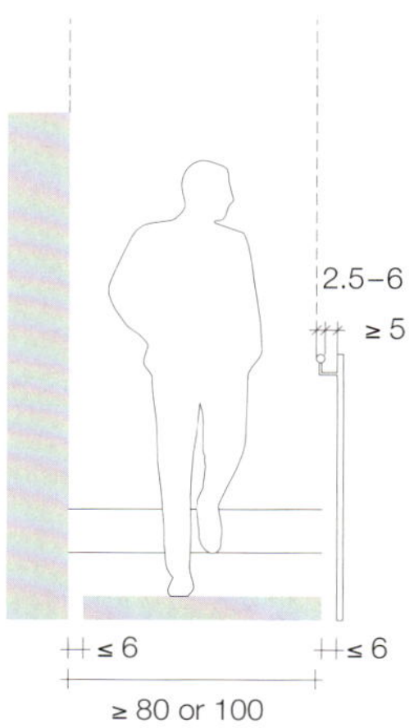

23

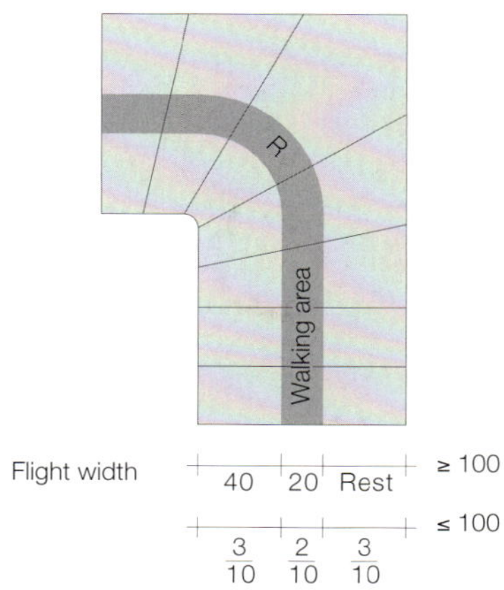

24

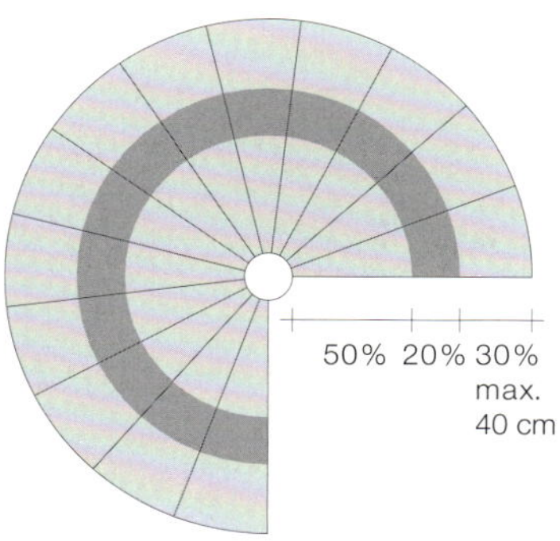

25

26

walking area (fig. 24). In the winding zone of the tread line, the tread equals the chord which results from the intersections of the curved tread line with the leading step edges. In a straight stair zone, the walking zone runs along the centre of the stair. For usable flight widths of up to 100 cm, the walking zone has a width of 20 % of the usable flight width and lies in the central zone of the stair. In the case of stairs with more than 100 cm of usable flight width, excepting newel stairs, the width of the walking zone is 20 cm. The distance of the walking zone to the inner boundary is 40 cm. [3]

Geometry and mounts

Multi-flight stairs, especially those of solid build (see "Solid base plate", p. 105), require careful planning of bend lines in order to take into account the different requirements of various load-bearing situations of flights of stairs at landings. Moreover, this allows for an orderly view of the underside of a staircase and a continuous progression of the handrail at a uniform height along the entire staircase.

The bend line is the intersecting line between the landing and the ascending or descending flights of stairs as seen from the underside of the flights of stairs and landings. In multi-flight stairs with half-turn landings (180° turns), the planning objective should be to have the bend lines of both flights of stairs meet at a single point on the landing.

The planning parameters influencing the bend line are the position of the exit step vis-à-vis the bottom step as well as the landing and base plate thicknesses. The position of the so-called zeroth step is of vital importance here. The zeroth step denotes the flush horizontal displacement in the landing area between the last rise of the descending flight of stairs and the first rise of the ascending one. As such, it lies on the landing level but adds to the usable landing depth. Fig. 27 shows three fundamentally different positions of the bottom and exit steps and hence of the zeroth step. Either the zeroth step divides itself in the landing area with one half on the ascending and the other half on the descending flight of stairs respectively (fig. 27 a), or it is fully assigned to either the ascending (fig. 27 b) or the descending flight of stairs (fig. 27 c).

Fig. 28 (p. 104) illustrates in greater detail the geometric consequences of the three described basic variants for landing thicknesses and handrail heights. Starting from the base plate thickness, the thinnest landing thickness is shown in fig. 28 c (p. 104) with d = base plate thickness/cos of stair gradient. In fig. 28 b, this measure is doubled with respect to fig. 28 c. The landing thickness increases in fig. 28 a with respect to fig. 28 c by a factor of 1.5.

On the one hand, the base plate and landing thicknesses play a major role in the aesthetics of a staircase, and on the other, have a decisive influence on the possibility of supporting the flight of stairs on the landing slabs in longitudinally set flights of stairs. The three depicted geometric variants are equally well-suited for the case of a continuous solid structure running from the landing slab to the base

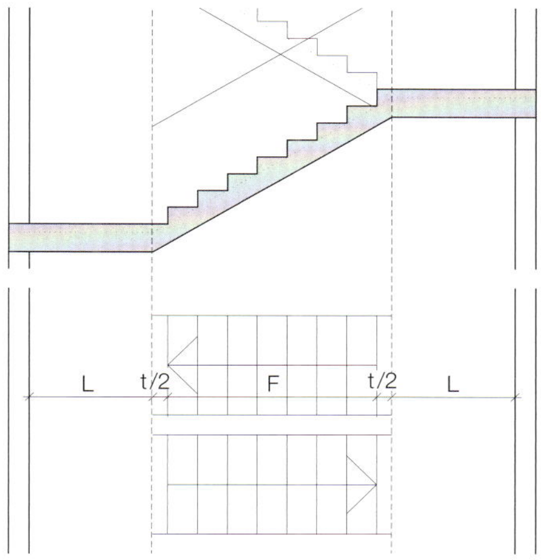

a

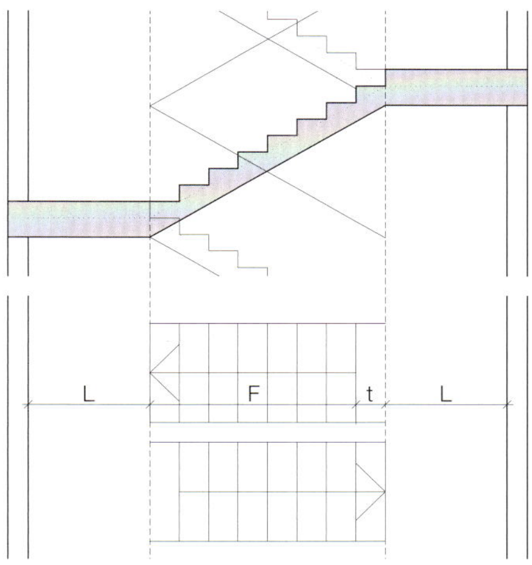

b

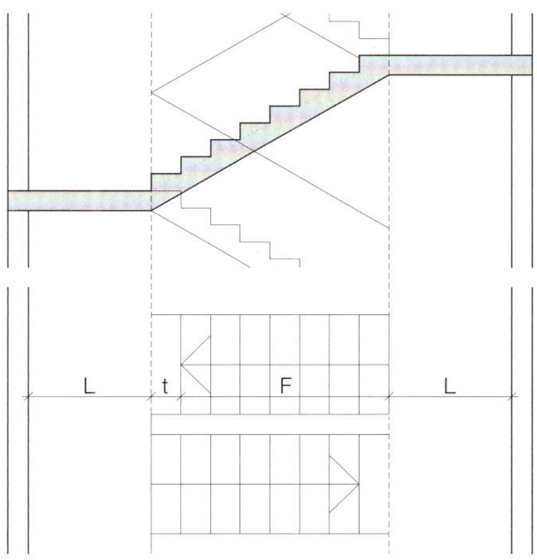

27 c

20 String in clearance diagram, flat in New York (US) 1999, Maya Lin with David Hotson
21 Spiralling stair of oak wood, holiday homes in Nossentin (DE) 2012, gmp
22 Clearance diagram (dimensions in cm)
23 Side clearance (dimensions in cm)
24 Walking area and tread line in spiral stairs (dimensions in cm)
25 Walking area and tread line in newel stairs (dimensions in cm)
26 Multifamily house in Zurich (CH) 2007, Graber Pulver Architekten
27 Bend line progression in two-flight stairs subject to the position of the "zeroth" step

30

31

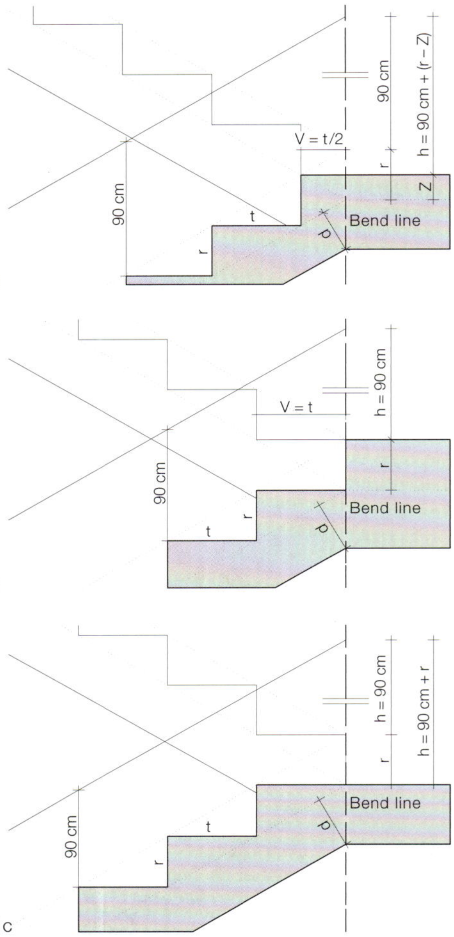

a

b

28c

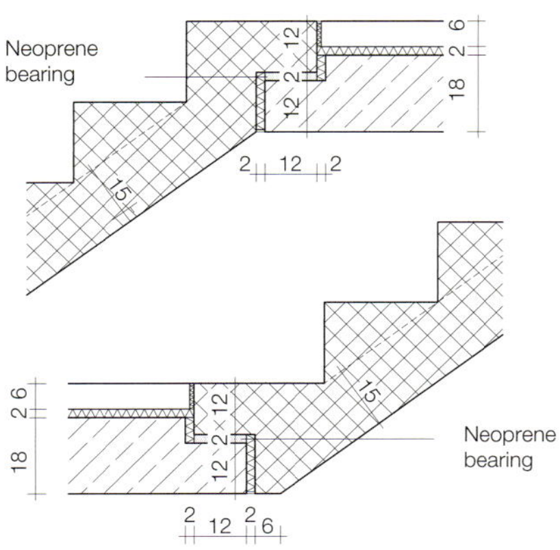

29

plate. In cases where construction physics-related requirements for sound insulation demand sound-decoupled flights of stairs, the bracket mounts needed for this purpose require a correspondingly large landing thickness, in order to accommodate two bracket thicknesses in height, as well as the thickness of the elastic support material. In cases where base plates are correspondingly thin, position c can no longer ensure this mount variant. Position b usually allows this without a problem. For position a, this mount possibility must be examined on an individual basis.

The handrail height in the landing or well hole area which results from the intersections of the handrails can likewise have various values depending on the variant. This must be taken into account when implementing a continuous handrail running along the entire staircase.

The preceding explanations illustrate the complex relationships of individual parameters and the influence of possible additional construction physics-related requirements on the space required for the staircase. The stairwell developed in conjunction with the building design and available in the further course of planning finally determines whether all parameters can be considered in such a way that the design idea can be implemented in a convincing manner. Planners should, at an early stage, endeavour to clarify these parameters with the related consequences for space requirement. Otherwise, there is the risk that retroactive requirements emerging in the course of further planning can negatively impact the design of the stair. In extreme cases, implementation of a planned stair within the available spatial situation in a design is no longer possible.

Types of construction

The basic principle underlying all stairs, consisting of an additive sequence of steps, is the same. Their appearance, however, is decisively shaped by both their basic geometric form and the type of construction, in combination with the related materials. The choice of construction type primarily depends on the aesthetic requirements of the staircase in the overall scheme of a building's design.

The type of construction is, in the first place, defined by the geometric relationship between the tread surfaces and the load-bearing elements, and furthermore by the derived position and design of the superordinate load-bearing elements of the stair. This results in the development of different load-bearing systems. All the parts of a stair (see "Stair parts", p. 96f.) fulfil specific structural requirements owing to the type of construction. Step mounts are differentiated in accordance with the respective load transmission. Roughly summarised, there are two groups of construction types: firstly, common types of construction, such as solid base plates, closed string stairs, open string stairs and individual steps; and secondly, the group of special types of construction, including spiral stairs, folded plate stairs, space frame stairs and suspended stairs. The distinctiveness of the construction type consists, on the one hand, in the combination of the principles of common types of construction, and on the other, in the development of novel, independent constructions. Once the construction type is determined, it defines the constructional requirements for the elements of the stair, which in turn and in the further course of planning, decisively influence the materials used for the staircase construction (see "Materials for stair construction", p. 107ff.).

Solid base plate

The construction type of the solid base plate refers to an inclined one-way slab. It stretches from the lower to the upper support, transmitting the loads in the area of the linear supports into the floor or landing slabs, which likewise are plate-shaped construction components. Stairs of this construction type are made of reinforced concrete, both as prefabricated and in-situ concrete stairs. The treads are usually made of the same material and integrated into the solid base plate or are formed by facings mounted on the base plate. In doing so, the mounts can be constructed in terms of a homogenous transition, like with a folded plate, or in the form of bracket mounts. The section "Sound insulation" (see p. 113) contains further information on this.

Closed string stair

In this type of stair, the laterally limiting strings act as inclined single-span beams with lower and upper mount points in the adjacent landing area, thus forming the main load-bearing structure. The steps, as individual load-bearing elements, are located in between, transmitting the loads via the lateral mount points in a static bond into the strings. This type of construction is widespread in wooden stair construction, and is realised using wooden steps which fit sideways into grooves mortised or milled into the

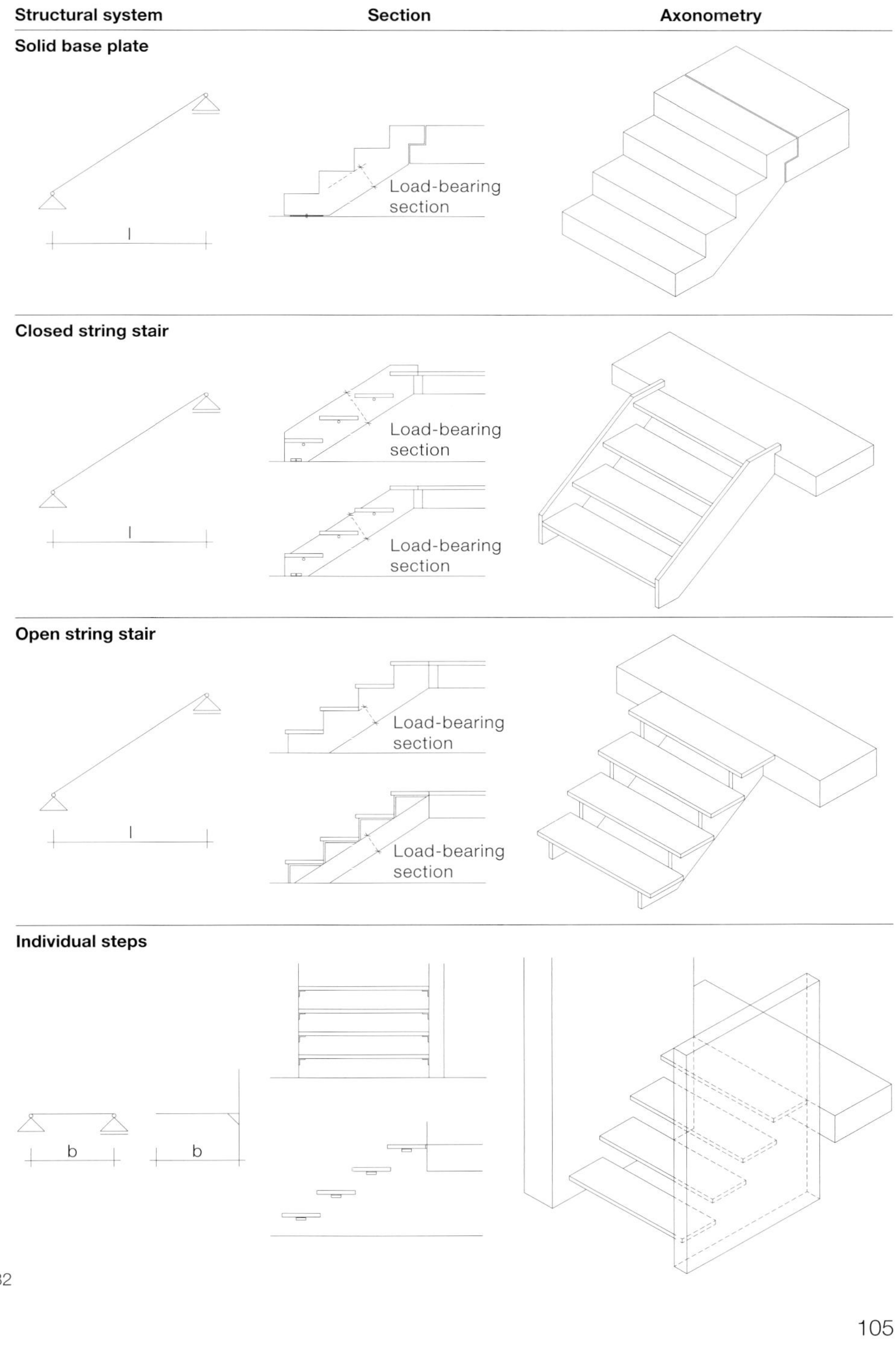

32

28 a–c Landing slab thickness of the three basic variants subject to the position of the "zeroth" step
29 Bracket mounts of the ascending and descending stair flights at the landing (dimensions in cm)
30 "Zeroth step" half/half, town hall extension, Aarhus (DK) 2002, 3XNielsen
31 "Zeroth step" at the exit of the stair, sports hall in Zug (CH) 2001, Bétrix & Consolascio Architekten with Eric Maier
32 Typology of construction types/load-bearing systems

33

34

33 Central string stair, residential building, Imabari (JP) 1999, Toru Murakami Architect & Associates
34 Several slender stringers, administration building in Struer (DK) 1998, KHR AS Architekten
35 Bent open string, office building, Bolzano (IT) 2007, Markus Scherer
36 Self-supporting steps
37 Folded plate stair, residential building in canton of Vaud (CH), Eligio Novello
38 Museum Küppersmühle, Duisburg (DE) 1999, Herzog & de Meuron
39 Residential building in London (GB) 1997, Seth Stein Architects
40 Clothing store in London (GB) 1997, David Chipperfield Architects

wooden string. Stair strings may not only be made of wood but also of steel. Steps can be manufactured to be self-supporting and made of wood, steel sheet, stone or laminated sheet glass, or be constructed with a load-bearing steel frame and planar filling.

Open string stair
Similar to the closed strings of a stair, open strings also, act as single-span beams with a lower and an upper mount. They either rest on adjacent landings, or in the case of bent open strings, incorporate landing surfaces into their horizontal sections. The steps and, if applicable, the landing slabs, too, rest on the open strings below, which is why an open string stair is also called a cut string stair. Due to their geometric position below the steps and landing slabs, it is possible to indent the strings with respect to the lateral step edges of a closed string stair so that the steps project out to the extent of the indentation. In extreme examples, the structure is reduced to one central string with embedded projecting steps (fig. 33). Fig. 34 shows a variation of the open string stair, where several open strings with highly reduced dimensions are positioned underneath the steps.

There are several possibilities for supporting steps on strings. In a stepped string, a so-called saw tooth, the steps directly rest on the stepped upper side of the string, while in the case of a straight upper string edge, the steps must be wedge-shaped. Straight strings can be supplemented by bracket-like mounts on which slab-shaped steps are attached. Stepwise bent strings consist of short individual steel rods which are rigidly joined together at their bending points (fig. 35).

The three above-mentioned construction types can be applied in straight stairs as well as spiral stairs, or combined straight and spiral stairs.

Individual steps
Several individual steps in a structurally self-contained element add up to form a stair. In doing so, the individual steps each represent a closed structural system that transmits the loads to building parts bounding the stair, such as walls and ceilings (fig. 36). As such, further structurally effective construction elements, such as closed or open strings, are not required.

Newel stair
Due to their specific geometry, newel stairs consist of a combination of different construction types. The newel, i.e. the vertical load-bearing element in the centre of a circular stair, is where the pointed steps meet. These may project out from the vertical pole comprising the newel, as in the case of steel structures. It is likewise possible to additionally enclose the steps at the outer edge by means of a load-bearing spiral-shaped closed string or an accompanying open string for support. Solid steps made of concrete or natural stone are spirally walled up while added conical newel segments form a newel. In doing so, the broad sides of the steps are embedded into a surrounding wall.

Folded plate stairs
Self-supporting folded plate stairs correspond to the structural principle of the folded single-span beam, which is used as a base plate (fig. 37). For this purpose, steel sheet plates are used, which are folded or consist of individual plates that are welded at the bending points.

Plate-shaped, wood-based materials can be rigidly joined by gluing, screw joints,

35

36

37

or bolting. Folded plate structures made of fibre-reinforced ultra-high performance concrete can be prefabricated in one piece without visible joints.

Space frame stairs
Stairs with complex basic geometry, such as with self-supporting, multiply curved, or bent runs, use the construction type of the structurally highly efficient space frame with embedded steps.

Suspended stairs
The steps of a suspended stair are fastened onto the ceiling of the above-lying floor using tensile rods or cables made of steel, which simultaneously form the railing (see "Residential building in Vrhovlje", p. 82ff.).

Materials for stair construction
In construction typology (p. 48ff.), the respective categorisation is usually derived from the materials used in the primary load-bearing structure. The following description goes the opposite way, assigning available stair part materials depending on the type of construction used. The great number of these materials and their possible processing cannot be fully described here, and the listing therefore limits itself to common applications and their appearance.

Primary load-bearing structure
In stairs with solid base plates, reinforced concrete is exclusively used as the material. This material, moreover, can meet demanding fire safety requirements at relatively minor constructional input.

In terms of their design, there is the possibility of manufacturing the basic structure as an exposed surface. For this purpose, the entire range of surface treatment of concrete, including influencing the composition of fresh concrete by varying the aggregates, is available. At the Museum Küppersmühle, Herzog & de Meuron gave the concrete stair a monolithic, organic form (fig. 38). With the exception of the subsequently applied floor covering made of terrazzo, all surfaces of exposed concrete display the surface image of the employed wooden board formwork. The concrete has been dyed and the banister surfaces have subsequently been polished.

In contrast, the reinforced concrete body can be constructed as a purely servient load-bearing structure which can then be completely concealed by coatings or the application of other surface materials.

Closed and open strings of stairs belonging to a particular construction type are usually also made of steel or wood. These stairs usually expose their construction material and per se have a filigree appearance. Reinforced concrete is rather rarely used for this purpose due to the large cross sections it requires. If closed or open strings are made of composite wood materials, these are, as a rule, also used for the steps due to the simple joining technology.

In stairs with closed or open strings of steel, steps of steel, as well as steps made of other materials, are often employed. The residential building staircase in London, by Seth Stein Architects, has glass steps enclosed by steel brackets in between closed steel strings (fig. 39).

The increasing technical possibilities for "laminating on" other materials in thin layers over the surface of steel components results in the fact that – though the filigree appearance is retained – steel as a material is often no longer used as a design-defining surface. The spiral

38

39

40

41 a 

b 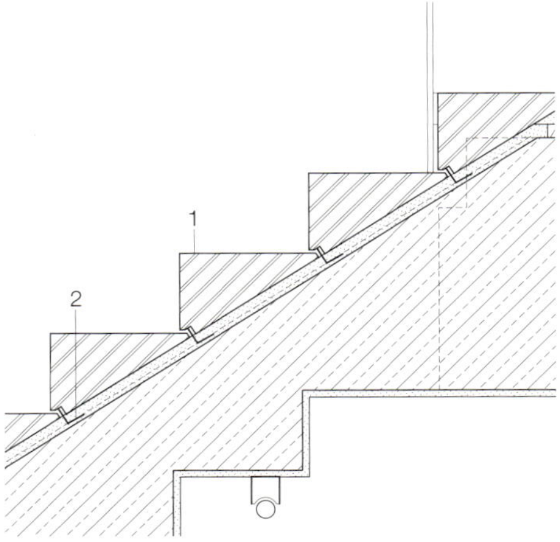

Section
Scale 1:20

1 Block step natural stone on 30 mm mortar bed Reinforced concrete Plaster 15 mm
2 Steel angles ∟ 40/40/5 mm Dowelled on concrete

stair in a clothing store in London by Chipperfield Architects, has an outer and inner closed string made of bent steel plates, which simultaneously serve as a railing and handrail (fig. 40, p. 107). The steel plates are, however, fully clad in coated plywood panels, covering the surface.

Projecting individual steps, clamped on one side only, are mostly constructed in steel, and more rarely using stone plates or solid wooden steps. Projecting steps with wooden surfaces usually have a load-bearing steel structure inside.

Individual steps, supported on both sides, are easy to construct using plate-shaped composite wood materials. Likewise, folded steel sheets or steel frames with fillings can be employed. Stone steps or self-supporting glass plates made of appropriate laminated glass are technically possible.

Step surfaces and fillings
There are two options for designing the step surfaces of stairs, provided the exposed surface is not already formed by the surface of the structure: either as a walkable covering applied to the steps of a stair, and made of reinforced concrete, steel sheet or composite wood materials; or using wedge-shaped components made of natural or artificial stone (fig. 41 b) that form the staircase geometry of risers and treads on inclined base plates. In both cases, the surfaces can consist of thin layers, such as textile or elastic coverings or liquid plastic, or of reinforcements using plate-shaped composite wood materials, ceramic or natural stone plates and compound materials (laminates).

In each case, steps made of circumferential steel frames require a flat filling of a self-supporting material to form a walkable covering (fig. 44).

Apart from purely aesthetic aspects, the improvement of technical and functional characteristics such as slip resistance or impact sound-reducing effects, determines the choice of material. The aesthetic freedom that becomes possible here is shown by the following examples: in the residential building in Morcote, Markus Wespi + Jérôme de Meuron constructed the step surfaces, for example, out of exposed brick (fig. 9, p. 50).

The treads of the folded plate-like, steel sheet stair in Skara Cathedral by AIX Architekter received step surfaces of corrugated rubber with underlying impact sound insulation (fig. 42; fig. 15, p. 52).

At the residential building in Kajagaya by Atelier Den, expanded metal serves as filling for both the steps and the railing (fig. 44). As a result, the stair acts as a transparent light filter. Similar effects can be achieved with step fillings of glass (fig. 39, p. 107).

Banister/fall protection
The load-bearing structure of the stair and the banister are often developed as a structural unit. In many cases, the banister – in the form of a step-bounding string – simultaneously takes on a load-bearing role. In doing so, the materials used in the basic construction of the stair also determine the materials used for the banister or of the sideward fall protection. At the Museum Küppersmühle, Herzog & de Meuron constructed the stair and banister in one pour out of red-dyed reinforced concrete (fig. 38, p. 107); with the steel staircase in the Juilliard School in New York by Diller, Scofidio +

42 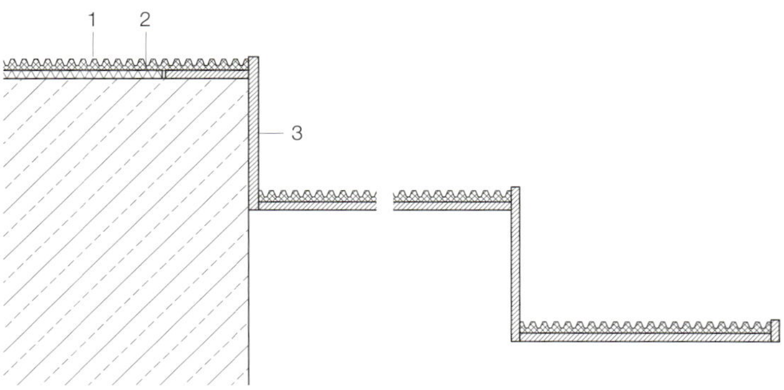

Section
Scale 1:10

1 Rubber cover, corrugated 15 mm
2 Impact sound insulation 10 mm
3 Flat steel 10 mm

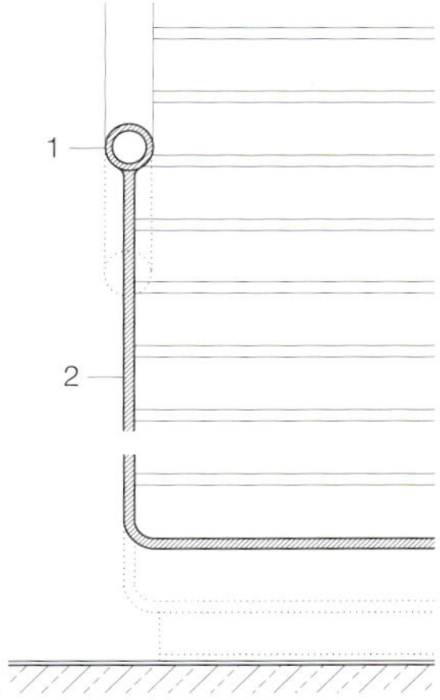

43 a

Section
Scale 1:20

1 Handrail: steel tube coated ∅ 76 mm
2 Side wall: steel panel coated 19 mm

b

Renfro / FXFOWLE, the steps and banister are formed by individual, 19 mm thick steel plates (fig. 43).

Frequently, the banister consists of a frame which is supplemented by vertical rods in a grid, with a maximum spacing of 12 cm, for the purpose of fall protection. Here too, there are no limits to the design, allowing the use of round or flat steel in various thicknesses by differentiating supporting and fill bars (fig. 45). For filling the spaces, all surface-covering materials, including metal, wood, plastics, glass or composite materials, as well as tensile structures, metal grills and grids or round bar mats are also suitable. The uppermost horizontal rod often forms the handrail at the same time. This can, however, also be mounted as an individual element.

Banisters with an independent structure and materials often stand in contrast to the staircase. A sideward fall protection made of self-supporting safety glass can, for example, reinforce the sculptural impact of the flight of stairs as it aesthetically recedes into the background (fig. 41 a).

Current development of new materials and technologies
The rapid development of special types of glass means that their application in staircase construction is close to becoming a standard technical solution. Safety glass consisting of several laminated panes or of hardened glass is available, either straight, or bent as formed components. Only the relatively high costs make this technology still somewhat exclusive.

Fibre-reinforced composites, such as high-strength carbon fibre reinforce concrete, or fibreglass-reinforced plastic, have in the meanwhile become ready-for-use technologies which are likely to become as pervasive as the special types of glass.

Adhesives and their processing possibilities are widespread today, with the result that laminated materials are available as mass-produced articles. Due to the layered combination of different materials, even thin plates have high load-bearing capacity and mechanical or weather resistance. The design of the surfaces is highly diverse, owing to pictographic reproductions and independently of the material. It remains to be seen, however, whether this leads to a separate material typology.

Regulatory framework / standardisation
National jurisdictions create numerous legal regulations and standards. It is not within the scope of this book to provide a comprehensive treatment of this subject. Therefore, the following consideration is to be viewed as exemplary, especially with respect to their relevance for public building law. The structuring of the subject and the content-related preparation provide a thematic overview, permitting orientation in the relevant legal framework of a respective project. In doing so, the level of detail of individual topics is subordinated for the sake of clarity.

State building codes
In federally constituted Germany, public building law is the duty of the federal states. The state building codes regulate the legal framework, which is obligatory for building construction in the respective state. The primary objective is to prevent danger to life and limb, amongst other objectives. For standardising the different state building codes, the Model Building Regulation was created as an overriding

41 Administration building, Munich (DE) 1998, Betz Architekten
   a Glass banisters
   b Stair treads made of wedge-shaped natural stones
42 Step treads made of steel sheet, Skara Cathedral, (SE) 2000, AIX Architekter
43 Juilliard School in New York (US) 2009, Diller Scofidio + Renfro / FXFOWLE
44 Stair treads and banisters made of expanded metal, residential building, Kajigaya (JP) 2001, Atelier Den
45 Differently dimensioned load-bearing and infill spindles of the stair banister, town hall extension, Aarhus (DK) 2001, 3XNielsen

44

45

46

47
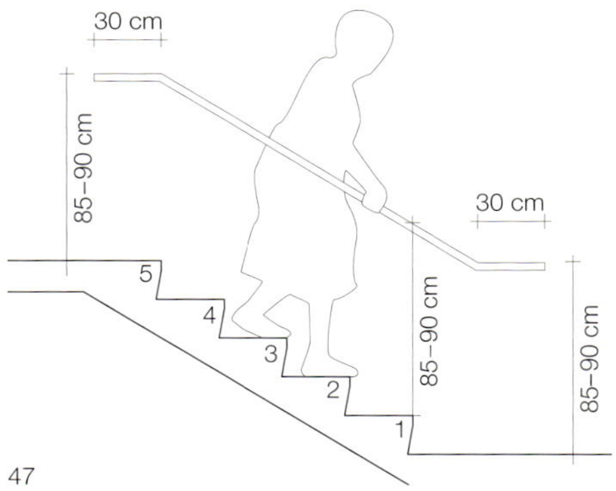

46 Research building in Dübendorf (CH) 2016, Gramazio Kohler Architects
47 Handrail height above leading step edges and landing surfaces, horizontal handrail endings. At the lower end of the stair flight, the inclined part of the handrail must be continued by one tread width to avoid a height offset when transitioning to the horizontal level.
48 Blavatnik School of Government in Oxford (GB) 2015, Herzog & de Meuron

orientation framework for all federal states. The state building codes therefore primarily contain congruent regulations with state-specific particularities. The concrete example presented below is the Bavarian Building Code (BayBO).

- Art. 2, "Begriffe" [Terms], Paragraph 3, regulates the building classes which have primary importance for the construction of stairs. Paragraph 4 regulates special constructions, which have further ordinances that also contain special stipulations on the construction of stairs. This pertains, for example, to high-rise buildings, shops, meeting places, restaurants, care facilities, hospitals, residential establishments, day care facilities, schools or college buildings.
- Art. 3, "Allgemeine Anforderungen" [General requirements] refers to the generally accepted rules of architecture and technology for the maintenance of public safety and order. In Paragraph 2, Clause 1, it regulates the technical building stipulations, which are introduced in a legally binding manner through public announcement.
- Section V, "Rettungswege, Öffnungen, Umwehrungen" [Emergency escape routes, openings, fencing], Art. 31–36, contains the principal stipulations for planning stairs.
- Art. 32, "Treppen" [Stairs] regulates the term "notwendige Treppe" [required stair], which is subject to and must meet various requirements depending on the class of building (see Art. 2).
- Art. 33, "Treppenräume" [Stairwells] regulates the prerequisites and requirements which are relevant for the construction of stairwells for required stairs.
- Art. 36, "Umwehrungen" [Fencing], Paragraph 3, regulates the requirements for fencing along open margins of stairs and landings.
- Section VII, "Nutzungsbedingte Anforderungen" [Requirements depending on use], Art. 48, once again underlines the importance of requirements for accessible architecture.

In their clauses and articles relating to stairs, the state building codes hardly make statements on specific requirements, such as dimensional specifications. Instead, they contain many general references to requirements whose scope only becomes fully accessible when further ordinances and technical building stipulations are studied in this regard.

Adopted technical building stipulations
Technical rules, such as DIN standards, first and foremost are private guidelines making recommendations. They obtain a generally binding character only by their adoption as technical building stipulation. The Bavarian Building Law regulates this procedure in Art. 3.2.1: following its announcement by the Bavarian Ministry of the Interior, the current version of January 2015 only states three technical rules under Section 7, "Technische Regeln als Planungsgrundlagen" [Technical rules as planning guide], including DIN 18065, Stairs in buildings, and DIN 18040, Parts 1 and 2, Construction of accessible buildings – Design principles. For application of the technical rules, explanations accompanying the announcement have been provided, by means of which parts can be excluded or particular aspects commented on in greater depth.

The adoption of DIN 18065 as a technical building regulation highlights the content-related significance of this extensive technical standard. For this reason, this publication closely follows the content of this DIN standard.

Ordinances
Ordinances substantiate individual contents in the state building code relating to special buildings or uses, and are generally binding. With respect to the planning and construction of stairs, the following should be referred to:

- Hochhausrichtlinie [High-rise building directive], issued on 21 April 2015
- Verkaufsstättenverordnung (VkV) [Ordinance on sales outlets], issued on 6 November 1997
- Versammlungsstättenverordnung (VStättV) [Ordinance on places of assembly], issued on 12 February 2012
- Beherbergungsstättenverordnung (BStättV) [Ordinance on accommodation], issued on 2 July 2007
- Arbeitsstättenverordnung (ArbStättV) [Ordinance on workplaces], issued on 12 August 2004
- Heimmindestbauverordnung (HeimMindBauV) [Ordinance on minimum building requirements for retirement homes, homes for the elderly, and care homes], issued on 3 May 1983

The above-mentioned laws, stipulations, and ordinances are not concerned with private law-related issues but with those of public building law. Moreover, issues relevant to planning in publicly funded building measures, which may include the prescribed condition of compliance with further recommendations and ordinances, are to be noted.

Accessibility
The following requirements for barrier-free stairs can be integrated into planning with relatively little effort and implemented in an economically justifiable manner. The need for persons with disabilities to move to a special facility may thus be deferred. Temporary or minor motor constraints

48

hence do not lead to the loss of self-sufficiency. The first goal of accessible construction should be to equip habitual surroundings in order to make them accessible in a barrier-free manner in daily life, and hence to preserve the self-sufficiency of the persons concerned in a user-friendly manner and for as long as possible.

The inclusion of a separate article or clause on accessible construction in the state building codes and the introduction of DIN 18040 "Construction of accessible buildings" as a technical building stipulation, illustrate the significance of this issue. The standard consists of three parts: Part 1 discusses publicly accessible buildings; Part 2 dwellings; and Part 3 public and open spaces.

Requirements for stairs are regulated by Paragraph 4.3.6, including four sub-items in Parts 1 and 2, respectively.

Item 1 points out that this paragraph is about measures for improved usability and higher safety for persons with limited motor constraints, as well as for blind and visually impaired persons.

Item 2 discusses the design of flights of stairs and the construction of steps. If a flight of stairs is not straight, it must have a correspondingly large inside radius larger than 100 cm in publicly accessible buildings, as per Part 1. A stair tread line at right angles to the step edges ensures safe placement of feet and a natural walking rhythm. Open string stairs without risers are unsuitable for accessible staircase design. Steps must not have nosings; risers can have a maximum slant of 2 cm across the entire step height.

Item 3 requires a double-sided positioning of the handrail at a height of between 85 and 90 cm, with mounts on the underside (fig. 47). Handrails are to proceed without interruption in stairwells and on landings. Their ends must continue horizontally for 30 cm at the start and end of a stair, and – in case they freely project into a space – must be rounded off. A round or oval shape ensures improved grip safety.

Item 4 describes measures for enhanced recognisability of stair elements by visually impaired persons. This is achieved by marking step edges by contrasting them with the other surfaces of the treads and risers. Handrails are also to display high contrast with respect to the background (fig. 48).

Fire safety

In the state building codes, stairs are first and foremost viewed as emergency escape routes in case of fire, alongside their function as a required access component in a building. The scope of contents of fire-safety issues in staircase construction illustrates the importance of this aspect. The following comments take into account the fire safety requirements in Germany, guided by the Model Building Regulation or the Bavarian Building Law.

Required stair

As per the state building code (such as the Bavarian Building Law, BayBO, Art. 32), a building's stair serves the purpose of providing user-friendly access to floors not located on ground level, and of ensuring the rescue of people in the case of fire and the fire-extinguishing operation. A stair thus forms the vertical component of an emergency route, and must lead to all connected floors in one go. Building law calls this stair a required stair.

Stairwell

The necessity and – where applicable – the type of construction of the stairwell is determined by the classification of buildings into building classes, as regulated by the state building code (see BayBO, Art. 2.3). Linked to this are also the requirements for the type of construction of the stair.

Number, distance and dimensioning of required stairs

The floor area of a building determines the number of required stairs. The stairwell of at least one required stair must be reachable within 35 m from every point of a habitable room. In the "Sonderbauverordnungen" [Ordinances on special buildings], this distance reduces depending on the type of use.

In school buildings, places of assembly and sales outlets, at least two required stairs are demanded. The minimum requirement for the usable stair width is defined by DIN 18065, while special buildings are subject to particular requirements. In places of assembly, for example, the number of users who depend on a stair determines the usable stair width: for every 150 users, at least 1 m of stair width is to be allocated.

If, subject to use, the transport of patients reclining on stretchers is required, their dimensions (2.26 m in length and 0.60 m in width, as per DIN 13024) must be taken into account by corresponding dimensions in the spatial design of the stair.

Fire resistance rating of required stairs and stairwells

Load-bearing parts of required stairs must be fireproof (90 min. period of fire resistance). In low-rise buildings (building class 3), they must be non-flammable or at least fire-retardant (30 min. period of fire resistance). This is to ensure that, in case of direct fire exposure, the stair remains passable.

Stairwell walls are to be constructed in a fireproof manner, and in low-rise buildings, as firewalls. As such, the stairwell forms a separate fire or smoke compartment, without having to meet the fire compartment requirements concerning stairwell enclosures. Stairwells can be designed to be internal or external.

Other requirements for stairwells
The ingress of smoke from adjacent floors is to be prevented by means of accordingly constructed doors as stairwell enclosures. Likewise, smoke must not be allowed to enter the building from the outside. Fire smoke ingress must be dissipated quickly. Safe walkability and the longest possible standing time are required in case of fire. Depending on the building class, the applied building elements and materials must have corresponding fire resistance. Due to applied materials and possible items of furniture, stairwells must not have fire loads of their own.

External stairwells
A required stairwell should normally lie along an exterior wall and have a direct exit leading outside. Consequently, the external stairwell is the rule. As such, it is possible to incorporate openings into the exterior wall for extracting smoke from the stairwell. For this purpose, an opening of at least 0.5 m^2 per floor is required.

Internal stairwells
As a deviation from the principle of the external stairwell, internal stairwells are also possible. In this case, first and foremost, a smoke outlet with a clearance cross section of 5% of the stairwell floor area, but at least 1 m^2 in size, is required.

Safety stair
In high-rise buildings, the rescue of people by ladders from the outside is no longer possible. Therefore, a second required stairwell, or alternatively, a single safety stair for two required stairwells is demanded. The safety stair must be effectively protected from smoke ingress. This can be ensured by an air lock positioned in an open air stream.

Emergency staircases
If a second emergency escape route is not possible, an outlying emergency staircase can alternatively be employed. These staircases must not be compromised by fire spread from adjacent building openings. Emergency staircases may be spiral stairs and must consist of non-flammable building materials. They are permitted to terminate on a safe waiting landing, from where further rescue is possible.

49

1 Natural stone cladding
2 Stair flight
3 Edge insulation strips
4 Elastic joint
5 Screed on separation layer
Impact sound insulation
Reinforced concrete ceiling
6 Bracket mount impact sound-insulated
7 Mount impact sound-insulated

Non-required stairs
Non-required stairs are often planned due to functional reasons and are open stairs without stairwells. In buildings starting from building class 3, they are permitted to connect a maximum of two floors with each other. The number and position of required stairs remains unaffected by this.

Sound insulation
Sound insulation is a major quality feature of a building. The minimum requirements necessary due to the acknowledged rules of technology are often insufficient to meet the expectations of users. There are many legal disputes on account of different perceptions of the promised and delivered degree of sound insulation. For this reason, a precise agreement on the desired sound insulation should be concluded with the client in a service contract. In doing so, the building stair must meet requirements for impact sound insulation. For this purpose, defined interfaces between the stair and delimiting components of the building, which are assessable in terms of sound insulation, are required. In solid constructions, the use of bracket mounts allows for relatively simple and effective measures (fig. 50). However, this requires certain geometric prerequisites to be met for supporting the base plate and the transmission of forces in the mount. If these are not available, only specially developed components can be employed for the mount of the stair. These structures are based on the principle of elastic mounts. Correspondingly mounting the bearing and contact points of the stair with surrounding components ensures decoupling of vibrations. Use-incurred frequencies are not transmitted to spaces in need of protection.

Both the planning and the construction of these connecting points requires great care. Already the smallest of weak points cause sound bridges, comprehensively risking the success of a measure.

Linked to the decoupling of flights of stairs, precise planning of the path of joints is required. On the one hand, the geometrical mounting requirements must be met, and on the other, exposed joints can also have an aesthetic impact.

Apart from sound decoupling an entire stair, there is the alternative possibility of acoustically separating the tread coverings at the mount points. For this purpose, the tread coverings are vibration-decoupled from the support by means of an underlying decoupling mat. Since the area involved is large, the risk of a constructional defect is high. If possible, sound decoupling of the entire base plate takes precedence over step decoupling.

In case of high impact sound protection requirements for stair constructions, it is recommended that a building physics specialist be consulted.

Notes
[1] DIN 18065:2015-0 Stairs in buildings – Terminology, measuring rules, main dimensions
[2] Bolleray, Franziska: Früher aus Holz, noch heute steiler als anderswo – die Treppe in den Niederlanden. In: Detail 2/1998, p. 141–146
[3] as per DIN 18065 Section 8

49 Emergency stairs located in front of a fireproof wall, Pleasure Dome entertainment centre in Vienna (AT) 2001, Rüdiger Lainer
50 Measures for sound decoupling (dimensions in cm), scale 1:20
a Upper junction stair flight to landing/floor
b Lower junction stair flight to landing/floor
c Junction stair flight to floor slab
51 Central string stair with concrete steps

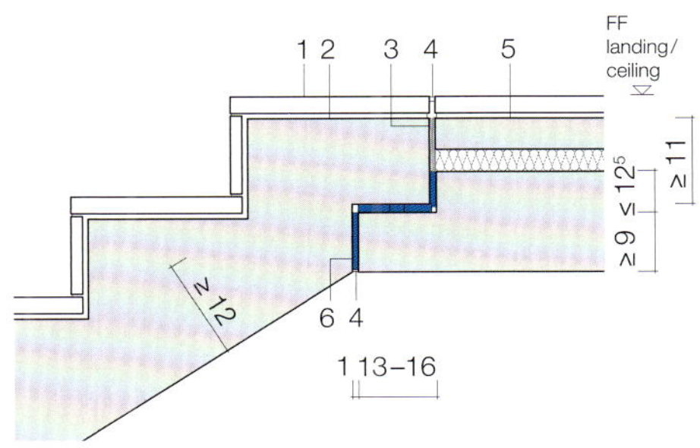

a

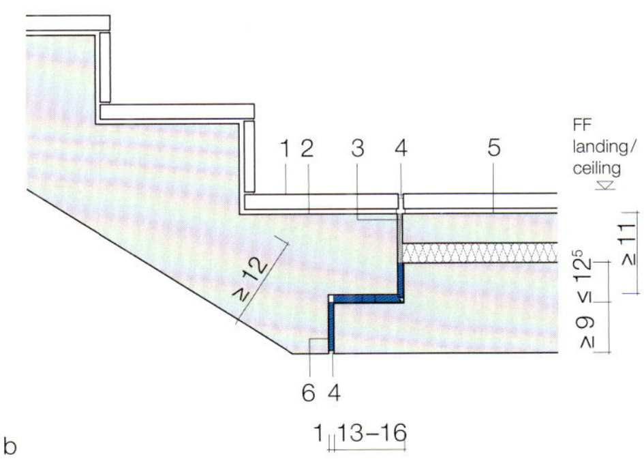

b

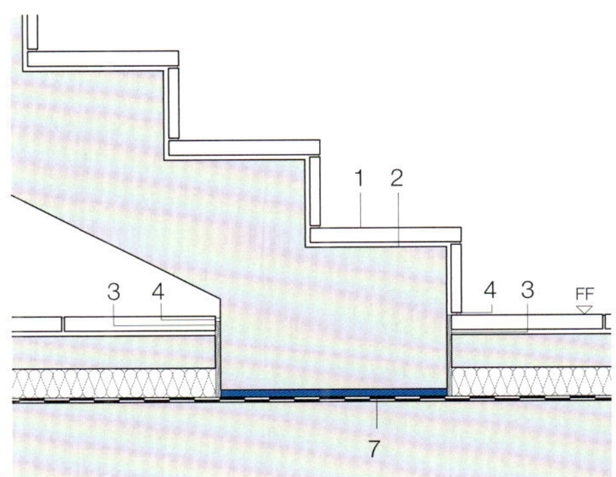

50 c

51

Step by step: Defining stair geometry

The following sample calculations show how the geometry of a single-flight or two-flight stair can be ascertained and defined in a step-by-step manner.

The example assumes a staircase in a residential building with more than three flats and a floor height of 2.85 m (2.50 m ceiling height + 35 cm ceiling structure). The rise/run ratio should not be more than 190/260, and the usable flight width at least 1.00 m.

1. *Ascertaining the number of stair steps:*
   To set a limit, the floor height is divided by the maximum possible rise (19 cm):
   285 cm : 19 cm = 15 steps (min.)
   ⟶ Choice of either 15 or 16 stair steps

2. *Calculating the rise r:*
   The floor height is divided by the number of stair steps:
   - For example, 285 cm : 15 steps = 19.0 cm
     ⟶ Rise r = 190 mm
   - For example, 285 cm : 16 steps = 17.8 cm
     ⟶ Rise r = 178 mm

3. *Defining the dimension of the tread t (including control of the tread line rule):*
   - For example, 15 risers 90/260
     ⟶ control: 2r + t = 2 · 190 + 260 mm = 640 mm ⟶ tread line rule fulfilled
   - For example, 16 risers 178/280
     ⟶ control: 2r + t = 2 · 178 + 280 mm = 636 mm ⟶ tread line rule fulfilled

4. *Ascertaining the stair flight length or run (single-flight stair):*
   The number of treads t (number of risers r – 1) is multiplied by the tread dimension.
   - For 15 risers: 14 (t) · 260 mm = 3,640 mm = 3.64 m stair flight length (run)

Single-flight stair
15 risers 190/260 ⟶ stair flight length (run): 3.64 m
16 risers 178/280 ⟶ stair flight length (run): 4.20 m

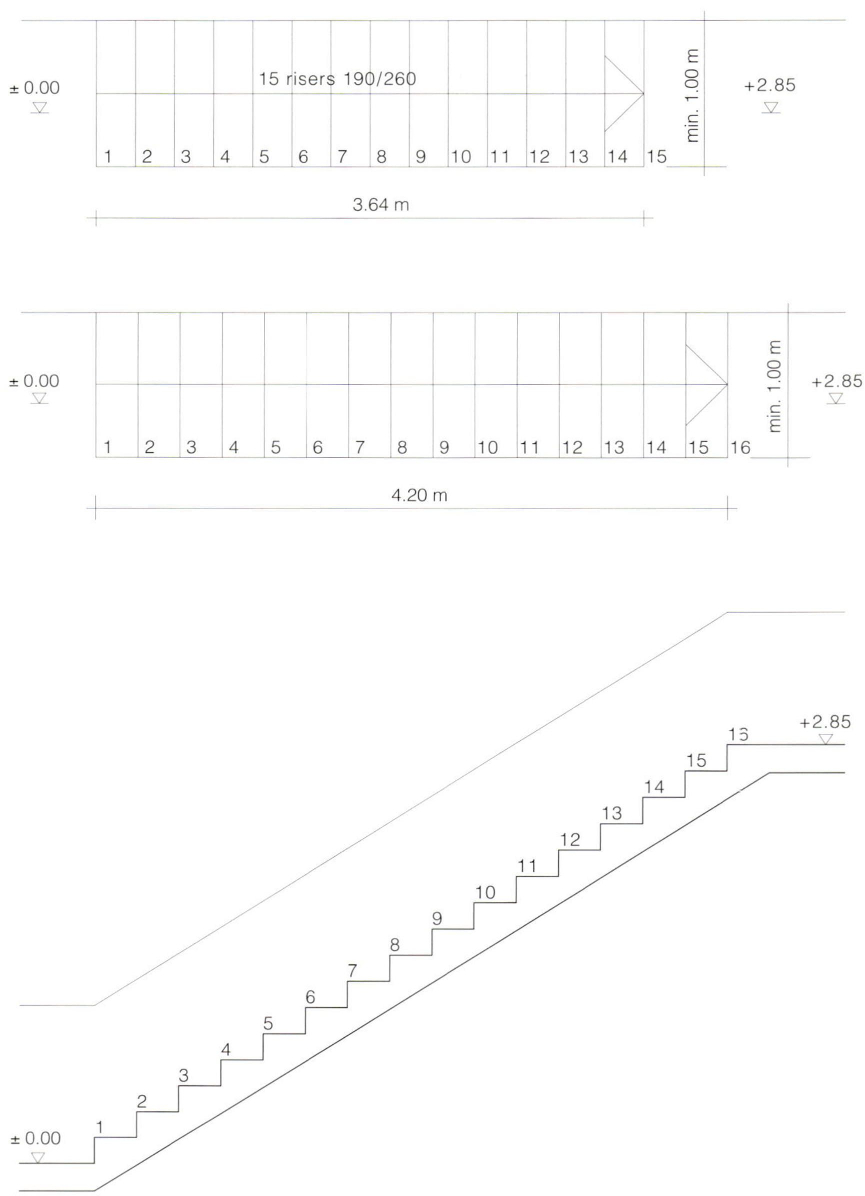

Two-flight stair
2× 8 risers 178/280 ⟶ stair flight length (run): 2.24 m

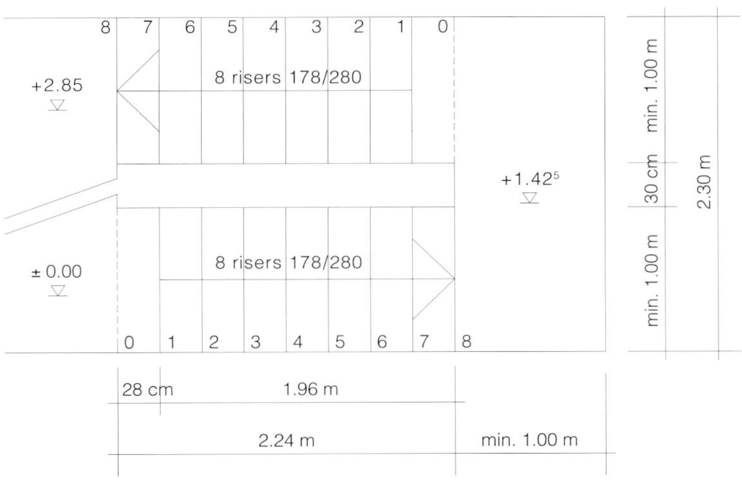

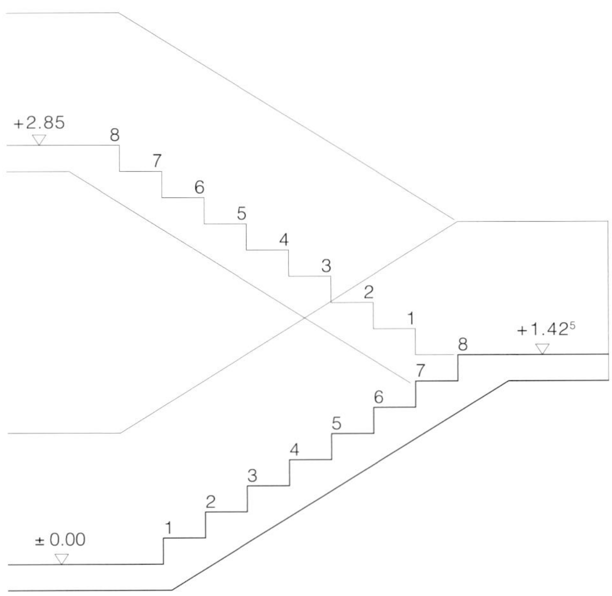

- For 16 risers:
  15 (t) · 280 mm = 4,200 mm
  = 4.20 m stair flight length (run)

4. *Ascertaining the stair flight length or run (two-flight stair):*
   16 risers 178/280 in two flights
   ⟶ 2× 8 risers 178/280:
   The number of treads t (number of risers r – 1) is multiplied by the tread dimension.
   For each flight, with 8 risers:
   7 (t) · 280 mm = 1,960 mm
   = 1.96 m stair flight length (run)

   If the handrail on the side of the well hole is to continue at a steady inclination without having to include a height offset, the bottom step must include a "zeroth" step at the level of the landing. The flight length (run) is thus extended by the width of one tread.

   For each flight, with 8 risers:
   7 (t) + 1 (t) · 280 mm = 2,240 mm
   = 2.24 m stair flight length (run)

   Depth of intermediate landing: at least 1.00 m between the handrails
   Well hole: size as per space / configuration of railing / aesthetic intention.

5. *Further specifications:*
   - Selection of load-bearing structure (solid base plate, open string, closed string, single projecting steps, etc.)
     ⟶ Dimensioning by means of statics
   - Material of the load-bearing structure (wood, steel, sheet metal, concrete, etc.)
     ⟶ Restriction due to fire safety requirement
   - Material of treads and risers (wood, steel, metal sheet, concrete, natural stone, glass, tiles, plastic, etc.)
   - Construction and material of the railing / handrail

Authors

Christian Peter
graduate architect (Dipl.-Ing. Architekt)
born in June 1960 in Heidenheim a. d. Brenz
until 1992, worked in various architectural practices in Munich and Stuttgart
1992–1995 lecturer at the University of Applied Sciences Munich
2010–2012 lecturer at the University of Applied Sciences Augsburg
since 1994, SPP Architekten + Ingenieure, together with Christine Peter and Wolfgang Sturm
since September 2012, professorship for building construction and design at the University of Applied Sciences Augsburg
Member of the Bavarian Chamber of Architects

Christine Peter
graduate architect (Dipl.-Ing. Architekt), BDA member
born in June 1963 in Stuttgart
1983 studied art history at the LMU Munich, graduation in 1988
1986 scholarship of the German Academic Scholarship Foundation
1988–1991 worked in various architectural practices in Munich and Freiburg
1992–1995 research assistant at the Chair of Building Construction and Architectural Design, Prof. Hugues, Technical University of Munich
1997–2001 tutor at the Chair of Building Construction, Prof. Schunck, Technical University of Munich
2010–2012 visiting professor at the University of Applied Sciences Munich
since 1994 SPP Architekten + Ingenieure, together with Christian Peter und Wolfgang Sturm
since 2001, various teaching assignments at the Universities of Applied Sciences in Munich and Augsburg
Member of the Bavarian Chamber of Architects and the BDA [Association of German Architects] Bavaria

Daniel Reisch
graduate architect (Dipl.-Ing. (FH) Architekt)
born in May 1974 in Stuttgart
1994–1995 studied German philology and Romance philology at the LMU Munich
studied architecture at the University of Applied Sciences Munich, graduation in 2002
2000–2004 worked at Herzog & de Meuron in Munich
2004–2006 worked at Herzog & de Meuron in Basel
2006–2012 research assistant at the Chair of Architectural Design and Building Construction at the Bauhaus University Weimar
2013–2014 research assistant at Studio Krucker Bates at Technical University of Munich
since 2010 collaboration with Katinka Temme at studio3
since 2015 freelance editor at Detail Business Information GmbH
since 2015 teaching assignments at the University of Applied Sciences Augsburg
Member of the Bavarian Chamber of Architects and the Federal Foundation of Baukultur

Katinka Temme
graduate architect (M. Arch.)
born in May 1976 in Hilden
studied architecture at the TH Karlsruhe and Arizona State University, USA, graduation in 2000
2001 worked at Gerber Architekten general planners in Dortmund
From 2001, worked at Kengo Kuma & Associates in Tokyo
2004–2005 worked at Herzog & de Meuron in Basel
2005–2011 project architect at Kengo Kuma & Associates
2011–2012 research assistant at the Technical University of Darmstadt, Department of Architecture, Chair of Architectural Design and Open Space Planning
since 2010, her own creative studio "kyLAB" in Tokyo
since 2010, collaboration with Daniel Reisch at studio3
since February 2013, professorship for Analogue Architecture & Design at the University of Applied Sciences Augsburg
teaching assignments at various national and international universities
Member of the Bavarian Chamber of Architects

Standards, Regulations

Standards
DIN 18040: 2010-10 Construction of accessible buildings – Design principles – Part 1: Publicly accessible buildings
DIN 18040: 2010-10 Construction of accessible buildings – Design principles – Part 2: Dwellings
DIN 18065: 2015-03 Stairs in buildings – Terminology, measuring rules, main dimensions

ÖNorm B 5371 Stairs, guard rails and parapets in buildings and landscapes – dimensions. Date of issue: 15 August 2011

Building codes of the federal states
Model Building Regulation in the version of 1 November 2002. Last amended by the resolution of 21 September 2012. Standard-setting body: federal government
Example: Bavarian Building Code in the version of the announcement of 14 August 2007 Last amended on 12 July 2017

Ordinances
Arbeitsstättenverordnung ArbStättV [Ordinance on workplaces]. Issued on 12 August 2004. Last amended on 30 November 2016. Published by the Federal Ministry of Labour and Social Affairs
Beherbergungsstättenverordnung BstättV [Ordinance on accommodation]. Issued on 2 July 2007. Last amended on 8 July 2009 example for the Free State of Bavaria
Heimmindestbauverordnung HeimMindBauV [Ordinance on minimum building requirements for retirement homes, homes for the elderly and care homes]. Issued on 3 May 1983. Last amended on 25 November 2003 (current version). Standard-setting body: federal government
Muster-Richtlinie über den Bau und Betrieb von Hochhäusern (Muster-Hochhaus-Richtlinie – MHHR) [Model directive on the construction and operation of high-rise buildings (Model directive on high-rise buildings)] in the version of 18 April 2008. Last amended by the resolution of the Building Supervision Commission of February 2012
Verkaufsstättenverordnung VkV [Ordinance on sales outlets]. Issued on 6 November 1997. Last amended on 29 November 2007 exemplarily for the Free State of Bavaria
Versammlungsstättenverordnung VstättV [Ordinance on places of assembly]. Issued on 2 November 2007. Last amended on 8 April 2013 example for the Free State of Bavaria

References

Daidalos, No. 9/1983 Treppen
Deplazes, Andrea (Ed.): Architektur konstruieren – vom Rohmaterial zum Bauwerk. Basel 2008
I Ging: Das Buch der Wandlungen, Translation by Richard Wilhelm. Düsseldorf 1999
Loidl, Hans; Bernard, Stefan: Freiräume. Entwerfen als Landschaftsarchitektur. Basel 2003
Los, Sergio: Carlo Scarpa. Cologne 1994
Mielke, Friedrich: Handbuch der Treppenkunde. Hanover 1993
Nerdinger, Winfried (Ed.): Konstruktion und Raum in der Architektur des 20. Jahrhunderts. Munich, Berlin, London, New York 2003
Norberg-Schulz, Christian: Logik der Baukunst. Braunschweig, Wiesbaden 1980
Rasmussen, Steen Eiler: Architektur Erlebnis. Stuttgart 1980
Schittich, Christian (Ed.): Designing Circulation Areas. Munich 2013
van der Laan, Hans: Der architektonische Raum. Leiden, New York, Cologne 1992

Photo credits

The authors and the publisher sincerely thank all persons who have supported the production of this book by giving approval for the printing of their master illustrations, issuing reproduction permission and providing information. All drawings in this work have been specially prepared. Unverified photos come from the archive of the architects or the archive of the journal Detail. In spite of intensive efforts, some of the authors of photos and illustrations could not be ascertained; the copyright, however, is maintained. We request to be informed accordingly.

Cover photo: Eva Schönbrunner

Design typology – Methodology

1, 2 Katinka Temme

Design typology – Jacob's ladder and Sculpture

1 Eva Schönbrunner
2 Carschten (CC BY-SA 3.0)
3 Zoonar GmbH/Alamy Stock Photo
4 Judith Stichtenoth
5 Daniel Schwen (CC BY-SA 4.0)
6 Sander Meisner
7 https://figosfromagio.wordpress.com/2013/05/20/huashan-the-most-wonderful-of-mountains-part-1/
8a Ei Katsumata/Alamy Stock Photo
8b as per: wikiwikiyarou
9 akg-images
10 from: Swarbrick, John: Robert Adam & his brothers: their lives, work & influence on English architecture, decoration and furniture. London 1915
11 Andy Ryan
12 Koji Okamoto
13b Francesco Martello
14b Juan Rodriguez
15b Hannes Henz
16b Walter Mair
18 Ruedi Walti
20a www.italianways.com/stairs-and-theater-at-palazzo-dello-spagnolo/
20b from: Daidalos 9/1983, p. 79
21 Garnier, Charles (1880). Le nouvel Opéra, vol. 2, plate 8. Paris: Ducher
22 Janine Mahler/IBA
23 Matevž Paternoster
24 Duccio Malagamba
25 Christian Richters
26 Hufton + Crow
27 Shen Zhonghai

Design typology – Stage and Landscape

1 Birgit Verwiebe (Ed.): Unter den Linden. Berlin 1997
2 Filmbildfundus Robert Fischer
3 http://evil.wikia.com/wiki/File:The_Illusionary_Maze.jpg
4 Film copies of the Film Museum Munich, Gerhard Ullmann
5 ApA © R. Roozen
6 Iwan Baan
7 Chen Hao
8 Jaime Navarro Soto
9 Atelier Bow-Wow
10 Thomas Jantscher
11 Therme Vals
12 Michael Bause
13 David Monniaux
14 Álvaro Leite Siza Vieira
15 Fernando Guerra
16 Hisao Suzuki
17 Erik Berg/Den Norske Opera & Ballett
18 Jean-Pierre Dalbéra
19 Simon King (CC BY-NC-ND 2.0)
20 Rosemie Callewaert
21 Hufton + Crow
22 Iwan Baan
23 Naoomi Kurozumi
24 Hal Chen
25 Li Xiaodong

Design typology – Aesthetics of technology vs Longing for the archetype

1 Michal Huniewicz
3 Åke E:son Lindman
4 Arturo Duarte jr.
5 Filip Šlapal
6a Andreas Keller
6b Bloomberg
7 Christian Richters
8 Giovanna Silva
9 Werner Kaligofsky
10 Mitsumasa Fujitsuka/helico
11 Katsuhisa Kida
12 jean claude braun
13 Cardaf
14 Beat Bühler
15b Filip Dujardin
16 John Mitchell/Alamy Stock Photo
17 Cristobal Palma
18 Helene Binet
19 Paula Herrero
20 Åke E:son Lindman
21 Lucia Degonda
22 Ruinelli Associati
23 Ruedi Walti
24, 25 Tomas Heimann

Design typology – Volume vs Continuity

1 Katsutoshi Sasaki + Associates
2 Addison Godel
3 Thomas Jantscher
4 Adolf Bereuter
5 Daniel Malhão/DMF
6 www.vanderlaanstichting.nl
7 Allard Bovenberg
9 Rainer Retzlaff
11b Juan Rodriguez
11c Juan Rodriguez
12b Iñigo Bujedo Aguirre
13 Roland Halbe
14 Steven Massart
15 Jens Weber
16 Marco Introini, Kengo Kuma & Associates
17 Mitsumasa Fujitsuka, Kengo Kuma & Associates

Design typology – Furniture and Addition

1 j l t
2 www.sundaymorning.it/House_in_pinewood.html
3a Kouji Okamoto/Techni Staff
3b Shinkenchiku-sha
4 Shinkenchiku-sha
5 Janez Marolt
6 Design + Weld Limited
7 Stéphane Chalmeau
8, 9 Roland Halbe
10 José Campos
11 Victoria Sambunaris/DAM Frankfurt
12 Stijn Poelstra
13 Bruno Klomfar
14 Christian Schittich
15 Andreas Meichsner
16a from: Fondazione Querini Stampalia Onlus (Ed.): Carlo Scarpa – la fondazione querini stampalia a venezia. Verona 2006, p. 52
16b from: Fondazione Querini Stampalia Onlus (Ed.): Carlo Scarpa – la fondazione querini stampalia a venezia. Verona 2006, p. 55
17 seier+seier
18 Luca Onniboni

Construction typology

1 Zoonar/Jürgen Vogt
2 R. Schweitzer
3 Florian Monheim/arturimages
4 Jens Hauspurg
6 Barbara Staubach/arturimages
8 Roberto Collovà
9 Hannes Henz
10 from: Behse, W. H.: Treppenwerk für Architekten, Zimmerleute und Tischler sowie für Baugewerk- und Gewerbeschulen. Plate 1. Weimar 1873
11 Filip Dujardin
12 Christian Schittich
13 Archives d'Architecture Moderne
14 Mitsuo Matsuoka
15 Åke E:son Lindman
16 Iwan Baan
17 Zooey Braun/arturimages
18 Lukas Roth
19 Andreas Keller
20 Ramon Prat

Project examples

p. 56 top left, 58–61 Hannes Henz
p. 56 bottom left, 62, 63 left Leonardo Finotti
p. 63 centre, 63 right, 64 Pietro Savorelli
p. 66 bottom Armin Linke
p. 67 bottom Michael Moran
p. 56 bottom centre, 68–70 Tuomas Uusheimo
p. 56 top right, 71–73 Nacasa & Partners
p. 56 bottom right, 74–76 Ralph Feiner
p. 77, 78 bottom Margot Gottschling
p. 57 top left, 78 top, 79 Annette Kisling
p. 57 bottom left, 80–81 Daici Ano
p. 57 top right, 82–84 Janez Marolt
p. 57 bottom right, 85, 86 top, 87 Alessandra Chemollo
p. 86 centre, bottom René Riller

Matrix

p. 88, image 1 Hannes Henz
p. 88, image 2 Paola de Pietri
p. 88, image 3 Francesco Martello
p. 88, image 4 Hannes Henz
p. 88, image 5 Leonardo Finotti
p. 88, image 6 Andy Ryan
p. 88, image 7 Ramon Prat
p. 89, image 2 Iwan Baan
p. 89, image 3 Chen Hao
p. 89, image 4 Jaime Navarro Soto
p. 89, image 5 Tuomas Uusheimo
p. 89, image 6 Naoomi Kurozumi
p. 89, image 7 Hal Chen
p. 89, image 8 Hisao Suzuki
p. 90, image 1 Nacasa & Partners
p. 90, image 2 Åke E:son Lindman
p. 90, image 3 Andreas Keller
p. 90, image 5 Ralph Feiner
p. 90, image 6 Helene Binet
p. 90, image 7 Beat Bühler
p. 90, image 8 Ruedi Walti
p. 91, image 1 Annette Kisling
p. 91, image 2 Simon Menges
p. 91, image 3 Thomas Jantscher
p. 91, image 4 Rainer Retzlaff
p. 91, image 5, 6 Daici Ano
p. 91, image 7 Roland Halbe
p. 91, image 8 Jens Weber
p. 92, image 1 Janez Marolt
p. 92, image 3 Bruno Klomfar
p. 92, image 4 www.sundaymorning.it/House_in_pinewood.html
p. 92, image 5 Alessandra Chemollo
p. 92, image 6 Andreas Meichsner
p. 92, image 7 Roland Halbe
p. 92, image 8 Luca Onniboni

Planning guide

1 Shinkenchiku-sha
2 Daici Ano
3 Gerhard Hagen
4 Sacha Geiser
5 Cosmin Dragomir
6 Hannes Henz
8 Lard Buurman
9 Simon Menges
12 David Matthiessen
17 Christine Peter
18 Nürnberger Nachrichten
20 Eric Schiller
21 Heiner Leiska
26 Walter Mair
33 Mitsuo Matsuoka
34 Ib Sørensen
35 Bruno Klomfar
36 fhs Treppen GmbH
37 François Bertin
38 Christian Richters
39 Richard Bryant/Arcaid
40 Hisao Suzuki
41a Jens Weber
43b Iwan Baan
45 Ivar Mjell
46 Roman Keller
48 Iwan Baan
50c as per: Schöck Bauteile GmbH, Planungshandbuch Treppen
51 Eva Schönbrunner

Photos introducing sections

Page 4: Heydar Aliyev Center, Baku (AZ) 2012, Zaha Hadid Architects
Photo: Hufton + Crow
Page 6: House NA, Tokyo (JP) 2010, Sou Fujimoto Architects
Photo: Iwan Baan
Page 54: Hotel in Obanazawa (JP) 2006, Kengo Kuma & Associates
Photo: Dacio Ano
Page 94: Gallery building in London (GB) 2015, Caruso St John Architects
Photo: Sabine Drey
Page 93: Cultural centre in the Azores, Ribera Grande (PT) 2014, Menos é Mais Arquitectos
Photo: José Campos
Page 116: Residential building in Tokyo (JP) 2007, Claus en Kaan Architecten mit Atelier IMAMU
Photo: Tomio Ohashi

Subject index

Index of persons